MRS SIDDONS
TRAGIC ACTRESS

Mrs Siddons as Mrs Haller in *The Stranger*

*From the portrait by Sir Thomas Lawrence
by Courtesy of the Trustees of the Tate Gallery*

YVONNE FFRENCH

MRS SIDDONS

Tragic Actress

DEREK VERSCHOYLE

LONDON

First published in 1936
This revised edition, entirely reset
first published in 1954 by
Derek Verschoyle Limited
12-14 Carlisle Street, Soho Square
· London W1

Made and printed in Great Britain by
William Clowes and Sons Ltd
London and Beccles

ACKNOWLEDGMENTS

THE original version of this book appeared before the war, but all the publisher's stock perished in the London blitz. A new edition has given me the opportunity of making certain revisions, and also of taking advantage of a considerable amount of fresh material previously inaccessible and of first importance to students of the period.

Mr Rupert Sissons has generously allowed me full use of a large mass of Kemble papers which he has collected over a long period; while the publication in recent years of the complete edition of Mrs Piozzi's *Thraliana* has provided some intimate and in certain respects invaluable additional detail concerning members of the Siddons family both in and out of the theatre. From this I have been allowed to quote extensively by the Clarendon Press. The Governors of the John Rylands Library gave me leave to include material from the Piozzi–Siddons correspondence. Mr Kenneth Garlick, of the Barber Institute of Fine Arts, Birmingham, drew my attention to some unfamiliar portraits by Sir Thomas Lawrence. Among the latter I am able to reproduce through the kindness of Mrs Fitzroy Newdegate the drawing at Arbury in her possession. To all these my grateful thanks are extended.

Acknowledgments must also be made to the Trustees of the British Museum, the National Gallery, the Tate Gallery and the Victoria and Albert Museum for leave to reproduce paintings, drawing or prints in their collections.

Y.ff.

CONTENTS

CONTENTS

ILLUSTRATIONS

PREFACE

THE news of Mrs Cibber's death, on 30th January 1766, was received by David Garrick with an outburst that was as significant as it was characteristic: 'Cibber dead! Then Tragedy has died with her . . .' Indeed, the loss of that fine actress, wife to Theophilus Cibber and sister to Dr Arne, appeared irreplaceable, and he could not foresee that Providence had already furnished in the form of a small girl of eleven, trudging through the Western Midlands of England with her father's troupe of players, the true successor to Susanna Cibber's throne. Hers was to be a long minority, the legitimacy of which Garrick himself only half acknowledged when the time arrived. The succession was assured, though it was not to be proved for sixteen years.

Throughout the earlier part of the century the Cibbers had had things much their own way. Colley Cibber, who may be said to have built the bridge between the Restoration Drama prevailing in the days of his youth and the polite comedies of the Georgian age, had written, acted, and for a lifetime dominated the affairs of Drury Lane until his rule had become an unpopular dictatorship. But ten years before his death in 1757 a new force appeared on the English stage: Garrick himself opened at Drury Lane with his co-manager Lacy. Reformation began in earnest.

The conditions he found were almost as primitive as during the preceding century. Theatres were still almost as small and quite as uncomfortable as in the rough days of the Restoration, while the population had increased and a new public had become conscious of the Drama. Accommodation was cramped, seating was restricted to plain benches, and, apart from whole boxes, the system of advance bookings was unknown.

Reforms were needed, and Garrick did his utmost to introduce them. Circumstances were not unfavourable, for the rise of the middle classes to a status of active participation, in pleasures formerly shared between aristocracy and people, had created a demand for cleaner conditions, more virtuous standards on the stage, and, in the auditorium, a larger measure of comfort.

A type of genteel comedy had latterly come into vogue, vulgarity had disappeared, indecency was banished and, apart from the traditional bawdiness of the Epilogue, was altogether tabooed. Refined manners ousted the broad, lusty humour of unpolished Britons. Gentility above all became the prevailing tone.

This drastic purging left the theatre more respectable than it had been for a very long while; it also left it in a state of sad anæmia. Important dramatists were lacking, so that for his repertory Garrick fell back to classics, reviving plays by Shakespeare, for a long while unfashionable, and adapting their texts as his fancy pleased him. Other adaptors followed suit, and mutilated Shakespeare came into vogue. Superb players formed Garrick's company; their names illuminate the history of the English Stage. Besides the celebrated Mrs Cibber, he had engaged Peg Woffington, Kitty Clive, the Spranger Barrys, husband and wife, and the classic Shakespearian actress Mrs Pritchard. Great names, but judged by what standards?

English acting had for long been subservient to the reserve which formed, as it still does, an important element in the national character. Garrick, of French descent, flashed vitality through all his work, discarding the conventions which transformed so many of his contemporaries into mere rhetorical dummies. But even so, under his galvanizing influence, teamwork was non-existent. Performances were individual, depending upon the quality of the one or two leading players, and a tedious monotony of voice production seems to have been common to most performers, if Thomas Holcroft's allusion is to be accepted, when he refers to the 'laborious strainings at false climaxes in which the tired voice reiterates one high tone beyond which it cannot reach'.

Performers, again, were strongly conscious of their audiences, going out of their way to ingratiate themselves by dropping curtseys at each burst of applause or, when idle, by nodding and smiling at their influential acquaintances in the boxes. Inattention was common among actors filling minor parts, and lack of co-operation was a normal standard in the performance of any piece.

Theatrical costume was that of contemporary fashion. The aged Macklin had appeared, it is true, with his supporting players in tartans for a performance of *Macbeth* in 1777, but this was an unheard-of innovation. During the greater part of the eighteenth century Garrick played all military rôles in the uniform of a British general or of a Hanoverian officer, while in adaptations from the Greek tragedies leading ladies wore their hair powdered, appearing in richly trimmed dresses with conventional hoops. The application of historical research to period dramas was still entirely unknown. For scenery Garrick had employed P. J. de Loutherbourg to design his settings, decorated with lavish taste. Lighting was improved. Make-up was carefully and conscientiously applied. The Italian traveller Riccoboni, a keen observer of standards throughout the theatres of Europe, noted the care that was expended on this art. He noted, too, that English actors were still in the grip of formality: strutting, mouthing, moving about stiffly, and often ungainly in manner. There was, for instance, much opening and tapping of snuff-boxes to cover up awkward moments, little spontaneous action, and little save rhetorical gesture.

This conventionalism accompanied the plays themselves, many of which were five-act, heroic dramas in the grand manner, admired by the aristocracy and ideal for the declamatory style. The taste of the bourgeoisie, to whom such fare would, it was feared, prove too advanced, was catered for by the provision of after pieces, light and often farcical burlesques, more palatable to these new recruits to the theatre public, and evidently more digestible.

The fare was mixed; so no doubt was the enjoyment. Impressive though the Playhouses in London and the larger provincial centres may have appeared from without, interior conditions were still barely tolerable. In the provinces and the smaller market-towns they would by present standards seem unendurable.

By the end of the seventeen-sixties Garrick's original team had faded from view. Most of his players had died; only Kitty Clive survived them, and even she had retired.

A vigorous chapter seemed about to close in the history of the English theatre when the majestic Kembles faced their London audiences for the first time.

Part One: The Road
1755-1782

'La noble figure et la profonde sensibilité de l'actrice captiv-
èrent tellement l'attention de Corinne, que pendant les
premiers actes ses yeux ne se détournèrent pas du théâtre. La
déclamation anglaise est plus propre qu'aucune autre à remuer
l'âme, quand un beau talent en fait sentir la force et l'origina-
lité. Il y a moins d'art, moins de convenu qu'en France;
l'impression qu'elle produit est plus immédiate; le désespoir
véritable s'exprimerait ainsi . . .

'. . . L'actrice la plus noble dans ses manières, Madame
Siddons, ne perd rien de sa dignité quand elle se prosterne
contre terre. Il n'y a rien qui ne puisse être admirable, quand
une émotion intime y entraîne.' – MME DE STAËL, *Corinne*

'Of actors Cooke was the most natural, Kemble the most
supernatural, Kean the medium between the two. But Mrs
Siddons was worth them all put together.' – BYRON, *Letters*

ONE

THEIR origin was modest, though their antecedents were by no means obscure. There is a strong traditional link with the ancient family which took its name from the Wiltshire village of Kemble, but later migrated in troublous times to Herefordshire. Stubbornly Catholic, devotedly Royalist, these land-owning Kembles had been persecuted on the one count and dispossessed on the other. Two members of the family were classed as Recusants and deprived of their property. Several were priests. The most venerable of these, Father John Kemble, was to survive the horrors of the Civil War and the bigotry of the Commonwealth only to be accused in extreme old age of complicity in the Titus Oates plot and, though innocent, to die a martyr's death.

Captain Richard Kemble, his nephew, distinguished himself at the battle of Worcester, and little remained to substantiate the claims of the famous Kembles of the succeeding century excepting the conviction that their Catholic religion and Hereford origin were derived from the Captain's seventh son who had been last heard of in that town in abject poverty.

It may hardly be a coincidence that the turn of the century saw the appearance at Hereford of a Roger Kemble, described as 'fatherless', whose own son Roger begat a generation remarkable for genius, talent, distinction of appearance and bearing.

Little is recorded of the second Roger Kemble's early years. He was born at Hereford in 1721, baptized a Catholic and is generally supposed to have begun life as a barber. He was very well favoured and possessed unmistakable breeding, good manners and a mild and somewhat jocular disposition. These qualifications forming his capital, at the age of thirty he threw in his lot with a disreputable company of strolling players, quarrelled with them, left them, wandered up and down the provinces until he came to Birmingham, and there fell in with Mr John Ward and his troupe of comedians. These he joined; and while he fulfilled the dual rôle of actor and company's barber the destiny of theatrical history was slowly moving in his direction.

For itinerant players in a century when the lowest branch of the profession was utterly degraded, the Wards were a reputable pair. John Ward, sometimes, though inaccurately, described as an Irishman, late of the Aungier Street theatre, had been Betterton's contemporary and a capable actor. But it was not his competence which gave him his superior reputation: it was his unquestionable respectability. He was a Methodist and he applied his principles both in and out of school with regularity. In former years his harshness had caused the flight of Peg Woffington from the Dublin theatre which he managed and where, as a girl of sixteen, she had already begun to captivate her audiences. But unable to endure his rigid discipline she had been frightened away to pleasanter surroundings.

By the time that Roger Kemble joined his company in 1752, Mr Ward had long been married, and his grown-up daughter, Sarah, was as strong willed as she was handsome. A year later Roger was asking permission to marry her. Ward and his wife, knowing their professional world, had other views for their Sally. An actress's life was the last into which they wished her to drift. But the daughter's will being at least as strong as her father's and having behind it the additional impetus of romance, she overcame the objections, won the battle, and a year later at Cirencester she married Roger Kemble.

John Ward slid out of his defeat with as much dignity as he could command and a side-thrust at his new son-in-law's professional competence. He resorted to casuistry hardly in accordance with Methodistical tenets: 'I forbade you,' he remarked to his daughter, 'to marry an actor. You have not disobeyed me since the man you have married neither is nor

[4]

ever can be an actor.' Having evaded this matrimonial issue, the Wards magnanimously presented the young couple with their theatrical company and so pass out of the story. They reappear many years later in a churchyard at Leominster, reposing beneath a Georgian tombstone; solid representatives of the Nonconformist conscience:

> *Here, waiting for the Saviour's great assize,*
> *And hoping through His merits hence to rise*
> *In glorious mode, in this dark closet lies*
> *John Ward, Gent.,*
> *Who died Oct. 30th, 1773, aged 69 years:*
> *Also*
> *Sarah, his wife,*
> *Who died Jan. 30th, 1786, aged 75 years.*

The Roger Kembles were now faced with independence and responsibility. They proposed to manage their company of players on the approved lines of Mr Ward and to continue on the same circuit. This particular circuit, as the itinerary of strolling actors was called, lay along the western midlands. It stretched from parts of Lancashire to the Welsh marches, and included Worcestershire, Warwickshire, Gloucestershire, Shropshire and Staffordshire.

The Drama had never quite recovered from the effects of Puritan discipline. Although the suppressed gaiety of the country had found an outlet with the Restoration, and the immense popularity of the theatre served as a safety valve for the curbed liberties of the public, the roots of restraint struck far too deep into national prejudices to be so easily torn up. London, however, with the King and the aristocracy to set a convivial example, had led the way in a return to the Drama, and one of Charles II's earliest actions had been to issue royal patents for the establishment of two London theatres. The first of these was in Drury Lane, and the second at the Cockpit. But if the seventeenth century had to contend with Puritanism, the succeeding century inherited Methodism, and there is small wonder if theatrical activities were mostly confined to the capital until well on in the eighteenth century. Even so in the provinces old conditions still held. A few fashionable resorts, such as Bath and Tunbridge Wells, were equipped with tolerable theatres, and gradually stock companies began to be formed among provincial players. In the county towns buildings appeared which served the purpose of these and the lesser touring companies. But for the country people and those in outlying districts there remained the strollers – troupes of raffish vagrants who trudged from town to village through dusty lanes in summer and through foul roads in winter. Their theatre was generally a barn; at best it was the courtyard of an inn. Their very existence depended on the goodwill of their public, for they had no recognized legal status of their own. Improvised performances, generally heralded by the beating of a drum, were liable to indictment, while under the Vagrancy Act of George II the players were subjected to the persecutions of any capricious municipality. This Act lumped them together with mountebanks and performing animals, denied them privileges and safeguards, and all performances at theatres not possessing a royal patent were liable to proscription. In cases where the law could not be enforced a fine was placed upon each performance.

Under the constant threat of indictment and always in the shadow of persecution, the strollers maintained a code of laws that had barely altered since Elizabethan times. The manager of a company was usually the member who possessed enough capital with which to fit the rest out with dresses and provide some meagre scenery. After expenses had been deducted the profits were divided into shares, one to each member of the troupe, and four 'dead shares' allowed to the manager in consideration of the properties. As his whole family was marshalled into the players' list he usually raked in half the profits: a state which created among the actors constant discontent and open rebellion. As a rule the strollers were an improvident, tippling and bedraggled crowd: welcomed on arrival at their circuit towns and hustled out of them by indignant tradesmen, bailiffs and landladies. Even as late as the close of the eighteenth century the conditions under which a company of players toured their circuit was pitiable. The manager or proprietor travelled easily enough, lumbering on ahead in his coach; but the weary company followed on foot, stumbling along in th wake of the long, top-heavy, overloaded wagons that strained over hills and snow-bound moors or crusted uneven roads, piled up with baggage and theatrical properties. At the end of the journey their reception would vary according to the convictions of the authorities. Worcester, for instance, at one time possessed a mayor who was a monster of inhumanity, ordering the expulsion of players with sticks and stones and threats of imprisonment.

There was a wide divergence in the standards of different companies: some were low; others, particularly that of the Kembles, preserved an unusually high reputation. This was more owing to the character of Mrs Kemble than to her amiable husband. Sally Kemble was a tartar. She was strong minded as a wife and despotic as an employer. Her black brows contracted in displeasure at any delinquencies in her company, and her superabundant vitality kept her in constant control of the business.

On 5th July 1755, at the Shoulder of Mutton, an old inn at Brecon, she was delivered of a daughter, her eldest child and the first of a family to whom she was to transmit such an astonishing combination of genius, talent and majesty. The Shoulder of Mutton still exists; its exterior has altered with the passage of time and its name has changed as the result of Mrs Kemble's confinement. It is now called The Siddons Wine Vaults. The child was christened a few days later by the curate of St Mary's Church at Brecon, whose inaccurate entry may still be read in the church register for that year: *July 14th Sarah Daughter of George Kemble a Commedian and Sarah his wife was baptized.*

She was, it will be noticed, baptized into the Protestant faith according to the prevailing agreement on the issue of mixed marriages, and her brothers, soon to follow, were brought up as Catholics in accordance with the Kemble tradition. Two years later, at Prescott in Lancashire, Mrs Kemble gave birth to a son, John Philip; and thereafter at regular intervals ten other children followed them. John Philip, Stephen, Frances, Elizabeth, Anne, Charles and Jane will play some part in their sister's history; but Mary, Catherine, Lucy and Henry Kemble died young and may be forgotten.

* * *

Sarah Kemble received a tolerable education. She was sent to good day-schools at most of the towns on the circuit, and while her parents were at Worcester she was placed in the charge of a Mrs Harris of Thornlea House, who received and instructed her for nothing. At first she was victimized. Snobbery was inherent in her companions, and they turned their backs on the player's daughter; but as soon as her histrionic experience proved useful in school theatricals she was considered an acquisition. The kind little creature came forward with offers of help and plenty of resourceful ideas. She suggested scenes, she was full of hints about production, and her chief accomplishment was the improvisation of a sack-back from a sheet of stiff sugar paper, by which means she procured acknowledgement as a social equal. It was consistently claimed by Roger Kemble that his daughter was not to be trained for the stage, but this seems to have been little more than a pleasant self-deception, for even during these periods of spasmodic education she was constantly being snatched away from her classes in order to participate in some performance where her abilities might shine.

It is impossible to give a clear account of her youth, so little is known of its details, and her first public appearance is a matter for pure conjecture. She is believed to have taken some part in *The Grecian Daughter* at Stourbridge, where she performed with some officers of the local militia, and is said to have infuriated the hero by an outburst of convulsive laughter during a romantic passage. She had certainly been acting, on and off, for most of her childhood, but few records of those rustic performances remain, and in after life she rarely spoke of her early years. It is said that her first appearance was as Leonora in *The Padlock*, but she must have been very small indeed when she was exhibited as a juvenile wonder during a benefit performance at Kington at which there was some sort of organized protest against infant exploitation: a curious occurrence for Georgian England. In any case her appearance produced an uproar. When she opened her mouth to recite her little piece the attempt was submerged by a noisy demonstration and she was temporarily disconcerted. At this point the blood of the Wards, pounding with principles, stirred within Mrs Kemble. She took her daughter by the hand and led her

[8]

down to the smoky footlights, where she abandoned her to impose herself upon the unruly audience. The child began to recite the fable of 'The Boy and the Frogs'.

> *'Tis death to us, though sport to you,*
> *Unthinking, cruel boy . . .*

The fierce training had begun.

*   *   *

At Worcester in 1767 the Kemble company announced a performance which, in view of contemporary persecution, throws some light upon the conditions under which they often practised their profession.

MR KEMBLE'S COMPANY OF COMEDIANS

At the Theatre *at the King's Head*, this evening will be performed

A Concert of Music

(To begin exactly at Six o'clock). Tickets to be had at the usual places.

Between the Parts of the Concert will be presented, *gratis*, a celebrated historical play (*never performed here*) called

CHARLES THE FIRST

The Characters to be dressed in ancient habits, *according to the fashion of those times.*

The numerous cast included the playing of General and Lady Fairfax by Mr and Mrs Kemble; James, Duke of York by Master J. Kemble, the Duke of Gloucester by Miss Frances Kemble, and the young Princess Elizabeth by Miss Kemble. Mr Siddons appears for the first time in the company's bills as the Duke of Richmond.

The subterfuge of calling the performance a concert with the play thrown in *gratis* was an evasion of the law in towns whose local authorities chose to assert their rights. Worcester's harsh mayor was out for blood, and Roger Kemble was always trying to outwit his vigilance. On another occasion at

[9]

Wolverhampton Mr Kemble advised the population that he proposed entertaining them with:

A Concert of Vocal and Instrumental Music,

which was to be divided into three parts, when during the intervals ('for the amusement of the town and further improvement of polite literature') was to be continued the Histrionic Academy at which the inhabitants were invited to display their various modes of elocution 'for their diversion, without fee, gain, hire, or reward'. The inhabitants were further instructed to pay no money on entering, but that at Mr Latham's, who would *sell* them tooth-powder, they would obtain their tickets *gratis*. The show concluded with *Love in a Village*, in which the five parts were distributed among the Kembles, the forecast of a family affair, in which Young Meadows was played by Mr S-dd-s and Rosetta by Miss K-mb-le. Another early performance of which details have been preserved was that of a celebrated comedy entitled '*The Tempest, or, the Enchanted Island*, with all the scenery, machinery, music, monsters, and the decorations proper to be given, entirely new'. In this production the part of Ariel was played by little Miss Kemble.

* * *

It was now apparent that the girl possessed unusual powers. Her elocution was remarkable, she had an amazing memory and learnt without effort, while her taste in literature was to a very high degree pure and elevated. Her early passion for Milton and the classic poets was encouraged by her parents, and her aptitude for music, especially her singing, was also being developed. Her mother supervised her musical education and taught her to play the harpsichord and to accompany herself to a voice that was true and, though small, very pleasing.

There was at this time, billeted at the public house at Wolverhampton, a strange Hogarthian character: a common soldier of anonymous identity whose parts, knowledge and invention had so delighted the customers of the tavern that he was proving a constant attraction. He had squandered a fortune, enlisted in the army, was enabled to obtain his discharge with a subscription fund raised by these local admirers and was given a benefit by Roger. At this function he promised to disclose his name. But the moment came and went; he made a comic speech, revealed himself to the audience as 'their most humble obedient servant' and retired. Roger Kemble was enchanted; he had an idea. He invited the adventurer to become his daughter's tutor. Instruction from the private soldier who could read Horace was an opportunity not to be missed. Kemble rushed home to inform his wife of this happy inspiration, but her perhaps not unexpected reply rather took the wind out of his sails. She promptly quashed the transaction, and the matter there ended. Many years afterwards Samuel Rogers made the acquaintance of William Combe. The eccentric author of the *Travels of Dr Syntax* had never forgotten the snub he had once received from the Kembles; Rogers noticed his unreasonable aversion to Mrs Siddons, then at the summit of her fame; and his malicious pleasure in recalling her as a child at Wolverhampton, a solitary figure in the draughty wings of the rustic theatre, banging a pair of snuffers against a candlestick to produce the monotonous sound of a windmill off the stage.

TWO

WHEN Sarah was about sixteen there was no longer any doubt as to her powers of attraction. She was beset by admirers. The Brecon audiences in particular owning, as it might have been, a proprietary interest, followed her fortunes attentively. She was passing out of the awkwardness of adolescence into glowing beauty of a rare, dark, rather Semitic quality which combined the magnificent symmetry of her mother with her father's air of distinction and breeding. The superb poise of the head and carriage that was later to contribute to her redoubtable personality was already characteristic, while the serenity of her spirit was reflected in her grave exterior calm.

Being much with her, William Siddons, who had been a member of the company for the past three or four years, fell deeply in love with his manager's daughter, and the impressionable girl of seventeen, seeing a hero instead of a most ordinary young man, returned his passion with all the ardour of first love in a setting of tinsel and paper decoration.

William Siddons was twenty-eight at the time. He came from Staffordshire, where his father had been a publican, landlord of the London Apprentice at Walsall, before meeting with an untimely death in a sparring match. Young Siddons, having acted once or twice in his native town as an amateur, was then apprenticed to a hairdresser but eventually gravitated to the stage again. He was an acquisition for a strollers' company. His good looks and excellent manners made him popular with provincial audiences, and, aided by a remarkable memory with which he could learn perfectly any part however long within twenty-four hours, he could perform any character from high tragedy to low buffoonery to the satisfaction of an undiscriminating public, and forget it directly afterward.

At first Roger Kemble and his wife may quite possibly have looked favourably at Siddons's pretensions. But they had no illusions with regard to his professional capabilities. They saw him as he was: mediocre as an actor, honest as a man, and as a son-in-law devoid of prospects. Against this bird in the hand there were about half a dozen others in the surrounding bushes, in one of which perched Mr Evans, a local squire of landed property and an income of £300. It was said that this Mr Evans had heard Sarah singing 'Robin, sweet Robin', had been devastated by the effect and had fallen madly in love on the spot. In Brecon it was thought he would marry her – in any case he now came forward with serious intentions. After mutual deliberation the Kembles decided in his favour and determined to encourage him. Sarah's attitude is uncertain. She may, for a moment, weighing duty against affection, have wavered; it would have been most unlike her; but in any case Siddons went to her in an agony of jealousy. He proposed an elopement, and when this invitation was declined rushed off and made a scene to her parents. Their reply was to give him his dismissal. But before he left the company Roger allowed him a farewell benefit performance; and then it was that the mediocre spirit of William Siddons prepared to justify itself at the expense of the Kembles, Sarah and his more fortunate rival.

The benefit was given to a full and curious house. The romance was the talk of Brecon, and speculation divided as to whether the manager's daughter would stick to the object of her choice or allow herself to be persuaded to marry against her inclinations. At the end of the play William Siddons, supposed no doubt to take leave in some sort of declamatory address, came down to the front of the stage and launched at the audience a rhymed complaint of his own composition, entitled 'The Discarded Lover'. It related to the assembly the course of the whole proceedings and appealed to the ladies of Brecon for sympathy. In eleven doggerel verses he exposed the

infamy of the jilt and the perfidy of her parents. *Dear Ladies,*
ran the penultimate verse,

> *. . . Avoid one indelible stain,*
> *Excuse me, I beg, if my verse is too plain;*
> *But a jilt is the devil, as has long been confess'd,*
> *Which a heart like poor Colin's is bound to detest.*

These highly personal revelations created a stir. Just as
William Siddons was never conspicuous for wisdom so now
tact was not his strong point.

He took his applause with confidence, and, triumphant with
self-justification, bowed himself off the stage. But he bowed
himself straight into the arms of Mrs Kemble, who was waiting
for him in the wings with indignation in her heart and revenge
in each hand. With these she soundly boxed his glowing ears,
and there was a first-class family scene. But out of the mist that
veils her early actions Sarah emerges for a moment resolute
with loyalty. In spite of his cavalier behaviour she now definitely
promised to marry William subject to the eventual approval
of her parents. If she reproached her lover at all, her criticism
was restricted and her heart touched with sympathy for his
wounded feelings. The awkward confession, stimulated by the
applause of Breconian friends, may even have seemed to her
like a heroic monologue.

*   *   *

A compromise was now reached in which it was decided to
send Sarah away from the scene of her entanglements, and even
perhaps from the temptations of the stage. Her father, with
his vague ideas about her upbringing, may now have formu-
lated some plan for her social advancement. She was
accordingly packed off to Guy's Cliffe in Warwickshire, the
home of Lady Mary Greatheed, whose service she entered as
some sort of dependant. Conjecture has always been busy as to
her exact capacity. Thomas Campbell, her official biographer,
called it 'humble but not servile', her principal employment
being 'to read to the elder Mr Greatheed'; while *The Secret
History of The Green Room*, an unreliable production edited some
years later by a contemporary busybody, declared her occupa-

tion to have been maid to Lady Mary at a salary of £10 a year. Whatever her exact position it seems obvious that being in a dependent capacity she was probably a combination of lady's maid and companion, her elocutionary powers being well suited to the purpose of reading to elderly gentlemen.

Lady Mary Greatheed was the daughter of the second Duke of Ancaster and the widow of Samuel Greatheed, a former Member of Parliament for Coventry. But as her husband had died six years before Sarah's arrival at Guy's Cliffe, Campbell's vague statement of her reading to 'the elder Mr Greatheed' may be disregarded. There was, however, a younger Mr Greatheed, Bertie, in 1771 a little boy of eleven, and it is quite likely that part of her employment was to read to or teach him.

Whether she arrived at Guy's Cliffe forlorn or self-possessed there is no means of knowing, but it was not long before she made herself thoroughly respected. Her enthusiasm for Milton's poetry almost amounted to an obsession, and was duly appreciated. When she accompanied her employer to the Duchess of Ancaster's in Lincolnshire she was overheard declaiming long passages from plays in the servants' hall; and Lord Robert Bertie, Lady Mary's brother, who attended the recitation with enthusiasm, duly reported it in the drawing-room. He was admonished and told not to encourage the girl to go on the stage; but even if Lady Mary had no suspicions that she was harbouring a prodigy she was enough impressed by her abilities to present her with a copy of Milton's works. There is even a tradition that during this period of her life Sarah received an audition from Garrick, then manager of Drury Lane, that she repeated passages from *Jane Shore* and that 'he seemed highly pleased with her elocution and deportment, wondered how she could have got rid of the provincial ti-tum-ti, but regretted he could do nothing for her, and wished her a good day'. But although there is no record of Sarah's ever having gone to London before 1775, there is a possibility that Garrick, an old friend of the Greatheeds, may have heard her recite when on a visit to Guy's Cliffe.

The surroundings in which she found herself were highly encouraging to romantic fancies. She could indulge her moods to the very limits of the imagination as she walked along the banks of the Avon. The site abounded in legends. The house itself was on an ancient foundation. In Leland's *Itinerary* it is mentioned as 'a praty house of stone for the Cantuary Prists. . . . It is a place of pleasure, an howse mete for the muses; there is silence, a praty wood . . . the river rollynge with a praty voice over the stones'. Ancient hermitages, holy springs and legends of Count Guy of Warwick were all grist to the mill of her growing sensibilities; but her expanding mind was chiefly occupied by its first contact with material comfort. In Mr Greatheed's elegant restoration of the old house she was confronted for the first time with cultivated life and was not slow in adapting herself to her new conditions. Lady Mary afterwards admitted that she was always seized with an overpowering inclination to get up from her chair whenever her superbly dignified companion came into the room.

Sarah had not forgotten William Siddons. Although she had been forcibly removed from distressing associations, there was evidently on the part of her parents a definite plan to detach their children from theatrical influences. Their eldest son, John Philip, was being trained for the priesthood at the English College at Douai, and the next two girls, Frances and Elizabeth, had been respectively apprenticed to a Worcester milliner and a Leominster dressmaker. During two years spent at Guy's Cliffe Sarah had had time to think. Reflection had increased her determination, and when William came over to see her, as he did from time to time whenever he was in the neighbourhood, he added entreaties to his vows and obtained impulsive renewals of her former promise.

The Kembles were still reluctant to give their consent to the union with young Siddons; but in front of such resolution they could do little. Rather than face the alternative elopement, they at last half-heartedly consented, and on 25th November 1773, Sarah and William were married at Trinity Church, Coventry. The witnesses were Roger Kemble and a Mary Godfrey, and the minister an assistant curate. The bride was eighteen, the bridegroom twenty-nine. The future seemed to contain little for them beyond each other: they were resigned to the prospect of poverty and to spending their lives in drudging round the circuit. Sarah may have had, even at this time of her life, some submerged consciousness of her superlative histrionic powers, but probably the limit of her ambitions was

Mrs Siddons

*From a portrait by an unknown artist
in the Victoria and Albert Museum*

that of a good position in a provincial theatre. The present was imperative and a living the first necessity. It was settled that they should, to begin with, work on the Kemble's circuit pending the turn of circumstances.

One of the first towns that they visited was Wolverhampton, with whose public they were already familiar attractions. There they were to have performed in the yard of the King's Head, but the hostility of an aggressive mayor caused the erection of a notice prohibiting the performance in general of any player, puppy or monkey, by which insulting combination will be seen the humiliations to which they were liable to be subjected. Meanwhile in Wolverhampton the competitive spirit was augmented by the arrival of other companies, three of which were, by Christmas time struggling for public favour. In the face of opposition the ban was eventually lifted, and, to the general satisfaction, Roger Kemble was able to announce *The West Indian* and *The Padlock*, in which his daughter was to play respectively Charlotte Rusport and Leonora. On 13th December 1773, the handbills advertised this double production and contained the first printed announcement of 'Mrs Siddons'. The occasion was that of her own farewell 'Bespeak',[1] in which, preparing for a sympathetic reception, she concluded by reciting one of the trashy effusions which at all times in her life she was so ready to compose and – perhaps modelling herself upon her husband – to inflict upon others. Only a verse or two will be given:

> *Ladies and Gentlemen – my spouse and I,*
> *Have had a squabble, and I'll tell you why –*
> *He said I must appear; nay, vowed t'was right,*
> *To give you thanks for favours shown to-night . . .*
>
> *He still insisted; and to win consent,*
> *Strove to o'ercome me with a compliment;*
> *Told me that I the favourite here had reigned,*
> *While he, but small, or no applause had gained . . .*

This indeed, was all too likely to occur to the unfortunate

[1] A variation of a 'Benefit' when proceeds of a performance were given to one or more members of a company.

man, although his wife in the exuberance of her spirits was far too large-minded to heed such a detail. She concluded with the classic topical ending:

> *First for a father, who on this fair ground,*
> *Has met with friendship seldom to be found,*
> *May th' All-good Power your every virtue nourish –*
> *Health, wealth and trade in Wolverhampton flourish!*

Some months later the Siddonses managed to disentangle themselves from the Kemble authority, and they joined the company of Messrs Chamberlain and Crump, two barnstorming partners of notorious rapacity. Their characteristics were made plain by their nicknames of Fox and Bruin. William Siddons performed some indefinite duties connected with management, and Sarah fulfilled the part of leading lady. They were still distressingly poor and in most lamentable circumstances when the company stopped at Cheltenham in the summer of 1774.

THREE

CHELTENHAM was beginning to be known as a watering-place. It was very small and quite undeveloped. Its one street was long, clean and well paved, crossing at intervals, by means of stepping-stones, a clear, bubbling stream which flowed through the small town. Its one wretched theatre, the haunt of raffish companies, was its only place of entertainment.

During that summer season some few persons of consequence were staying there to take the waters. Among these were Lord Bruce, subsequently Earl of Ailesbury, his stepdaughter, the Hon. Henrietta Boyle, and a party of their friends. Miss Boyle was a modern and intelligent young woman. She had written several pleasing poems, among which an 'Ode to a Poppy' had met with approval in a London journal, and she took great interest in the intellectual and cultural fashions of her time. One day when she was out walking with her friends, they stopped outside the little local theatre to read the announcement that that evening would be played the grand old tragedy of *Venice Preserved*. The promise of such an exquisite burlesque was too good to be missed; the temptation to have a laugh at the expense of a third-rate troupe of red-nosed comedians hiccoughing their way through Otway's rich lines was too strong to be resisted. At the box-office, they accordingly took their seats for the evening performance.

In the miserable dressing-room, divided from that of the actors by a torn blanket, sat Sarah Siddons preparing for her part. Someone with more interference than discretion had informed her of the distinguished company from London that was coming to the theatre to scoff at the torments of Belvidera, and she was in a state of melancholy and bitter resentment. In the course of the evening as she stormed through the play her mortification was increased by the behaviour of a party in one of the boxes. She could not see but she could hear. And the explosive sounds that reached her were doubtless those of mirth; insulting, insolent; crueller for their being unsuppressed. That night she went to bed in a state of indescribable distress and wounded pride.

The next day the truth was out. William Siddons was waylaid in the street by Lord Bruce, complimented on his wife's superb performance, and informed of the disastrous effects of her acting on the ladies of his party. They were apparently still disfigured with weeping and so racked with headaches that they had not yet been able to leave their rooms. William, in Campbell's phraseology, 'hastened home to gladden his fair spouse with this intelligence'. The intelligence, which she badly needed, was immediately followed up by a visit from Miss Boyle in person, who, being a practical young woman, at once set about the work of helping and encouraging Mrs Siddons by every means in her power. She supplied her with dresses, rich stuffs, shawls, lace and drapery; fitted her out with all sorts of necessities, and so initiated a friendship that lasted until the end of their lives.

The practical value of this new and influential acquaintance was of immense importance to Mrs Siddons. Lord Bruce told Garrick of his discovery in the mean little Cheltenham theatre, and Garrick, invariably reacting to aristocratic patronage, at once sent off as his agent the well-known actor King, to assess the value of the pearl in the Cheltenham oyster. King arrived there in time to see the pearl go through the part of Calista and, unobserved, returned to London and reported to Garrick. He was interested and impressed, and he advised Garrick to engage her. But Garrick was doubtful. Afraid of a rash investment, he was unable to decide without another opinion. In the end he did nothing active about the matter but let it slide from his overburdened hands. He already had more than enough to keep him occupied in London, but he knew that the time was not far distant when the acquisition of a new actress of merit for Drury Lane would be a matter of policy. The following spring proved that the time for action was approaching. He had kept track of his quarry and knew where to mark her down when he needed her. In a letter to Moody, then playing at Liverpool, he inquired: 'Have you heard of a woman Siddons who is strolling about somewhere near you?' And at Liverpool the Siddonses were: they had lately gone there to join Younger's company.

*   *   *

In the meantime Sarah had become a mother. Her eldest child, Henry, had been born at Wolverhampton in the preceding autumn, and she now had to provide for him as well as for her husband. She was still far from realizing the scope of her immense abilities. Necessity added to a passion for poetry, and love of acting provided the impetus for work and the burning desire to improve her condition. She had besides inherited her mother's tremendous energy. Until this time her talents, remarkable though they were in a strolling actress, were entirely unformed, and she had no conception of acting other than to reel off the words of her part and deliver them according to her unerring intuition. She was as yet unconscious of any intellectual process. The false dawn of what her friend and biographer Boaden described as 'the fiery markings of her intellect' perhaps began to be discernible when, some time during the course of this year, she began to study the part of Lady Macbeth. In her old age she described this experience in her memoranda.

She was twenty. She was full of confidence and secure in the conviction that little remained for her to learn in the nature of theatrical experience. She shut herself up to study the character of the Lady, according to her custom, when the household had retired for the night. She was to appear in the part the following evening, and knowing it to be a short one decided to make quick work of it. 'I believed . . . that little more was necessary than to get the words into my head, for the necessity of discrimination, and the development of character, at that time of my life, had scarcely entered into my imagination,' she wrote in after years.

While it grew late and the silence around her intensified, she studied the assassination. The experience was unendurable. She was seized with panic fear. She picked up her candle and, terrified by the rustling of her silk dress, crept up the stairs fancying herself pursued. Her imagination was undergoing its first wild reaction to the working of her mind. She reached her room at last: and found her placid husband sound asleep, but, 'I clapt my candlestick down upon the table, without the power of putting the candle out, and I threw myself on my bed, without daring to stay even to take off my clothes.' And though she rose at daybreak to continue her study, she knew little of her part that evening, but she had learnt that interpretation required something more than could be gained from superficial memorizing. This experience altered her methods of study and influenced the whole course of her subsequent creative genius.

*   *   *

The spring passed, summer was ending and Garrick still delayed. But with August and the dog-days he decided to act. He sent off another delegate, this time the Rev. Henry Bate, to inspect and report on 'the woman Siddons'. Mr Bate was many things besides being the proprietor of the *Morning Post*. He was a sporting parson, a duellist and a notorious bruiser. He vigorously imposed his opinions and prejudices on the world in the columns of his paper and defended them with his fists and pistols. He was therefore in a position to exact respect. But in spite of all his heavy artillery he had a weakness. He fancied himself as a critic of the theatre and was flattered by Garrick's friendship. Garrick accordingly slipped him into his pocket along with other persons likely to be useful.

Bate, pleased and proud with his mission, set off with Mrs Bate, posting along some of the worst roads in the country before reaching Worcester where Younger's troupe was now playing. Here he found his objective, and throughout the whole negotiation he maintained an amusing and spirited correspondence with Garrick. The evening he arrived he slipped into the wings of the barnlike theatre in time for a performance of *As You Like It*, and watched Sarah Siddons playing Rosalind on a stage measuring not much more than three yards wide.

She was again pregnant and it was obvious. But Bate, discounting this drawback, was very pleased with what he observed. He was, in fact, enthusiastic. And as he heard that other delegations, including one from Covent Garden, were hovering in the neighbourhood with the express intention of making overtures to seduce her from Younger, he felt that there was no time to lose in securing this promising young woman for Drury Lane. First of all Bate approached William Siddons and then sat down and wrote to Garrick. His letter assured the manager that the young couple were very docile and entirely willing to leave all business arrangements to his discretion. That his new discovery was a remarkably good-looking woman, who, considering her present inconveniences, should ordinarily have a very fine figure. Her face was for stage effect the most strikingly beautiful he had ever seen, but her appearance was as nothing to her action upon the stage and her distinguished deportment. He at once spotted her astonishing aptitude for quick transitions of emotion, and noted their variety and suitable expression. He considered she did more with the humbug scene with Orlando than anyone else in his recollection, Mrs Barry not excepted. But he described poor William as 'a damned rascally player'. The young woman had 'a very good breeches figure', he thought, and although her voice was dissonant and apt to sound grating in unimpassioned scenes, he concluded by venturing to prophesy that she might end by making 'the proudest *she* of either house tremble in genteel comedy'.

Although this is not what actually transpired it was exactly what Garrick had been hoping for.

David Garrick had had nearly forty years of public life. His phenomenal career as an actor and as a manager was soon to end; and although he wished to retire as gracefully as possible he was not unwilling to do so on a becoming triumphal cloud. He was a sick man and had had much to harass him during his last years of office. He was gradually losing hold of the reins with which he drove the theatrical coach. Worse, however, than ill health, and harder to bear than advancing years, were the humours of the wildest team that he had ever conducted at Drury Lane. The uncontrolled passions of three termagants: the jealousy of Mrs Abington, the envy of Mrs Yates and the vanity of Miss Younge, were the causes of his rapid and visible decay. His trump card for the farewell season was in the nature of a foil to these ungovernable women. From the depths of the provinces he produced an untutored genius, a raw girl against whom their rage and spite might concentrate and so leave him a little peace. His team became a four-in-hand.

*   *   *

Bate, having been invested with full powers, went ahead with the transaction. He followed up his letter to Garrick with another one written a few days later. He had now altered his opinion with regard to William. He had seen him as Young Marlow and had found some merit in the performance. Still, it was hard to know what was to be done with him. He was anxious for any sort of stage employment, and Bate's idea was that it would be possible 'to station him so as to satisfy the man without burdening the property'. He was plainly to become the white elephant of Drury Lane. One of William's uses, however, was as an amanuensis. He undertook the rest of the correspondence with Drury Lane. He wrote gratefully to Bate and obsequiously to Garrick and accepted for himself and his wife an engagement at £5 a week. He asked indeed 'no more than what I think we may decently subsist on, and appear with some credit to the profession – that is, £3 for Mrs Siddons, and £2 for myself. This I flatter myself we shall both be found worthy of the first year; after that we shall wish to rise as our merits shall demand.' So far as he was concerned he certainly flattered himself. '*Our* merits . . . *We* shall *both* be found worthy. . . .' William Siddons at the outset of his married life had no notion of what he had taken on as a partner. The day was to come when the sense of his inferiority, his inadequacy in talent and his lack of character was to make him retire into the domestic background with the resigned cry of a saddened husband: 'She is too grand a thing for me.'

Very naturally there were a few obstacles to hinder the smooth passage of the engagement. For one thing Younger was suspicious and indignant at the attempt to lure his best actress away to London, while the lurking emissaries from Covent Garden also attempted to embarrass the proceedings. They had made tentative proposals just before Bate's arrival and quick settlement; they now decided to assert their rights

to the first refusal of Mrs Siddons's services, and were prepared
to consider such rights as being infringed by the Drury Lane
management. There was some understanding between the two
patent theatres regarding priority when treating with players,
and the Siddonses, hovering undecidedly between two stools,
narrowly missed an undignified collapse. But the difficulties
were overcome and Garrick was pleased with the energy of his
representative. Besides welcoming the idea of a talented novice,
he promised that if she would be wholly guided by him he
would make her theatrical fortune. And 'if any lady begins to
play tricks,' he had written to Bate, 'I will immediately play
off my masked battery of Siddons against her.' The situation
appealed to him immensely.

There was now nothing further to do than wait. The pair
were urgently in need of money to cover expenses between this
and the time when Mrs Siddons would be strong enough to
travel to London. William became very agitated. He entreated
Garrick for money to cover their immediate needs, and pressed
for employment for himself 'in *any* situation where he is likely
to be useful'. This question had so far been left undebated, and
he was too thick-skinned to perceive an intentional omission to
nominate his duties. This accounts for the conceited tone that
he adopted throughout the correspondence. He grew more and
more fussy at the inevitable little delays. He foresaw untold
disasters and endless anxieties. He thought that they might not
even then have secured the engagement. Mr Garrick had,
after all, never seen them, and London was a long way off.
They were tied to the neighbourhood for the next two months,
and it seemed just possible that the whole fabric of the engagement was insecure and might fall to pieces. He had given
notice to his manager, 'so that if anything had happened and
we had not been engaged it would have proved a very unlucky
circumstance'.

His small petitions were endorsed by Bate; Garrick forwarded
a remittance of £20, and on 5th November 1775, immediately
after playing at Gloucester, Mrs Siddons was suddenly taken
ill and brought to bed of a daughter, Sarah Martha. While
waiting for the birth of her child she had prepared a select list
of her characters for Garrick to see. There were twenty-three
of them, and of these she underlined seven as being particularly

suitable for her first London appearance. These selections were: Alicia, Euphrasia, Belvidera, Lady Townly, Portia, Rosalind, and Widow Brady.

Thus, out of her special choice four parts were in comedy and three in tragedy. Only two were Shakespearian. Bate had been enchanted with her Rosalind and had urged her to make her début in that part. And she herself, besides her admirers, was convinced that comedy was her speciality. It was therefore mainly as a comic actress that she was engaged to appear at Drury Lane.[1]

*   *   *

It is certain that Mrs Siddons's ill-timed confinement was a cause of the disappointments which were now to take place. Garrick's original intention had been to open the season at Drury Lane by presenting his new actress, but as the season began early in September this plan was clearly impossible. As things turned out she was not in London before the end of November and was far from strong when, with her husband and two infants, she arrived in the capital on trial for her career.

Garrick had studied the choice of parts that she had made out for him, and decided to start her off in *The Merchant of Venice*. A few days after Christmas she was to appear on the great stage of Drury Lane as Portia. He had clearly sized her up to perfection. He admired her appearance, paid her many compliments and promptly placed her in the category to which she belonged: promising, inexperienced, and with everything to learn. But he was far from letting her notice his doubts. 'His praises were most liberally conferred upon me,' she afterwards wrote. He was waiting for the verdict of the public. It came soon enough.

An audience beaming with Christmas exuberance crowded to Drury Lane on the night of 29th December 1775. Bills of the performance had been printed in the *Public Advertiser* and the *Gazetteer*, and they revealed that Shylock was to be played by Tom King, the popular creator of Lord Ogleby, and the man who had first discovered Sarah at Cheltenham. They also stated that Portia was to be played by 'A Young Lady – Her

[1] Others seem to have seen her in this light. Notably John Downman who observed, 'Off the stage I thought her face more inclined to the comic.'

[26]

first appearance'. There was some curiosity about the young lady until she made her entry. Then the sad truth was undisguised.

Portia tottered on to the stage in a state of panic. Her voice quavered, her tones faltered; each sentence she spoke died off in a whisper that she alone could have heard. She was almost inaudible, and in such a state of nerves that she forgot where to stand or what to look at. An ugly, faded garment of salmon pink did little to improve her appearance which was in any case pale and fragile. In a word, the young and promising Mrs Siddons, who had been so sure of herself a little while before in the country, had shrunk to the proportions of a timid girl.

By the trial scene she had somehow got hold of herself and delivered her speech with 'critical propriety', as one of the critics said. But the audience was not impressed by this lamentable exhibition of self-consciousness, and the next day's papers lost no time in confirming the popular opinion.

All but one they denounced her. Condemnation was almost universal. Had it not been that the part was one of her own selections she might have been justified in her subsequent reproach of Garrick with having introduced her as Portia intending to cause her failure, for this was a thankless part in which to initiate the appearance of an emotional actress. The scintillation, the bright jets of elocution, afforded no scope for displaying the passions; and the even balance of the emotions was chiefly suited to the arts of a player well versed in a thousand tricks of skilled delivery.

Her voice, too, was thought to be lacking in pleasant tones. Bate certainly had made this point his only criticism when he saw her at Worcester, and now the *Gazetteer* found 'a vulgarity in her tones'. The *Morning Post* was the only paper to notice her with any sort of toleration, and when it is remembered that this was Bate's paper it is not surprising to find it making the best of a bad job. A young lady had appeared, it seemed, whose name the critic understood was Siddons; and that, 'allowing for her great natural diffidence, we see no unpromising presage of her future excellence. We think it one of the most respectable first essays we ever saw in either Theatre Royal.' It went on to praise her appearance, her deportment and graceful action, and admired her art of driving home her author's points by

[27]

'an emphatic though easy art, almost peculiar to herself'. The *Morning Chronicle* printed an article by the incorruptible Mr Woodfall, in criticism stern yet acute. He was not to be blustered into praise on Garrick's account, and he retraced the career of the new actress. He admired her appearance but condemned her in a qualified statement. He advised her to be more spirited in her performance, and thought that she could not be too early advised 'that on the stage nothing is so barren as a *cold correctness*'.

These statements bit into her feelings like prussic acid. She felt them to be unjust and utterly lacking in perception. She was incapable of sprightliness at a moment when her entire constitution was suffering from nervous and physical exhaustion: lack of self-confidence had let her down severely. Four nights later she repeated the performance. The effect she made was as poor as on the first occasion, but this time she was encouraged by the appearance of a letter in the *Morning Chronicle* in which her improvement was noticed.

Mrs Siddons was up against a towering wall of ill-luck. In addition to her theatrical disappointment she was treated to the malicious rivalry of the three elderly sirens of Drury Lane. An epigram which was current at the time is an indication of the notoriety which was given to these professional scandals.

> *I have no nerves, says Y——g; I cannot act.*
> *I've lost my limbs, cries A——n; 'tis fact.*
> *Y——s screams, I've lost my voice, my throat's so sore.*
> *Garrick declares he'll play the fool no more.*
> *Without nerves, limbs, and voice, no show that's certain.*
> *Here, prompter, ring the bell, and drop the curtain.*

Mrs Abington was the unrivalled interpreter of ladies in polite society. No other actress had been able to compete with her virtuosity in drawing-room comedies. She glittered with a cold and fashionable brilliance in her inimitable playing of Lady Racket or Lady Fanciful; and she delighted her audiences with her dashing portrait of Miss Hoyden. Gay, easy, elegant and accomplished, she was the acknowledged queen of light comedy. Mrs Yates had a commanding appearance and excited admiration. She was still under fifty, and though her early reputation had been one for meekness she had undergone an astonishing change, having become notorious for the violence of her temper. She had inherited public favour after the death of Mrs Cibber, and she was considered unrivalled. Her strength, thought the public, was recitation; her weakness, envy. As for Miss Younge, she was not in the same class with either Mrs Abington or Mrs Yates, but for any deficiency in talent she atoned with an overflowing measure of conceit. Her pretensions indeed were said to be comparable with those of the most spoiled favourite. All three women possessed ungovernable passions, and their displays of temper were celebrated throughout London.

Garrick's plan for self-protection was working out well. The envy of Yates and the pretentiousness of Younge were now thoroughly roused, and no opportunity was lost by either in showing Sarah how unpleasant life could be made for her. In the green-room, where he received homage that was more than regal, their feelings were enraged at seeing Garrick honour Mrs Siddons with the most distinguished attention. He would sometimes hand her to a chair next to his own and favour her with smiles and compliments. He enjoyed the situation. At the time Mrs Siddons was rather green. When he confided to her that on account of their jealousy he dared not advance her in a more prominent part, lest out of envy one or other of her rivals might poison her, she believed the story. She also believed him when he told her that on this account he had cast her for Portia, a character in which she was unlikely to create a sensation, and that thus she had been merely tolerated. When the awakening came it made her exceedingly bitter. The remembrance of how Garrick had exploited her remained with her throughout her after life. She saw herself as an innocent and trusting victim whose early career had been sacrificed to appease personal quarrels.

The season was nearly half-way over and Garrick still continued to push her. The characters he chose were for the most part uninteresting, though they were certainly not inconsiderable. *The Jubilee* had recently been revived as an afterpiece: the spectacular pageant that had been ruined by bad weather a few years before at Stratford on Avon. In the procession, a conglomeration of Shakespearian characters and allegorical figures, Mrs Siddons was chosen to represent Venus. '*Garrick's* Venus' she instantly became to her tormentors; and in the last scene, a massed grouping of the cast, her rivals attempted a concerted rush to crowd her out of the picture. But Garrick kindly came forward and, taking his disconcerted Venus in one hand and her little Cupid in the other, led them down to the front of the stage where they belonged; otherwise, thought Mrs Siddons, they might have as well been in the Island of Paphos at that moment. The little Cupid afterwards grew up to be Thomas Dibdin, the composer's son, and the author of some amusing memoirs. He clearly remembered the occasion. Mrs Siddons had bribed him into preserving a proper cherubic expression by a reiterated promise of sugar-plums. He recorded that she was as good as her word. She was adjusting his wings in her dressing-room when he heard her speak for the first time. 'Ma'am,' she called to Mrs Garrick's maid, 'could you favour me with a pin?' And on one occasion when Tom Dibdin was ill and absent, and was understudied by another child, he was gripped by jealousy. 'I could have killed that boy,' he thought, until Mrs Siddons had reassured his return to work with, 'I did not like Master Mills half as well as I do you.'

*   *   *

On 13th January 1776, Mrs Siddons took part in Colman's adaptation of Jonson's *Silent Woman*, with no success; and on 1st February she was cast for the part of Julia in a foolish play of Bate's, *The Blackamoor Wash'd White*, a piece of no value whatever. It was lavishly produced to Loutherbourg's scenery, and lawns, lodges, avenues and vistas formed part of the elaborate setting. The chief failure in the opinion of the Press was Mrs Siddons, who, remarked the austere Woodfall, 'having no comedy in her nature, she rendered that ridiculous which the authors evidently designed to be pleasant'. *Having no comedy in her nature!* One critic at least was on the right path. Woodfall's hint, however, passed unobserved among the flood of general censure, and no one cared to embark upon a debate concerning the future of Mrs Siddons in comedy.

After being washed white for three nights, the *Blackamoor* was hooted off the stage by the audience. In an uproarious

[30]

evening of rowdy demonstration the theatre was stormed by roughs, hirelings of Bate, who laid about them till disapproval was quashed. Officers occupying the boxes took on gods and pittites, and each box was a cockpit from which dismayed ladies scrambled, hoops permitting, into the corridors in an undignified retreat. Garrick came down to the footlights and addressed the wild assembly. Someone aimed an orange at him. He raised his hands and invoked the audience with admirable tact. He invited the public to state its will but held himself bound to protect the author's property. He begged to be allowed to close his professional life in peace. After this King came forward and attempted to read a paper from Bate announcing the play's withdrawal; a lighted candle whizzed past him. At midnight Garrick, the incarnation of patience, returned, announcing the departure of both author and play. What piece, he inquired, would the public choose now? His tact won the day. The audience, mollified, dispersed and slowly went home.

Such disasters as these did little to strengthen the nerve of a young and delicate actress. The unsettling effect of such a reception at Drury Lane only further ruined her confidence. To begin with, the great house paralysed her with fright. But Garrick either refused to accept the public's verdict that she was no actress, or, if he believed it himself, he continued to back his early opinion by bringing her forward in various plays. On 17th February she was Emily in *The Runaway*, by Mrs Cowley, the pseudonymous 'Anna Matilda' then mystifying the world of sensibility by a gush of Della Cruscan verse. In *The Runaway* the best part was given to Miss Younge, who played Bella and was the grand attraction of the piece; whereas Emily – a lovely fugitive – was, although the heroine, not calculated to enlist the enthusiasm of spectators. Maria, in Vaughan's *Love's Metamorphoses*, was her next unsuccessful attempt, and until the end of May she accomplished nothing further.

FOUR

THE time was coming for Garrick to take his final curtain and make his last exit from the stage which he had embellished for the past thirty years. He chose to revive the admired old comedy of *The Suspicious Husband*, where, in the character of Ranger, he was accustomed to let off some of his brightest fireworks. Once again he selected Mrs Siddons, this time to play with him; and on this occasion she was given a line to herself in the playbill. *Mrs Strickland* = Mrs Siddons. In this performance she was considered pathetic.

The end of May saw a revival of *Richard III*, which had always been one of Garrick's most illuminating achievements; and now he again chose Sarah to play with him as Lady Anne. Her second London venture in Shakespeare was hardly more encouraging than her first. Admittedly, here was an opportunity for her to show herself off in tragedy, but on an occasion when the greatest actor of the century was staggering his audiences by the terrific realism of his art it was unlikely that much attention would be given to the women in the play – especially in the case of a novice in whom interest had totally lapsed. *Richard III* was played three times, the third occasion being a command performance before the Royal Family. Mrs Siddons was ignored by the critics to a man; the *London Magazine* alone mentioned her. Amongst other things it found that the female parts were wretchedly performed; the Queen was ungracious, the Duchess frightful 'and Mrs Siddons a lamentable Lady Anne'.

Pit Entrance 1790

From a print in the British Museum

Garrick had actually taken a good deal of trouble in instructing Sarah to play opposite him. He had criticized the awkward movements of her arms, which she was at that time inclined to use stiffly; but she did not take correction well, and her pride, always on the defensive, made her at once imagine him to be jealous of her.[1] Then she had a dose of him in one of his very worst moments. He had told her to move away from his couch in the ghost scene so that the audience might have a full view of the variety of expressions which at that moment convulsed his face. But on the night she was so impressed by his acting that she forgot his instructions and he was obliged to turn his head. The glare he gave her was so terrifying that she could never afterwards remember it without confusion. The same effect of paralysing a fellow-actor by sheer realism afterwards became one of her own characteristics. She had plenty of opportunities to study Garrick's methods. On her spare evenings he liked her to watch his performances, and, seated in the darkness of the box that he set apart for her, she absorbed incalculable benefit from his playing. Incredible in versatility and illuminating in realistic acting, Garrick was a living example of his advice to beginners: 'If you cannot give a speech or make love to a table, chair, or marble, as well as to the finest woman in the world, you are not, nor ever will be, a great actor.'

Five nights later he took leave of the public as Don Felix in *The Wonder*. The two greatest players in the nation's history had thus for a few weeks appeared, like stars, in conjunction. Nobody was aware of the event. The one was vanishing in an apotheosis of public recognition, while the other was still indistinguishable in the mass of outer nebulæ.

Garrick was thankful to resign his responsibilities to the new management consisting of Sheridan, Linley and Forde; for his former partner and co-patentee, Lacy, had died three years before, leaving him to inherit the entire managerial work. His administration of Drury Lane had been both significant and unique. He had instituted reforms, ended abuses and directed affairs with the energy of genius. The condition of the stage had improved beyond all recognition during his term of office; its scattered forces had been galvanized into an efficient and

[1] 'I found I must not shade the tip of his nose,' was the remark she made to Lady Maria Waldegrave.

disciplined unit, and he had been progressive in his innovations from the Continent. The old hoop-frames hung with candles, irritating the spectators' eyes, had disappeared after 1762, and in their place had come modified footlights, protecting the audience from the glare by indirect lighting.

A revolution had been brought about three years later when Garrick had abolished once and for all the time-honoured occupation of seats upon the stage by aristocratic and otherwise privileged spectators. Occasions had even been known when a distinguished patron, finding the leading lady irresistible, had leaped from his chair and squeezing her round the waist had prevented her from continuing her part in the piece. The custom, almost feudal in conception, was one of the last of the conventions linking aristocratic culture to the players' mode of life. Thereafter, if the stage was cleared of distinguished impedimenta, it was cleared for the benefit of the wealthy, rising, fashionable middle classes, and to this type of spectator dramatic literature was gradually becoming adapted.

*   *   *

The new management inherited office with the zeal of new brooms. Automatically the engagements for the past season now lapsed, the company dissolved, and the Siddonses among them departed to play in the provinces. They had known earlier in the year that a change of management was expected, and William, once again full of apprehensions, had written an abject letter to Garrick beseeching him to recommend them both to his successors, otherwise they might be 'left to those who perhaps may not have an opportunity of observing us'. It is unfortunate that Sarah's pride was apparently as active as her husband's conceit. She should have made a personal application to Garrick and not have left William to grovel before the departing manager when there is no record even of his own occupation at Drury Lane. That he felt worthy of his hire there is no doubt at all. He asked for a continuation of the engagement at the rate of £3 a week for his wife and £2 for himself. He was desperate. Without influence, he felt, their situation might well be pitiful.

Garrick evidently set their minds at rest with smiles and assurances, for when they set off with their babies for the provincial tour, backed by the prestige of Drury Lane, they had no doubts as to the certainty of the coming engagement for the next winter.

They first of all went to Birmingham, engaged by Yates of the New Street theatre; and at Birmingham the blow fell. They received an intimation from the prompter of Drury Lane informing them that the management had no further use for the services of Mr and Mrs Siddons. Sarah was crushed by the sudden and overwhelming disaster. She fell ill – it was thought that she would not recover. The blow was twofold. It struck at her pride and it struck at her material future. The promise of regular employment had seemed so certain at last that the sordid struggles she had undergone were rapidly fading into the background of the past from which they might reasonably have been expected never to emerge. The letter from Drury Lane put a period to these happy speculations. Once more the youthful Mrs Siddons, as sensitive as a nerve and as proud as Lucifer, was confronted with the prospect of returning to the provinces with a family to support and the future to reconstruct.

She was ill for a long time. 'For a year and a half I was supposed to be hastening to a decline,' she afterwards wrote. But she worked on fiercely all the same. She blamed Garrick for everything: for being jealous of her, for suppressing her, for not showing her off in suitable parts, for depreciating her talents to his successors, for not telling the world what a surpassing genius she was. In short she blamed him because she knew that she had failed and that her failure, unlucky though it had been, was attributable to herself alone.

It never occurred to her to consider whether her record during that disastrous season could justify an engagement by new managers who would be bound to move cautiously at the outset of their joint undertaking. She saw herself the victim of malevolence, but she was the victim of her own pride and honesty. She was herself incapable of intrigue or subterfuge. Her one fault was a tendency to resentment and bitter feeling. Her ungratefulness to Garrick, from whom she had learnt so much that was of value, was a prejudice confined solely to private scores. She never denied her debt to his artistic experience, and of his professional gifts she spoke only with profound admiration. Garrick from her point of view had

[35]

flattered her, promised to make her career, had been jealous of her and had let her drop like a brick. 'I was at that time good-looking,' she wrote in her old age, 'and certainly, all things considered, an actress well worth my poor five pounds a week.' To add to this impression, Sheridan in after years mischievously told her that Garrick had gone about belittling her talents. The thought of this humiliation rankled within her for the remainder of her life. It was too strong ever to be overcome by the great generosity and warmth of which she was capable. She was a prey to self-pity. She was hypersensitive.

The reflections that embittered her heart were to a certain extent subordinated by the need for energetic action. Although she was supposed to be wilting under the shock, and no doubt was looking pale and wretched, she pulled herself together for the sake of her dependent children and her not very useful husband, and with characteristic moral stamina set to work with redoubled industry. She turned to the provinces with a resolution backed by desperate need. Here, at least, her reputation was enhanced. She had acted with the great Garrick and never again would return to the old, despised condition of the stroller.

With the autumn came the opening of the season and the inauguration of the new management at Drury Lane. As there was much to contend with, it is unlikely that anyone cared to remember Mrs Siddons and her curt dismissal. One wise voice, surprisingly enough, was raised in protest – one voice only. It was that of Mrs Abington: 'You are all fools,' she said.

*   *   *

The chief provincial theatres were considered highly respectable. Having been granted patents they were safe from the legal persecution that threatened so many of the unofficial play-houses. Bath was second only to London, with a standard almost as high, audiences equally discriminating, and its approval an important recommendation. It was followed by York with a nice judgement in acting; Edinburgh, Hull, Norwich, Liverpool and a few more succeeded in due order.

It was therefore a consolation to Mrs Siddons that while she was at Birmingham she played all the leading parts and won a good deal of admiring notice. She acted with Henderson, whose reputation was immense but who had fallen foul of Garrick through having mistakenly been pushed forward as his rival. Both players were therefore able to indulge a mutual grievance in the other's company while at Birmingham, and John Henderson was so impressed with his leading lady that he at once wrote off to Palmer, the manager of the Bath Theatre, advising him to engage her. Palmer, presumably having secured his whole company for the season, found the suggestion inconvenient and let the matter drop for the moment; so Sarah passed on to Liverpool under her old manager Younger, and from Liverpool she went to Manchester. There she played *Hamlet* and became 'the leader of theatrical fashion' according to a contemporary.

She now returned to her old reliable stock of non-Shakespearian tragedies. She acted in *The Grecian Daughter*, *Jane Shore*, and *Douglas*. Her unusual refinement and air of breeding once more distinguished her from her meretricious surroundings, and before she knew what was happening, she was again, as she had been at Cheltenham, the centre of a circle of exceptional and engaging people. The power of drawing to herself unusual friends was automatic. By being herself she attracted the few; again, by being herself she sometimes repelled the many. She was too natural to make social compromises, so that when, some years later, she became the greatest lioness of a generation itself distinguished for its race of celebrities, she took her place among them with ease and discrimination.

At Liverpool she increased her reputation by her intellectual performance of *Hamlet*, in which her pallor and melancholy became her well. She had not dared to undertake the risk of her benefit and had shared it with another actor on account of the heavy expenses. She need not have feared. Her *Hamlet* yielded nearly one hundred pounds. Earlier in the summer she had been preceded at Liverpool by her old bugbear Miss Younge. The result had not been satisfactory. The effect of starring in the provinces had been to overflow the theatre during the actress's expensive visit and to impoverish it for weeks to come while the normal companies played to deserted houses. This time the management decided to have no more 'exotics' as Sarah called them in a letter to Elizabeth Inchbald, 'so that

Liverpool must from this time forth be content with such homely fare as we *small folks* can furnish to its delicate sense'. She could afford to be sarcastic about Miss Younge.

Mr and Mrs Inchbald had between them survived a fair number of experiences and adventures, and when they first met the Siddonses both women were playing at Liverpool. The friendship was therefore recent; it had succeeded a critical phase in the relations between elderly Mr Inchbald and his clever young wife, and was responsible for the appearance of a new influence, that of John Philip Kemble, fresh from college and newly dedicated to a stage career. In a mild, semi-detached way young Kemble had gravitated toward his sister and these new intimates. Soon after the reconciliation of the Inchbalds, the whole party left Liverpool together for a brief holiday. In a farmhouse on Russell Moor, near Appledurcombe, the strong moorland air should have restored the lustre to Sarah's black hair and the clarity to her dark and expressive eyes. She washed, she ironed, she sewed for her family; and as she worked she sang. The afternoons were spent in long walks, the evenings at cards. There was an occasional frolic with 'blind man's buff' or 'puss in the corner' – with Mr Inchbald, doubtless, as the blind man. For while he painted, his talented wife with her bewitching stammer read from the classic poets with Sarah's young brother, and John Philip Kemble thought her then, as he did for the rest of his life, the most enchanting woman that could be known.

The rest was of short duration, for on 15th April when the York Races began, Mrs Siddons, who had been engaged until after Whitsun by Tate Wilkinson, the most enterprising and influential of provincial managers, made her first bow to a York audience as Euphrasia in *The Grecian Daughter*. Her recent holiday had apparently done little to revive her wan appearance, for Wilkinson thought her looking so frail from illness that he trembled lest she should collapse under the strain of her agitating part. She had a rival at York – a Mrs Hudson, whose friends were concentrating their hopes on a defeat for the newcomer. But Sarah was lucky. She won the approval of Mr Cornelius Swan, a self-styled authority in matters of theatrical taste and a former manager of the Aungier Street theatre in Dublin. At York he led the way in praise or condemnation,

[38]

and York respectfully waited to see which way the cat would jump before deciding upon the fate of a new player. But Mr Swan, having seen Mrs Siddons as Euphrasia, Alicia, Matilda, Lady Townly and Lady Alton, was so enthusiastic that she instantaneously became the acknowledged favourite; so much so that an unfortunate Miss Glassington, also making the same bid for success, was eclipsed and forced to retire in confusion. Sarah went on from strength to strength. She still played in comedy: she played Rosalind and the Widow Brady; but this seems not to have disturbed local sensibilities, where the general opinion was one of astonishment that such a marvel should have been neglected by London and restrained by Garrick.

*　　　　*　　　　*

After the Whitsun engagement the Siddonses prepared to leave York. Wilkinson for a frenzied moment hoped to retain Sarah as a permanent actress. He tried to bribe her from fulfilling her new provincial engagements with promises of a wardrobe of elegant finery. 'What lady likes it not?' he artfully reasoned, and, as he felt that he could produce something more effective than fat Younger of Liverpool, he showed Mrs Siddons what he could do by rigging her out in a 'most elegant full sack, with a large hoop . . . and that sack was really elegantly adorned with silver trimmings'. But though she so far succumbed to this temptation as to declare that it made her so happy that she wished she could take the sacque with her to Manchester, the silver trimmings were not strong enough to bind her permanently to York and Mr Wilkinson's theatre. So back to Manchester they went, and from Manchester to Birmingham. There they were more or less constantly with the Inchbalds. By June 1778, they were at Liverpool, where Younger had to apologize to the audience for presenting them with a company that had not performed before the King – a privilege due to provincial self-respect.

The despotism of eighteenth- and early nineteenth-century audiences was an expression of their smug and conscious superiority. Generation after generation, the middle classes had been taught to look upon players with contempt and to assert their respectability by exacting servile obedience from the theatrical profession. With the rise of the bourgeoisie the close relations that had formerly existed between the aristocracy and the stage underwent a gradual change, and it was the triumph of the middle class to be now able to establish itself upon a basis of patronage with regard to the profession. Garrick's prestige had prepared the road along which the Kembles would soon travel with such massive dignity towards an improvement of the social status of actors, but in the meantime, the public, unimpressed by individual distinctions, continued to ignore all influences ulterior to its own will. So William Siddons was pelted when he walked on at Liverpool bearing Younger's placarded apology, and Mrs Kniveton fell down upon the boards in convulsions. The uproarious audience extinguished the lights, stormed the stage, reclaimed their money and went home. Mrs Siddons merely showed scorn. But she was sensitive about situations of this sort; they reminded her of London, whither she fully intended never to return. Woodfall had gratuitously advised her to confine herself to provincial theatres in which her limited powers of voice would be better displayed than in the larger auditoriums of the capital. Judging by eventual results, his opinion appears curiously at fault, but the slow process of Sarah's growth was almost entomological. She was still in the chrysalis stage, and it was impossible to foresee the creature of sweeping strength that would emerge from the fragile shell. At present she was satisfied with the country; she enjoyed touring; she was popular and successful wherever she went. Her one drawback was her health, still so indifferent as to show no promise of recuperation.

FIVE

DURING the last three decades of the century Bath had surpassed its own reputation. Social genius, combined with natural advantages and municipal energy, had created a hotbed of fashion, elegance and scandal unparalleled even by London standards.

Among its principal purveyors of entertainment two of the most remarkable were the elder and the younger Palmer. John Palmer, senior, a wealthy brewer, had founded the famous theatre in Orchard Street thirty years before Mrs Siddons's arrival, and his son had recently spent at least £1,000 on enlarging and redecorating in the approved classical taste the house which his father had struggled to establish. In addition he had petitioned Parliament for an Act by which the King might grant him letters patent, and when in 1768 the Act was passed, Bath had become the first provincial city to own a Theatre Royal. So, what with the energy of Palmer and his enthusiasm for the stage, his theatre became second in importance only to London, and in excellence to none. In conjunction with that at Bath he ran a theatre at Bristol twelve miles away and on alternate nights hurried his exhausted company from the one place to the other in special fast coaches, forerunners of the great system of stage coaches which he was later, as first Comptroller-General of the Post Office, to inaugurate all over the country. Every year he toured England in search of new talent for his theatre, and each tour further exposed the infamy of British road travel. The lumbering mail carts took two days to reach London from Bath; there were no attempts at stages and no method in transport.

In 1778, mindful of Henderson's earlier recommendation and supported by the opinion of his prompter, Floor, who had seen her at Liverpool, Palmer engaged Sarah Siddons for the coming winter season. She was to receive a salary of £3 a week: a sum neither affluent nor beggarly but the usual figure for a performer who was not a star. Henderson's recommendation of her talents, an echo of what had been said of the rising Garrick years before, was worthy to have been her epitaph. She was an actress, he had said, 'who never had had an equal nor would ever have a superior'.

She arrived, with her family, in time for the beginning of the autumn season. It was September, and the place was opening to receive the dyspeptic, the gouty, the frivolous and the idle. The tyrannical influence of Nash, long dead, had seceded to a reign of amiable dilettantism and cultivated sensibility which prepared the way for Mrs Siddons's successes just as much as her art was to heighten the rage for the emotions which soon set in. In 1778 *The Rivals* was only three years old: the brilliance of the Sheridans and the fascination of the Linleys were still topics for curiosity and speculation.

*   *   *

At the theatre there were, of course, other actresses – leading ladies to whom priority was due – and Mrs Siddons was asked to play on Thursday nights, well known to be the dullest in the week, when all able-bodied Bathonians contributed to mutual suffocation down at the Lower Rooms where the Cotillon Balls were held. Thursday nights in Orchard Street were consequently meagre and unattended, and Mrs Siddons seemed likely to have recourse to her old grievance. Indeed she wrote: 'I had the mortification of being obliged to personate many subordinate characters in comedy, the first being, by contract, in the possession of another Lady'. Mortification or none, she made her first bow to a Bath audience on 24th October as Lady Townly in *The Provoked Husband*. Three days later she was Mrs Candour, although no serious notice was taken of either of these comic efforts. But on 3rd November she played Elwina in Hannah More's tragedy, *Percy*. This shook

[42]

a terrific compliment out of the *Bath Chronicle*. It considered that her Elwina established her 'in the judgement of the town, as the most capital actress that has performed here these many years'. After this high praise the wheel of approval began revolving towards her. She began to be noticed by the most critical public in the kingdom.

Her success was sure and universal. Week by week, as returning Thursdays proved, the attendance at the Cotillon Balls grew thinner while that at Orchard Street increased. The most critical of audiences, having closed languid and atrabilious eyes to all but the most superficial pleasures, opened them with a start and opened them wide. It saw High Tragedy, long ignored, return to favour on the wings of a dark young woman with classical proportions, an interminable nose and volcanic powers of stirring the heart.

Her greatest characteristic at this time was the indescribable pathos of her acting. It communicated itself so surely to her spectators that they were invariably reduced to tears. John Taylor saw her that winter and in a fever of enthusiasm wrote off to Garrick, saying he thought her 'as much a mistress of her business as ever female I saw'. She was in his opinion the ultimate point that he could reach in imagination, and her pathetic parts were 'exquisitely fine'. David Garrick, ageing in his Hampton villa, disordered by ulcers and gall-stones, probably thought the stage well lost after his years of servitude. It is doubtful whether he did more than raise an eyebrow at Taylor's panegyric.

The range of Sarah's characters was extraordinary. She played, during this season, Lady Townly, Mrs Candour, Mrs Lovemore, Belvidera, Lady Brumpton, the Queen in *Hamlet*, Portia, Countess of Salisbury, Euphrasia, Juliet, Emmeline, Elwina, Lady Jane, Millwood, Rosamond, the Queen in *The Spanish Friar*, Imoinda, Bellario, Imogen, Miss Aubrey, the Queen in *Richard III*, Indiana, Sigismunda, Lady Randolph, Jane Shore, Emmelina and the Princess in *The Law of Lombardy*. And twice she recited Sheridan's monody on Garrick, which she found excessively moving: 'I never yet was able to read that lovely poem without weeping,' she wrote to a friend.

*　　　*　　　*

At this time, and indeed throughout all her professional life, her industry was astonishing. On Mondays, after a morning rehearsal at Bath, she had to play the same evening at Bristol, returning to Bath the following day in order to give a performance there at night. Sometimes her luggage was mislaid and failed to turn up in time for the play. Tuesdays, Thursdays and Saturdays were allotted to Bath, while Bristol had alternate evenings in the week. Sarah, although she shone on her own tragic Thursdays, had also, through the terms of her contract, to play subordinate parts in comedy or else to forfeit part of her salary. But in spite of exhausting work she was making many valuable friends, receiving generous applause and earning the first fruits of a great reputation.

Her worries were chiefly domestic. Another daughter, Maria, was born on the first of July 1779, and even when she shut herself away to study her parts she had to attend to the demands imposed upon her by three young children. Her husband seemed very small beer indeed. He fussed about, played minor characters in an indifferent manner, but was a very good judge of acting and an ogre at drilling his wife in her parts, being 'very cross with her when she did not act to please him,' said a Mrs Summers who played tragedy confidantes to Sarah.

The leading hero at Bath was Dimond, an excellent actor, and with him Mrs Siddons usually played. But she also acted with Lee and with the great Henderson when he returned to the nursery of his career as a guest performer for a few nights. Henderson, having been instrumental in obtaining her Bath engagement, took a great interest in her success; allowed her to play Beatrice to his Benedick, Portia to his Shylock and Gertrude to his Hamlet. He even praised her in comedy and on his return to London extolled her to the autocrats of Drury Lane. 'He was a fine actor,' she afterwards wrote in her MS memoranda, 'with no great personal advantages indeed; but he was the soul of feeling and intelligence.'

Her first Bath season finished gloriously on the first of June 1779. The second reopened at the end of September and continued until the middle of the following July. Her popularity was greater and her success more assured during this year. On 12th February 1780, she and Dimond played *Edward and*

[44]

Eleanora, the occasion being her benefit, and Master Henry and Miss Sally Siddons appeared as Eleanora's children. The end of June brought her a benefit at Bristol with *Isabella* and *Edgar and Emmeline*. Her benefits were beginning to bring in money which was at once given over to William and administered by him. Throughout her life Sarah Siddons, with contemporaneous docility, was accustomed to receive a quarterly allowance from her husband – a tithe of the earnings for which she wore herself out.

* * *

During the four seasons that Mrs Siddons played at Bath, her genius, unlike the spontaneous achievements of Garrick and Kean, matured slowly with the gradual development of her intellectual powers. The deliberate process of her thought, the gift of superhuman concentration, the masculine strength of mind and the feminine tenderness of feeling, joined to unprecedented histrionic ability, were by a slow, inward fermentation producing an artist whose conception of acting was purely and absolutely original. As she claimed it herself, her art was derived directly from nature; and any character that was not true to nature she rejected on account of its insincerity. Although the stage at that moment was at no great level of excellence, she had had opportunities in London and elsewhere to assimilate the best that her contemporaries could give. She had been influenced by none of these. She had formed and was still forming her own conclusions about representation. Yates, Younge and Crawford were only so many runners-up before the overwhelming power of her genius. From them she learnt how not to act. She was entirely creative.

Her work was arduous and incessant. After a performance ending at midnight she would sometimes study at home until three o'clock in the morning. She took no chances with herself. She was as dependent upon humours in her work as she was reliable in her private life; and though she never failed her management, she was not proof against the exacting moods of her temperament. With her the urgency of creativeness raged against the reserve of her nature. The irresistible passion to express herself on the stage in every variety of mood and action was in constant conflict with her abhorrence of publicity

[45]

and her dislike of strangers. Yet even when she strove to please particularly for the benefit of special friends, she was at the mercy of her mood and of her artistic conscience, and, as she wrote to the Whalleys, to whom she had lately become attached and before whom she wished to do herself more than justice at the play: 'Sorry am I to say I have often observed, that I have performed worst when I most ardently wished to do better than ever. Strange perverseness! And this leads me to observe. . . . that those who act mechanically, are sure to be in some sort right, while we who trust to nature (if we do not happen to be in the humour, which, however, Heaven be praised, seldom happens) are dull as anything can be imagined, because we cannot feign.'

The Whalleys had become rather important to Mrs Siddons, for from them she obtained all the affection, sensibility and friendship for which she craved in the wilderness of her tough professional life. Through their warmth of feeling they supplied her with self-confidence: an inner stimulus which she herself was inclined to lack on account of the tremendous barriers of shyness that obstructed her personal relationships. To these people she found that she could talk and be herself. They were the first of the inner circle that she was subsequently to draw round her and include in her private life.

The Rev. Thomas Sedgewick Whalley was a clergyman by calling and an absentee by preference. An unhealthy living in an obscure Lincolnshire fen had procured him a comfortable stipend, while the Bishop of Ely provided him with a suitable curate, who for a consideration gladly undertook to perform his duties. Mr Whalley had therefore leisure to reside in the centre house of the Royal Crescent at Bath where, supported by a succession of rich wives, he devoted himself to the fine arts and earned a local celebrity. Although once on a visit to the French Court he had been referred to by Marie-Antoinette as 'le bel Anglais', Miss Burney, when she met him, was not so impressed. She dismembered him unsparingly, laughed at his affectations and sentimental pathos and ridiculed the tones of languishing dread in which he complained of the sharp winds that blew across the Crescent. His conversation, she recorded, was chiefly about amiable motives and his own feelings.

This curious product was the last word in contemporary

[46]

affectation. He practised all the snobberies of his time. He had the travel mania, the culture mania, and, very violently, the building and collecting mania; he had, in fact, the whole total of literary dilettantisms and artistic pretensions that were committed by eighteenth-century *cognoscenti* in the name of Taste. The best thing that Mr Whalley ever did during his lengthy and rather absurd existence was to befriend Mrs Siddons; and to their mutual honour the friendship continued unblemished through the rest of their lives.

The society that the Whalleys gathered round them at Bath, and whenever possible at their 'Alpine habitation' in the Mendips, included Miss Sophia Weston, 'the leader of a knot of ingenious and charming females at Ludlow,' Mrs Thrale, Hannah More and, in the spirit if not often in the flesh, Anna Seward. That remarkable mixture of gush and sincerity, worth and affectation, the 'Swan of Lichfield', had discovered Mr Whalley for herself a few years earlier when his poem *Edwy and Edilda* had appeared; and with this literary introduction the languishing clergyman had become the Edwy of Miss Seward's correspondence. 'Edwy, my dear Edwy, teach thy Amelia and thy Siddons to love me!' the Swan had rapturously written. 'Sophia's heart, that mine of mental wealth, is affianced to me already, if my horrid figure and embarrassed dialect do not blot the fair compact!' It was, to be sure, an extravagant way of expressing her feelings, but Miss Seward, although she later lost patience with poor, foolish Sophia Weston, retained her admiration for Mrs Siddons throughout her life.

Unfortunately, however, one member of the circle presided over by Whalley turned out to be a sad disappointment. A certain Samuel Jackson Pratt, known pseudonymously as 'Courtenay' and 'Melmoth', had, after being a failure in the Church and equally unsuccessful on the stage, become a lecturing bookseller at Bath. He was tall and genteel and something of a literary charlatan, and had locally acquired a nebulous prestige among the more susceptible elements of the population. He inclined to the society of dowagers and neglected women and was remarkable for his powers of flattery. He had written ten undistinguished plays, but his 'Sympathy', a poem, enjoyed some success, 'on account of the sensibility which was the soul of its production'. So it was that he seized upon Mrs

Siddons, who was always rather impressed by plausible persons, and although she later detected his baseness, she at that time obtained great benefit from his teaching and responded whole-heartedly to his proffered friendship and valuable advice.

One of Pratt's plays was *The Fair Circassian*. This he particularly hoped that she would be able to perform in, but the part was eventually given to Miss Farren. It ran for nineteen nights and Sarah followed its fortune with not the slightest tinge of resentment.

Some time in 1780 she was seen by Thomas Sheridan, who had come to Bath for his health. He remembered her poor exhibition at Drury Lane in *The Runaway*; he also remembered Garrick's observation that 'she possessed enough powers to delight and electrify an audience'. And although he saw her playing after one of her hurried returns from Bristol, when her luggage had failed to arrive and she acted in day clothes, 'no disadvantage of dress could conceal her transcendental merit' from the elder Sheridan's discerning eye. He rushed round to the green-room, full of felicitation and advice. He heard her story, listened to her hesitations, sponsored her cause and, on returning to London, brought all his persuasions to bear on his powerful son at Drury Lane. During that year Richard Brinsley Sheridan certainly tried to engage her for London but apparently with no success. Sarah was happy at Bath and fully occupied, with a secure position and immense popularity. She gave birth to, but lost in infancy, another daughter, Frances Emilia, who died on 26th April and is registered in Bath Abbey. She was bringing in much money to Palmer who again improved his theatre and raised his prices as the result of her profitable acting. She introduced her sister, Frances Kemble, on the Bath stage, and in fact had become so much a resident that she felt she could stay there for ever. Economically considered, a successful position at Bath was a security set beside the gamble of a London venture. But she had calculated without destiny or her professional conscience. The machinery which had been set in motion by Sheridan's correspondence caught her up in its wheels, and during the season of 1781–82, when she was apparently ensconced for good in the hearts of Bath audiences as their most shining ornament, she closed with the offer to revisit Drury Lane. 'This was,' she wrote, 'to me a triumphant moment.' The opportunity to rehabilitate herself upon the scene of her previous mortifications was, after all, the opportunity of her life. She accepted it with enthusiasm, and all too late a movement was set on foot to retain her services a little longer for Bath. Palmer, hitherto apathetic, now offered her an increased salary, and the papers printed a statement to the effect that he was doing his best to secure her for another year from the grasp of Sheridan.

*   *   *

The courage shown by Mrs Siddons was characteristic. She was staking an enviable provincial position for a wild uncertainty in London. At Bath she was known, admired and adored; in London she would have to start afresh, risking again the odds of rivalry and intrigue, worldly machinations to fight against which she was ill-equipped. Enthusiasts had certainly praised her in London, and the combined trumpetings of Henderson, old Sheridan and the Duchess of Devonshire, who had become her ardent supporter, had each a decided effect in their respective spheres.

The Bathonians were beyond measure distressed at Sarah's resolution. 'Remember me to your charming Mrs Siddons,' wrote Miss Weston to Whalley. 'I should imagine her loss and Lord North's new tax, when they both fall, must inevitably ruin Palmer's new theatre. . . . What a pity this man did not sooner become sensible to Mrs Siddons's value and his own interest! The terms he has now offered, were she at liberty to accept them, would be such a security to her ease and happiness (which, with all her merit, I am afraid is not so certain in town), that one cannot help lamenting such perverse infatuation.'

There was no looking backward for the Siddonses, and the negotiations were completed. On 9th February 1782, Sarah took her first benefit as Zara in *The Mourning Bride*. She followed it up with Nell in *The Devil to Pay* as an afterpiece. As in the previous year, the occasion called for special arrangements and the crowds were so overwhelming that the pit was turned into stalls, the pittites pushed up into a section of the gallery and in the box office subscriptions were entered up to twenty guineas. The benefit brought in £146 – but it was quite eclipsed in sensation by the farewell benefit given to Mrs Siddons on 21st May. She had determined to make it a memorable occasion and was to play *The Distressed Mother*, Phillips's version of *Andromaque*. The title was aptly chosen, as the audience were presently to learn. The advertisement of the performance announced that: '*At the end of the Play Mrs Siddons will deliver a Poetical Address (written by herself) in the course of which she will produce to the Audience* THREE REASONS *for her quitting this Theatre.*'

This performance was to be followed by a Holiday Fête and the Farce *The Devil to Pay* – '*Nell, (by particular desire,) Mrs Siddons.*' A footnote added that William Siddons begged leave to say that the Entertainments between the Address and Farce were '*not only calculated to please, but to fill up the time, while Mrs Siddons dresses, which otherwise would hang very heavy on the audience.*'

This intimation was all that the public was permitted to know, and Sarah kept her secret well. Not an actor or a scene-shifter knew what was coming. When the play was over she came down to the front of the stage and began her address. It is curious enough to be reproduced in full.

MRS SIDDONS'S THREE REASONS

Have I not raised some expectation here? –
Wrote by herself? – What! authoress and player?
True, we have heard her, – thus I guess'd you'd say,
With decency recite another's lay;
But never heard, nor ever could we dream
Herself had sipp'd the Heliconian stream.
Perhaps you farther said – Excuse me pray,
For thus supposing all that you might say –
What will she treat of in this same address,
Is it to shew her learning? – Can you guess?
Here let me answer – No; far different views
Possess'd my soul, and fir'd my virgin Muse;
'Twas honest gratitude, at whose request
Shamed be the heart that will not do its best.
The time draws nigh when I must bid adieu
To this delightful spot – nay even to you –

To you, whose fost'ring kindness rear'd my name,
O'erlooked my faults, but magnified my fame.
How shall I bear the parting? Well I know
Anticipation here is daily woe.
Oh! could kind Fortune, where I next am thrown,
Bestow but half the candour you have shewn.
Envy o'ercome, will hurl her pointless dart,
And critic gall be shed without its smart,
The numerous doubts and fears I entertain
Be idle all – as all possessed in vain. –
But to my promise. If I thus am blessed,
In friendship link'd, beyond my worth caress'd –
Why don't I here, you'll say, content remain,
Nor seek uncertainties for certain gain?
What can compensate for the risks you run;
And what your reasons? Surely you have none.
To argue here would but your time abuse:
I keep my word – my reason I produce.

At this information Mrs Siddons, herself far advanced in
yet another pregnancy, went to the wings and returned with
her three children; Maria, no doubt, in her arms, Henry and
Sally clinging to her on either side.

These, she declaimed,
       are the moles that bear me from your side;
Where I was rooted – where I could have died.
Stand forth, ye elves, and plead your Mother's cause;
Ye little magnets, whose soft influence draws
Me from a point where every gentle breeze
Wafted my bark to happiness and ease –
Sends me adventurous on a larger main,
In hopes that you may profit by my gain.
Have I been hasty? Am I then to blame;
Answer, all ye who own a parent's name?
Thus have I tried you with an untaught Muse,
Who for your favour still most humbly sues,
That you, for classic learning will receive
My soul's best wishes, which I freely give –
For polished periods round, and touched with art, –
The fervent offering of my grateful heart.

[51]

This effort at composition produced less surprise than the nature of its revelation. The address created a sensation; and when at her Bristol benefit she again produced her *Three Reasons* there was a not unexpected reaction in the professional world. It was thought that, what with her husband and children, Mrs Siddons was rather overdoing it; and two local actresses were heard to declare their intention of producing *Reasons* for not leaving the Bristol stage.

This last profitable season yielded Mrs Siddons £393 in benefits alone, while in addition a group of gentlemen had presented her with sixty guineas in order to ensure themselves seats in anticipation of the expected rush for places. She considered that this was a most gratifying gesture. Mr Whalley had forestalled events by composing a set of verses on her being engaged at Drury Lane in 1781, and, although the attempt was slightly premature, it had gone to press on the wings of his enthusiasm.

*   *   *

The farewell at Bath was over. Sarah, whose fifth child Elizabeth Ann had been born on 2nd June, had given her last performance on 19th June as Mrs Belville in *The School for Wives*. The next three months were spent in mild touring and in holiday-making. She still had doubts with regard to Drury Lane. The old bogy of her inadequate voice-production, Woodfall's original criticism, once again reared its head, and the apprehension was fostered by her friends. Her voice had sounded limited at the Orchard Street house, and the reason for this, the bad construction of the theatre, had apparently occurred to nobody.

In July she played at Bristol, and in August she set out for Weymouth to rejoin her husband and children who had gone there for the sea air. Her letter to Mrs Whalley describing the journey and the occupants of the coach is a strong proof of her often disputed sense of humour; a sense peculiarly her own. Throughout the caricaturing description Sarah Siddons is present as a spectator. She can be felt sitting back in the coach, silent and darkly dignified, observing every detail through her large, melancholy eyes; preserving subconsciously every characteristic of her fellow travellers.

[52]

'We were,' she wrote, 'five of us in the machine, all females but one, a youth of about sixteen, and the most civilized being you can conceive, a native of Bristol, too.

'One of the ladies was, I believe, verily a little insane; her dress was the most peculiar, and manner the most offensive, I ever remember to have met with; her person was taller and more thin than you can imagine, her hair raven black, drawn as tight as possible over her cushion before and behind, and at the top of her head was placed a solitary fly-cap of the last century, composed of materials of about twenty sorts, and as dirty as the ground; her neck, which was a thin scrag of a quarter of a yard long, and the colour of a walnut, she wore uncovered for the solace of all beholders, her Circassian was an olive-coloured cotton of three several sorts, about two breadths wide in the skirt, and tied up exactly in the middle in one place only. She had a black petticoat, spotted with red, and over that a very thin white muslin one, with a long black gauze apron, and without the least hoop. I never in my life saw so odd an appearance, and my opinion was not singular, for whenever we stopped, she inspired either mirth or amazement, but was quite innocent of it herself. On taking her seat amongst us at Bristol, she flew into a violent passion on seeing one of the windows down; I said I would put it up if she pleased. "To be sure," said she. "I have no ambition to catch my death." No sooner had she done with me, but she began to scold the woman who sat opposite to her for touching her foot: "You have not been used to riding in a coach, I *fancy*, good woman!" She met in this lady a little more spirit than she had found in me, and we were obliged to her for keeping this unhappy woman in tolerable order the remainder of the day. Bless me! I had almost forgot to tell you that I was desired to make tea at breakfast. Vain were my endeavours to please this strange creature; she had desired to have her tea in a basin, and I followed her directions as near as it was possible in the making her tea, but she had no sooner tasted it than she bounced to the window and threw it out, declaring she had never met with a set of such awkward, ill-bred people; what could be expected in a stage-coach, indeed? She snatched the canister from me, poured a great quantity into the basin, with sugar, cream and water, and drank it altogether.

[53]

'. . . The remaining part of our journey was made almost intolerable by her fretfulness; one minute she was screaming out that the coachman should overturn us; she was sure he would, because she would not give him anything for neglecting to keep her trunk dry; and, though it was immoderately hot, we were obliged very often to sit with the windows up, for she had been told that the air was pestilential after sunset, and that however other people liked it, she did not choose to hazard her life by sitting with the windows open. All were disposed, for the sake of peace, to let her have her own way, except the person whom we were really obliged to for quieting her every now and then. She had been handsome, but was now, I suppose, sixty years old. I pity her temper, and am sorry for her situation, which I have set down as a disappointed old maid.'

While Sarah was at Weymouth, there was actually some question of deferring her London appearance. The reason is not very clear. Linley thought that a 'partial' appearance would do justice neither to herself nor to her management. The veteran Mrs Crawford was giving them a good deal of trouble, and of this old lady Sarah hoped the coast would soon be clear.

Part Two: Drury Lane
1782–1802

In private life she shines as on the stage;
Is both the favorite of the town and age.
Describes in each a great, a glorious course,
Gives life to language, or to morals force.
Ye critics, say, where most does Siddons shine,
In love or virtue, or in parts divine?

THE ACTOR'S BUDGET 1811

'. . . Were a Wild Indian to ask me, What was like a queen? I
would have bade him look at Mrs Siddons.' – TATE WILKINSON

TOWARDS the end of September 1782 – 'the year Mrs Siddons came to London and raised the price of salts and hartshorn,' as Tate Wilkinson said – laconic hints of her return to the London stage began to creep into the Drury Lane bills. They announced that 'Mrs Siddons (From the Theatre Royal, Bath) will shortly make her appearance at this Theatre in a Capital Character in Tragedy'. She and her family were at last in London, and actually settled in lodgings at 149, Strand. There had been some doubt as to which of her parts would create the best impression. She, at first, had felt like letting herself go in the vehemence of *The Grecian Daughter*, but the soberer judgement of her friend, the elder Mr Sheridan, was strongly in favour of her playing Isabella, her most successful pathetic rôle, and one that he had seen her perform countless times at Bath, where its never-failing effect upon members of the audience had been to rend their hearts and, so far as was physically possible, to dissolve their eyes. *Isabella, or The Fatal Marriage*, was consequently decided upon and was billed for 10th October, and for the fortnight preceding her début Mrs Siddons ran through the whole gamut of suspense. By the time that she was ready for the event she was only barely in command of herself.

Thomas Sheridan accompanied her to rehearsals, for she had told him that only on the stage itself would she be able to show him what she could do with her part. Her assimilation of a character was invariably made through solitary study,

Hours of concentration on the text of a play would form their slow deposit in her mind, and there germinate until the rehearsal. Then, and only then, did she create aloud the character that had been so gradually conceived.

When she was called to rehearse *Isabella* she was in a state of panic. Remembering the pessimistic warnings of her friends, she hardly dared to speak loudly for fear of the consequences; but gradually losing herself in the part, she warmed up and unconsciously threw out her voice. It carried magnificently into every part of the house. She next noticed that her companions were beginning to cry, which, for her, was always a sign that things were going well. The second, and last, rehearsal, on 8th October, 'was even more affecting than the first,' she wrote in her notes. Tom King, at that time manager of Drury Lane, was enthusiastic in his applause, and even her small eight-year-old son Henry, playing Isabella's child, was deceived by the realism of his mother's acting. In the scene of her death-bed she revealed such mortal agonies that Master Harry wailed and wept in a flood of tears at the distressing sight. But that evening on returning home she was appalled with a discovery. She found that she was losing her voice. A hoarseness, entirely due to nerves, had set in which redoubled her fears and worries. The next morning, after a succession of dull, dark days, the sun was out, and the voice slightly better. She had slept, and from sheer exhaustion did not wake until midday. She missed her last rehearsal, and was allowed to sleep on. The sun and her voice were both in the best form on the morning of 10th October. Mrs Siddons always attached importance to omens. A bright day was an omen and to her on this day of all others a most auspicious one. She passed it, however, in worry and fearful uncertainty, in spite of the successful rehearsals, and with the evening Roger Kemble came round to give her moral support and to escort her to Drury Lane. William was in one of his useless agitations and kept far away from the theatre.

Mrs Siddons, left alone in her dressing-room, was seized by a mood peculiar to her deeply reserved nature. In her own words, 'I, in one of what I call my desperate tranquillities, which usually impress me under terrific circumstances, there completed my dress, to the astonishment of my attendants, without uttering one word, though often sighing most profoundly.' Her indomitable heart was for once in her boots. As she passed on her way to the wings she met her father hovering behind the scenes in an equal state of emotion and uncertainty. A moment later she was on the stage, facing 'the awful consciousness that one is the sole object of attention to that immense space, lined as it were with human intellect from top to bottom, and all around. . . .' To her the occasion was indescribable and unforgettable.

The evening made theatrical history. It was only comparable with Garrick's first appearance, and only equalled by that of Kean many years later. Sarah Siddons as Isabella made such a tremendous impression upon her audience that the house was drowned out in tears, while one miserable woman, having unsuccessfully endeavoured to suppress her distress, went into convulsions and, according to one paper, 'continued in that miserable state for a considerable time after the curtain dropt.' In *The Fatal Marriage* the principal note was grief, and eighteenth-century audiences found themselves chilled with horror at being witnesses of innocence in such desperate straits. For here innocence and tenderness were betrayed into the darkest alleys of guilt, bigamy and suicide. All spectators underwent the strongest feelings of horror and compassion, and the part gave Sarah a magnificent opportunity for displaying her moving pathos and simplicity. She was well supported on the stage by 'Gentleman' Smith as Biron, and Palmer as Villeroy; while Packer, Farren and Wrighten were the other chief players.

Tumultuous acclamations from the audience broke out before the play had come to its conclusion; the curtain came down upon a scene of wild enthusiasm, and, as Mrs Siddons triumphantly wrote to Whalley, 'I thought they would not suffer Mr Packer to end the play.' But the heroine of the night was too overcome to do more than conclude her part. She left unrecited the epilogue that had been specially composed for her by Pratt, and she returned home more dead than alive. She was speechless, exhausted and in her most solemn mood. The occasion affected her deeply.

At home with her husband and father she sat down to a 'frugal neat supper' in silence; the meal being only punctuated at intervals by hysterical interjections from William who was unable to believe in this sudden turn of the wheel of fortune. Old Kemble from time to time gave way to tears of joy, and an immense relief surrounded the family party. Sarah that night lay long awake and turned over in her mind the events of the miraculous evening. Her thoughts, untroubled for the first time for weeks, were characteristic. 'Who can conceive,' she gravely wrote in her memoranda, 'the intenseness of that reverie?' It is a wonder that she slept at all; what with the reverberating echoes of applause, and the vast impression of multitudes revolving kaleidoscopically in her memory among wigs and wings and sets and lights and machinery across the large dimensions of the stage that she occupied with such conspicuous effect. She did sleep, however, deeply, until late in the next day, when any doubts that she might possibly have entertained as to her overwhelming triumph in every class of opinion were dispelled by the arrival of the newspapers.

The critics had gone to the theatre prepared, if not to condemn, at least to be well on their guard. The preliminary puffing of Mrs Siddons which for weeks past had filled the Press, although a usual form of publicity, had this time been pushed to extremes. For this William was responsible, whose zeal in the matter, as in others, outdid his discretion; and it is only owing to his wife's shining ability that there was not an organized campaign against her. As things were the papers were disarmed. The *Morning Chronicle* was tamed by her excellence, noting incessant applause during the fourth and fifth acts; and the *Morning Post* placed her above the great Mrs Cibber, dwelt in detail upon her 'minute beauties' in playing, 'necessary to complete a great actress', and considered that her control over Isabella's conflicting passions 'absolutely beggared praise'. The panegyric concluded with the following sentence: 'A late hour prevents us from dwelling on the merits of this accomplished woman who beyond all comparison is the first tragic actress now on the English Stage.'

* * *

At the end of her first season in London, Thomas Holcroft, in an article in the *English Review* for 1783, discussed her at considerable length. The conclusion at which he arrived was that Isabella was so far her greatest success. The remarkable

[60]

powers of her acting were shown in the immense range and variety of her ability to express the thousand complex moods in which Isabella confronts perplexing situations. Her shading, distinct and admirable, of the varying states of madness and reason as they rapidly succeeded each other, can have been nothing less than a masterpiece. She was, too, in the prime of her life, and easily in appearance one of the most imposing women of her time, although she surpassed her own standards later on, when with years and the added weight of her consequence she became regal in her impressive bearing. But Mrs Siddons at twenty-seven was above the average height, slender, and well covered enough to round off any angles, without the least tendency to robustness. Perfect proportions and well-modelled limbs revealed her graceful movements in any and every attitude – she was always remarkable for her stage falls – and her carriage itself was a lesson in deportment. Her head with its small, Attic shape was later to be disencumbered of its powdered and feathered burdens, for she was to be the first actress to discard convention and adopt the new fashion from Jacobinical France, seeing the necessity for returning to the neo-classic lines based on antiquity. Her features were strong without being coarse, and fascinating in animation. Passion rendered her extremely beautiful, and for the interpretation of all emotions, she brought into play the most irresistible of her many attractions – her formidable, dark, expressive and compelling eyes. These and the flexibility of her brows were perhaps the outer signs, the fingerprints of genius. 'Her eye is large and marking,' wrote Holcroft, 'and her brow capable of contracting to disdain, or dilating with the emotions of sympathy or pity; her memory is tenacious, and her articulation clear, distinct, and penetrating.'

She acted in *The Fatal Marriage* twenty-four times between October and the following June. Horace Walpole, who was persuaded to see the wonder of Drury Lane as Isabella, took pleasure in disagreeing with the friends in his box as to her merits. He by no means thought her the best actress he ever saw; he found her nose and chin trespassed across the prescribed Grecian limits; he hated the 'red powder'[1] on her hair; he

1 But was it powder? There is some evidence for believing that her hair was naturally auburn.

considered that her voice lacked modulation, and deplored the absence of gentility in the movements of her arms. His criticism was evidently provoked by the rhapsodies of his friends, for he lived to become one of her most fervent admirers.

The day after the ordeal she had written to her beloved Mr Whalley, in order that he and his wife should not miss one instant more than was necessary in sharing her joy. She hardly knew what to make of her feelings. She was in a great rush – dining at Linley's – being made much of – rehearsing a new prose tragedy, and being guided by Pratt, whom she believed to be one of her truest friends: 'Never, never let me forget his goodness to me.' The artful Pratt's goodness was delivered chiefly with the view to stand well with an actress who was certain to become an influence in the theatre. He was, after all, the author of plays as well as epilogues; but her impulsive wishes were not yet to be rewarded by her management. 'They won't let me play in Pratty's comedy. How cruel! I am sadly grieved about it.'

The second performance saw a stampede of the *ton* and those who were determined to be in the right place at the right time. In the lobbies there was jostling of very distinguished persons. Lord North and Lady Shelburne were seen; so was Lady Essex; and Mr Sheridan wiped his streaming eyes from the box where he sat surrounded by a galaxy of Linleys. The enormous success of *Isabella* was strengthened by the almost daily improvement of Mrs Siddons's playing. After the first performance her fears were allayed, her habitual calm returned, and she settled down to the business with her accustomed concentration. Her triumph met with its reward at the hands of her employers. The management decided that she was inadequately quartered at the theatre, and instead of dressing in the bowels of the earth she was allotted Garrick's former dressing-room on the stage level. She was overcome at the honour and very gratified. She could now prepare herself at the mirror that had reflected those incomparable grimaces, and she was in no mood to detract from his memory. Indeed, regarding the mirror, she was possessed by 'a vague fanciful hope of a little degree of inspiration from it'. There was, as yet, however, no mention of an increase of salary, and she had only been engaged for the sum of ten guineas a week. She faithfully kept the

Whalleys informed of her successes, and her letters glowed with warmth and exuberance.

'Just at this moment are you, my dear sir, sitting down to supper, and "every guest's a friend." Oh! that I were with you for one half hour. "Oh! God forbid!" says my dear Mrs Whalley; "for he would talk so loud and so fast, that he would throw himself into a fever, and die of unsatisfied curiosity into the bargain." Do I flatter myself, my dear sir? Oh! no; you have both done me the honour to assure me that you love me, and I would not forego the blessed idea for the world. . . .

'I did receive all your letters, and thank you for them a thousand times; one line of them is worth all the acclamations of ten thousand shouting theatres. . . . I have yours and my dear Mrs Whalley's hair in a ring, set round with small gold beads; it looks neat and quiet.'

In her correspondence she found an outlet for the suppressed emotionalism of her temperament. In her ordinary manner she was so far removed from being ecstatic that she was apt to give offence. She had developed a blunt directness, a habit of saying exactly what she thought, so that at first sight she was found disconcerting by strangers, for sensibility, the most cultivated flower in the garden of Georgian graces, left her indifferent unless she was sincerely affected. So it was that she came to be looked upon as a cold and formal woman in private life; hard of feeling, and only able to reproduce the passions on the stage. Her tears, some years later, at Burke's eloquence during the trial of Warren Hastings, were even doubted to be genuine, and were promptly set down by malicious witnesses as exercises in theatrical behaviour.

*   *   *

Public infatuation for Mrs Siddons was immediate and immense. It had one uncommon characteristic: it never abated to any serious degree, notwithstanding short periods of unpopularity, until her death nearly fifty years later. Like Lord Byron she awoke one morning to find herself famous, and famous she remained for the rest of her days. 'To have seen Mrs Siddons,' wrote Hazlitt when she was sixty-one, 'was an event in everyone's life.' Lengthy poetical addresses to her and about her were poured into every corner of the Press. On every side admirers hastened to publish interminable heroics revealing their appreciation of her astounding qualities. From being the fashion she became the rage. She was the most important topic that the newspapers had known for a long time. She was imitated in elegant circles, discussed by the *dilettanti* and mobbed by the common public. Her clothes, her movements and her salary became outstandingly interesting, and the crowning event of the season was the presentation, in November, by one hundred gentlemen of the Bar, of a purse of one hundred guineas on the occasion of her first benefit. To this compliment Mrs Siddons replied in a gracious manifesto, sent to the papers, in which she referred with some wit to the elegant tribute as the most shining circumstance of her whole life.

On 30th October she appeared as Euphrasia in *The Grecian Daughter*. Murphy's play, set in 'A Wild Romantick scene amidst overhanging Rocks', although popular enough, was chiefly built upon the reputation of Mrs Crawford, for whom, in her heyday, it had been written. It was given to Sarah to snatch the diadem from the brows of her elderly rival, and as Euphrasia to astonish crowds by her inspiring loftiness. There was a sensational moment in the play when, with her veil streaming behind her, she rushed upon the stage exhorting the Greeks with the stirring cry of:

War on, Ye heroes!

This moment was, on Campbell's authority, very precious in the recollection of old playgoers, whose faces would glow with pleasure at the recital of the thrilling occasion. But *The Grecian Daughter*, like many of the plays in which she performed, was only a sow's ear woven with artistry into a most presentable silken purse by Mrs Siddons. It was not much more than a superior thriller. It had the effect of producing suspense upon the spectators which could hardly be borne and which, if prolonged, would have been quite intolerable. *The Grecian Daughter* was succeeded on 8th November by *Jane Shore* with Sarah Siddons in the name part – a deeply affecting one in which audiences surrendered immediately and unconditionally, for her acting, said Campbell, was terrible and perfect. It presented the former mistress of Edward IV in the full swing

[64]

of repentance and retribution. Hounded by her enemies, driven from door to door, the starving creature was discovered paying dearly for former gaieties. Penitence, affliction and uncomplaining resignation were the prevailing notes in this sentimental production, and Mrs Siddons played upon them with such verisimilitude that 'A Lady of Distinction writing to her friend in the country' determined that, '*Belvidera, Isabella,* all were obliterated from my mind, and I alone beheld in her the beautiful Magdalen'. Here, as in many other references, one can understand the fascination of her acting. She lost her own identity in that of her interpretation. She was unrecognizable as herself. She became another character each time she re-created a part. The horrible realism in *Jane Shore* of her death by starvation, her emaciated appearance and faintness were depicted by her with such success that the women who saw her went off into hysterics, the men sobbed, and, once more to quote Campbell, 'fainting fits were long and frequent in the house'. Her death scene was apparently 'a succession of astonishing changes. Her eagle eye, obedient to its will, at times parted with its lustre, and, though open, looked sightless and bewildered. . . .' All the same it is not wholly surprising that Mrs Siddons eventually switched over to the part of the shameless Alicia in the same play, more interesting, active and purposeful. Jane Shore's character must have been nauseating to an actress whose intellect was now becoming paramount to her emotions.

On 16th November she appeared as Mrs Montague in *The Fatal Interview*; a prose play which did not survive three performances and was the one unfortunate slip in a triumphant season. She spoke a frivolous epilogue in her comic vein, which was only politely acknowledged, and the offence was withdrawn at once. It was on Sheridan's side an admitted mistake.

A fortnight later, in rivalry to Mrs Yates across the way at Covent Garden, who was playing the same character, Sarah performed the part of Calista in *The Fair Penitent*, one of Rowe's 'she-tragedies' which seemed as though it had been written expressly for her. In this play she was given a magnificent chance for displaying the haughty demeanour that had never been surpassed by any other actress. She exhibited a greater precipitation in all her movements, and an acceleration of nervous gesture. And her eyes moved restlessly and suspiciously. As Calista she scored another triumph. 'Such acting as Mrs Siddons's had never been brought to Rowe's poetry at least during the last century,' volunteered Campbell, although the brilliance of the original cast could hardly have been excelled: it had contained Betterton, Elizabeth Barry and the divine Mrs Bracegirdle. But now Sarah eclipsed every tradition of recent greatness in this popular tragedy, and shattered the reputations of Mrs Cibber, Mrs Yates, Mrs Crawford and Mrs Woffington into a thousand particles.

The chief event of the season was still, however, to come. Her first benefit was given on 14th December, and for this important occasion she chose to play Belvidera in *Venice Preserved*. The audience was tremendously distinguished. Most of the pit was laid into boxes, and the benefit was described as the most remunerative on record. Eight hundred pounds was received on account of subscriptions and presentations which, of course, included the hundred guineas subscribed by the barristers who have already been mentioned, and to whom she enthusiastically referred as 'The whole body of the Law'.

Venice Preserved was a great favourite. Its action is pregnant with violent situations in which horror, anger, love, passion and sacrifice followed each other with heart-stirring rapidity. Mrs Siddons's tempestuous Belvidera was characterized by quick transitions of emotion particularly remarkable for their versatility of expression in her face and attitudes, where the finest shades were registered, yet under complete control. Her voice, too, melted with a limpid tenderness which was remarkable, and her meticulous attention to detail was consistent with the part: a positive instance of being 'in nature'. Otway's tragedy, recently revived, remains rich in poetic imagery; and as a medium for her grand, heroic manner no play can have done more in the way of showing off her extraordinary power to fascinate her audience. Her eyes were seen to glare or sparkle at an immense distance from the stage; while the muscular movements of her forehead commanded her expression, conveying her feelings before she had even given utterance to a line of her text.

There exists a copy of *Venice Preserved* in which all the lines emphasized by Mrs Siddons have been heavily scored by her in blue pencil. Her habit was to hand the copy to some person whose judgement she could trust, and who would hear her repeat her part and report on its effect in various corners of the theatre. A specimen is given below of her reading of Belvidera, of which the emotional value of the italicized text in the prompter's copy has been heightened by her own scorings:

> *Oh! give me daggers, fire, or water:*
> *How I could bleed, how burn, how drown, the waves*
> Huzzing and foaming round my sinking head,
> *Till I descended to the peaceful bottom*
> *Oh! there's all quiet,* here *all rage and fury:*
> *The air's too thin and pierces my weak brain;*
> *I long for thick substantial sleep:* Hell! hell!
> Burst from the centre, rage and roar aloud
> *If thou art half so hot, so mad as I am.*

Among the passages marked as though to be omitted in the manager's copy are the lyrical lines into which Belvidera suddenly changes with the wandering of madness:

> *Murmuring streams, soft shades, and springing flowers!*
> *Lutes, laurels, seas of milk, and ships of amber!*

But the real moment for which the audience waited so breathlessly was that in which Mrs Siddons, in her softest and tenderest tones, repeated her assignation:

> *Farewell! Remember Twelve!*

For this moment the house was absolutely hushed – but it invariably broke into a roar of enthusiasm as the words died gently away through the remotest arches of the auditorium.

*   *   *

Apart from its prestige as a play-house Drury Lane was not conspicuous for the practicability of its design. Its chief inconvenience lay in the planning of the various entrances, those to the pit lying close to the orchestra. Here the door-keepers maintained an officious control by means of the box-screw into which they clamped late arrivals. The effect of this operation was to admit with the newcomer a blast of polar air on to the mass within, and this, according to Boaden, 'occasioned *fits* among the women and *fights* among the men,' during which pandemonium the entire proceedings on the stage were suspended, and actors and audience transferred their attention to the struggles in the pit. On these occasions the behaviour of the stars furnished an interesting commentary on their characters. The exquisite Miss Farren, for instance, was apt to glance at her acquaintance in the boxes for commiseration and sympathy; Mrs Jordan, on the other hand, always took her cue with unfailing accuracy, breaking into one of her devastating peals of laughter the moment that order was restored. But Mrs Siddons was accustomed to commotion; she could never be quite sure whether the struggle in the pit was occasioned by the rush to see her, or resulted from the fits of hysterics that overtook so many of her admirers. It is, however, a fact that during her first great London season the sums drawn into the Drury Lane treasury exceeded all former receipts; and the management, as well it might, decided upon giving her an extra benefit.

SEVEN

THE insensate popularity which Mrs Siddons enjoyed might well have been expected to turn her head. Voices were not wanting to warn the public against idolatry, against disloyalty to the honourable dead. Tom Davies was determined not to be swept up by the resistless torrent of adulation. His moderation was excellent and admirable, but it had no effect. He praised the public's fervour, and hoped it would be lasting; but he continued: 'I hope without that impatience to their old servants which will make their passion for Mrs Siddons less valuable, as it will convey a warning to her that a new face may possibly erase the impression which she has so anxiously studied to form, and so happily made.'

Mrs Siddons, on her part, was overwhelmed by her reception. She hastened to assure her admirers that she was unlikely to abuse their confidence, and after the excitements of *Venice Preserved*, and its enormous emoluments, she felt that an acknowledgement was called for. She wrote a letter to the papers in which she declared that: 'She knows the danger arising from extraordinary and unmerited favours, and will carefully guard against any approach of pride, too often their attendant. Happy shall she esteem herself if, by the utmost assiduity, and constant execution of her poor abilities, she shall be able to lessen, though hopeless ever to discharge, the vast debt she owes to the public.' It was an unnecessarily servile method of expressing a full heart, but it was sincere recognition all the same.

*　　　*　　　*

Mrs Siddons began the New Year of 1783 with intentions as laudable as they were unwise; for on 6th January she pushed forward her sister, Frances Kemble, into the limelight of Drury Lane by introducing her as Alicia to her own Jane Shore. It was an unfortunate instance of family clannishness. As it was known that Miss Kemble was very like her sister in personal appearance there had been a good deal of excitement about the début. Public curiosity was indescribable; and by three o'clock in the afternoon there was no means of approach to the theatre. The doors finally opened, admitting a hysterical crowd that stampeded the entrances; crushing many women, laming others, and picking the pockets of most. The better part was obtained by the thousands who were turned away from the theatre. They missed nothing. Miss Kemble's resemblance to her sister was as that of an empty shell. The audience were polite and encouraging, but the Press insisted that she had no merits at all. She limped through a few seasons on the strength of her connexions, and eventually vanished from Drury Lane on her marriage to Francis Twiss, the dramatic critic. She had, said Tate Wilkinson, a well-informed mind and a sound understanding. But her talents were destined to be put to a more scholarly use than in the theatre. Some years later, she opened at Bath a select academy for the education of young ladies. It proved to be a most successful and popular institution. In 1807, when she was firmly established and being sought out by refined mothers with delicate blossoms to be educated, her advertisement was most genteel:

'Mrs Twiss, No 24, Camden Place, Bath, receives under her care young ladies from the age of fourteen to twenty. Board 100 guineas per annum. Entrance five guineas. The young ladies may be introduced into the best company, and the utmost attention will be paid to their morals, conduct, and manners. Masters will be provided to teach such accomplishments as may be thought necessary. Mrs Twiss has no objection to taking a few young ladies of any age under twelve. Board and washing, English, French, Italian, writing, and arithmetic, 100 guineas per annum. Entrance five guineas. In each year one vacation only, which will last six weeks. Three months' notice will be required on the removal of any young lady.' Mrs Twiss did not add to her prospectus, as her younger sister, Anne, would have done, that she was 'sister to the celebrated Mrs Siddons', for this fact was known to the whole of Bath, and Mrs Siddons as a relative was an unqualified asset. One of the girls at 24, Camden Place was an adopted daughter of the Prince of Wales; but then, 'Aunt Twiss's School', as Fanny Kemble wrote in her memoirs, 'participated in the favour which everything even remotely associated with Mrs Siddons received from the public'.

Not satisfied with having forced the elder of her sisters upon London, Mrs Siddons managed to have the next, Elizabeth, introduced at Drury Lane as Portia, with even less success than that of Frances. The most that could be said for her was remarked by the *General Advertiser*, which journal considered that, although she merited encouragement, 'she was not entitled to applause'.

*   *   *

The final seal upon Sarah's authenticity had been set by the Royal Family. Early in 1783 they went to see her play, and so impressed were the King and Queen by the performance of the new tragic actress that the royal prejudice to Mr Sheridan and his politics was overlooked, and they went a second time. They then insisted on seeing Mrs Siddons in all her parts. The tender heart of George III was invariably touched at her poignant passages. The tears that filled his eyes were noted by Mrs Siddons with composed satisfaction, and when she became too realistic Queen Charlotte was sometimes obliged to turn her back to the stage, finding the effect upon her emotions 'indeed doo disagreble', as she herself told the actress in her Teutonic English. But the King had some independent views about the drama and about acting, and when he sent for Mrs Siddons to read to the Royal Family, it was to tell her among compliments that he had tried to catch her out in a single note of false emphasis, and had failed; whereas he had found Smith constantly to be falsely emphasizing. He praised her repose on the stage, a quality which he had thought lacking in Garrick, for 'he was a great fidget – he never could stand still'. But when the King wished Miss Burney to share his enthusiasm for Mrs Siddons he met with steady and persistent discouragement, for she pettishly hung back: she disagreed with every word he said.

[71]

And when pressed to reply to the royal criticism by a kindly 'What! What!' – 'I still said nothing,' she confided to her diary, 'for I could not concur where I thought so differently, and to enter into an argument was quite impossible.'

Both the King and the Queen were convinced of the superior qualities of Mrs Siddons, and they gave her a Court appointment. It was only nominal but it was full of honour. She was made Preceptress in English Reading to the Princesses, and was therefore commanded to Buckingham House. She arrived at the palace in a ceremonial sacque without which it was not permissible to appear before the Queen. In addition to its formal inconveniences it was trammelled by a hoop, treble ruffles and lappets. For purposes of declamation she felt that her style might well become cramped. At first she waited in an antechamber, chatting with some people she already knew; and presently from the drawing-room emerged George III, engaged in the innocuous pleasure of drawing along in a little wicker chair his youngest daughter, the three-year-old Princess Amelia. The child, left to trot about the room while the King embarked on a conversation with one of the guests, made straight for Mrs Siddons, attracted by the flowers in her bosom. Sarah was touched and pleased, and wished to kiss her. But the pretty little creature, remembering her rank, extended her hand to the actress's lips. The rebuke was accepted and the hint complied with. Here was a lesson in royalty to be absorbed.

With the Queen's arrival the reading began. Mrs Siddons, conscious of her court dress, was horribly nervous. She read on and on. She refused to take any refreshment and she was prepared to stand there till she collapsed. The truth was that she dared not risk an attempt to back away from the royal presence in her cumbersome hoop upon the highly polished floor. The Queen found that she behaved with great decorum and self-confidence, but when this was repeated to her Sarah was rather surprised. Queenly dignity came to her easily and naturally, and, 'At any rate,' she commented, 'I had frequently personated queens.' But royal interest pursued its new favourite even further. The King was told that Mrs Siddons was accustomed to use white paint upon her face and neck in the theatre; an impression due probably to the magnolia-like pallor of her skin. He sent her a message through Sir Charles Hotham to warn her of its evil effects. She was gratified by the personal solicitude of her Sovereign but she was incensed at being under suspicion of a practice she considered disgusting; she denied the charge with a certain indignation.

*   *   *

At the end of March Miss Seward took a holiday from her valetudinarian existence at Lichfield, and came up to London mainly with the object of seeing Mrs Siddons in some of her great tragic parts. On arrival she found it impossible to get into any part of the theatre. She had to wait a few days, after which her experience at Drury Lane was duly retailed in a gushingly enthusiastic letter to Whalley. Her 'Siddonian idolatry' had led her to undergo the discomforts of a crushed and stampeding crowd. She had found the experience well worth the trouble. 'Every attempt fruitless to procure boxes,' she wrote. 'I saw her for the first time, at the hazard of my life, by struggling through the terrible, fierce, maddening crowd into the pit. She only could have recompensed the terrors and dangers of the attempt; and the recompense was full! She far outstrips that ideal perfection which, through life, I have vainly searched for in the theatre. Her energy, her pathos, her majestic scorn, is inspired by the same sensibility and nobleness of soul which produces all the varied expressions of those passions in Giovanni's singing, and casts the Yates, the Crawfords and the Younges at the same immeasurable distance, at which he throws every other singer in the world. I have seen her in *Jane Shore* and in *Calista* – conceive with what rapture, for it is impossible to describe it. I am as devoted to her as yourself, and my affection keeps pace with my astonishment and delight; for I have conversed with her, hung upon every word which fell from that charming lip; but I never felt myself so awed in my life. The most awkward embarrassment was the consequence.'

In London indeed it had become the right thing to be acquainted with Mrs Siddons. Partly from curiosity, mostly because it was the fashion, and a little from genuine interest, a run had begun on her lodgings. Her carriage was mobbed by crowds upon her entrances and exits, and coaches, chaises and phætons were seen day after day, wedged together in the universal rush to the Strand. Their occupants greatly hoped to obtain a near sight of the goddess who had brought back tears and tragedies into such prominence. Hostesses gone mad with lionizing struggled to obtain her as their guest of honour; but, approvingly wrote Horace Walpole, she was modest and sensible. 'She declines great dinners, and says the business and cares of her family take her whole time.' But there were occasions on which she was dissuaded from her resolution, experiences which were usually bitterly repented. One of these was the famous evening at Miss Monckton's. This young lady was a curiosity. She was a 'Blue'; she was vivacious, she was eccentric and she was grotesque. Her short, squat body, her diamonds, her excessive rouge and her towering head-dresses made her general appearance so close to one of Rowlandson's corpulent and plumed monstrosities that, when she later became Countess of Cork and Orrery, she was compared by Jekyll to a shuttlecock – all Cork and feathers. At this time she was still living in a lively and eccentric manner at her mother's house in Charles Street, in which, according to Boswell, she used to entertain the finest 'bit of blue' in the country. To add to her collection she very naturally pursued Mrs Siddons. Mrs Siddons, on the explicit understanding that only a very few ladies of her acquaintance were to be bidden, accepted the invitation, and with her little boy, Harry, arrived at eight o'clock in a most modest toilette, determined to leave early in the evening.

There were, as she had expected, three or four mutual friends; and the evening looked like passing off quietly enough, when, just as she was rising to leave, on the door of that house where guests arrived unannounced, came a tremendous thundering. A host of people poured in – a ceaseless influx. They filled the house, they overflowed the reception-rooms, and for Mrs Siddons there was absolutely no way of escape. She was desperate. She sat down again and resigned herself to a situation that exasperated and appalled her. There seemed to be no end to the perfidy of Miss Monckton. The room became so full that the visitors clambered on to chairs in order to stare over the heads of others at the guest of the evening. When there was no rule to guide them, the vaunted manners of Georgian society hardly bore inspection. The only person in the room who seems to have been at all useful was Thomas Erskine,[1] whose 'benevolent politeness' eased the situation for Sarah; and even he was tactless enough to discuss her and her acting under her very nose with another woman without once deferring to her opinion. She was then sacrificed to a group of learned ladies who plied her with earnest questions which she thought were ridiculous. And she was natural and frank enough to admit that she could understand very little of what they were talking about so profoundly. When it transpired that they were 'Blues' the occasion was laughed at all over London for the rest of the winter.

It was at this alarming evening that Miss Burney first met Mrs Siddons, recording in her most condescending style that she behaved with great propriety, and was calm, modest and unaffected. But she found 'a steadiness in her manner and deportment by no means engaging'. It is plain that Sarah made not the least attempt to conceal her feelings. Mrs Thrale, who was sitting quite near at the time, was also astonished at the silence of this distinguished statue. 'Why,' she cried gaily, 'this is a leaden goddess we are all worshipping! However, we shall soon gild it.' The comfortable optimism with which she was upholstered made difficulties lessen considerably for Mrs Thrale. But the unfortunate victim was plainly at a disadvantage. She answered her admirers brusquely. All her defences were up, and she would have given worlds to have escaped the ordeal. Cumberland, in his *Observer*, satirized the whole affair. It culminated with the presentation of 'a young muse' to Mrs Siddons: 'a girl in a white frock with a fillet of flowers tied round her hair, which hung down her back in flowing curls. The young muse made a low obeisance and, with the most unembarrassed voice and countenance, whilst the poor actress was covered with blushes, and suffering torture from the eyes of all in the room, broke forth as follows:

> *O thou, whom Nature's goodness calls her own,*
> *Pride of the stage and favourite of the town!'*

It is not surprising that Mrs Siddons preferred declining invitations.

[1] Thomas, later 1st Baron Erskine.

She was also invaded in her most private moments. On one occasion in spite of repeated denials, a party of five ladies had themselves ushered into her drawing-room. They were headed by a tall, distinguished and delicate-looking woman, a person, discreetly wrote Sarah, 'of very high rank', who spoke in broad Scots, and had come to stare at her. She was, it appeared, too ill to go to the theatre, and her doctor had advised her to inspect Mrs Siddons in her own home. She sat down, stared at the actress until she could stare no longer, and after a few embarrassing moments rose and apologized. Mrs Siddons quite rightly felt that such insolence could not be overlooked. She allowed the distinguished visitor to depart as gracefully as she might without helping her out of her situation by so much as a single word. To her own considerate mind a great lack of breeding had been exhibited.

These incidents, painful and embarrassing though they might have been, were compensated for by the attention and homage which were paid to her by men of the greatest influence and intellectual weight. Night after night to the theatre came the wits and the statesmen. Burke and Sheridan, Reynolds and Windham, Gibbon and Fox, constantly occupied seats in the orchestra; and Fox's saturnine and swarthy face was more often than not suffused in tears. Sometimes they would be joined by the Prince of Wales; at others he accompanied them round to her dressing-room. It was thought that the Prince dared at one moment to fancy his chances with her. But, as a malicious wit remarked, 'One would as soon think of making love to Mrs Siddons as to the Archbishop of Canterbury.'

The brilliant season closed on 5th June with a final performance of *Isabella*. From a repertory of seven plays, Mrs Siddons had altogether given eighty performances within eight months: an average of three a week. And if the feat may appear moderate when judged by contemporary records, it should be remembered that she was expected to play different parts on alternate nights, and not in a sequence of 'runs'. *Isabella* alone had been acted twenty-two times. She had played for the benefit of the Theatrical Fund in May, and again for the benefits of the four leading Tragedy actors: Palmer, Smith, Bensley and Brereton. A period of repose might therefore reasonably have been expected. But Mrs

Siddons, reasonable in most things, was completely irrational as a bread-winner. As a haymaker she made the most of the dazzling sunlight. Her energy was incalculable. Four days after the dust sheets enveloped the Theatre Royal, Drury Lane, she set off for Holyhead to fulfil an engagement in Ireland. With her in the postchaise went her husband, her sister Frances, Mr and Mrs Brereton and Francis Aickin, who joined them on the way. In Dublin she was to meet her brother, John Philip Kemble, who, after a period of great popularity over there, had just signed a three-year contract with Drury Lane.

William Brereton had never distinguished himself as an actor until, during the season that had just ended, Mrs Siddons had chosen him to play Jaffier to her Belvidera. If the result of this selection was thrilling for the audience, it was disastrous for poor Brereton. Swept off his feet by the headlong rush of her passionate acting, his imagination had been so fired by the impact of her personality that he rose almost to her own level of playing, and became the ideal Jaffier. The effect it had upon him proved to be his downfall. He subsequently went raving mad, tried to kill his wife, was removed to Hoxton as a lunatic and there died in 1787. And the malicious attributed the tragedy to the heartlessness of Mrs Siddons.

The journey to Ireland in the late eighteenth century was at the best uncomfortable, but a bad crossing must have been unendurable. Sarah Siddons, with her powerful imagination, felt that she was in for a great adventure; she had a terrible crossing. But the dawn of the Romantic revival was throwing a faint glow in the sultry sky; and 'I was awed, but not terrified' – she wrote to Mr Whalley. 'We were lifted mountains high, and sank again as low in an instant. Good God! how tremendous, how wonderful! A pleasing terror took hold on me, which it is impossible to describe, and I never felt the majesty of the Divine Creator so fully before. I was dreadfully sick, and so were my poor sister and Mr Brereton.' And she discovered a great and useful truth. 'Always,' she advised, 'go to bed the instant you go on board, for by lying horizontally, and keeping very quiet, you cheat the sea of half its influence.'

It was long after midnight on 16th June when they arrived in Dublin. Mrs Siddons formed a very poor idea of the country.

To begin with, she was detained by the Customs and shut up for the occasion in a smelly room. At last, when, by two o'clock, they were released and forced to wander about the streets on foot and in the rain in search of lodgings, the women were refused beds in all the taverns. After some difficulty they were finally admitted to some sort of rest through the good offices of Brereton, whose father had come to meet him. But this reception did more to turn Sarah's face against Ireland than any other experience. Dublin she found filthy. The half-naked and distressing objects that infested the streets appalled her, and she disliked the Irish people. 'They are all ostentation and insincerity,' she bluntly wrote, 'and in their ideas of finery very like the French, but not so cleanly; and they not only speak but think coarsely.' From the pecuniary point of view, however, she can have had little to complain of her Irish season. She netted over a thousand pounds and was obliged to admit, though somewhat grudgingly, that she would always be under an obligation to the inhabitants although she could not love them. They disgusted her.

She began her season at Dublin at the Smock Alley theatre under the management of Richard Daly, the unprepossessing seducer of Dora Jordan, and one of the most unscrupulous men in the theatrical business. *Isabella* was performed on 21st June to a brilliant house at extravagant prices, and although she was always certain of admiration from the distinguished elements of the audience, she possessed neither the ease nor the confiding self-assurance which to the intuitive Irish populace was so necessary. She was unable to get into touch with them or to establish the direct personal contact that in a flash would dispel the barrier of the footlights. In Dublin and in Cork she was made to feel that she had enemies. Inimical articles began to appear in the Irish and the English Press, and William Siddons wrote back to England commenting upon there certainly being 'malice on both sides the water', the attacks being ascribed to the pen of envy. At Smock Alley she was exposed to a campaign of hostility. Her temperament was unlikely to appeal to the demonstrative emotionalism of the public, and comments from the gallery were of a familiarity to which she was unaccustomed. Frankly, at cries of 'Sally, me jewel! how are ye?' Mrs Siddons, like another great lady, was not amused.

[78]

The Press sensed her frigid demeanour and began to be insulting. Reviewing a performance of *Isabella* the facetiousness of Peter Seguin was given full rein. 'One hundred and nine ladies fainted! forty-six went into fits! and ninety-five had strong hysterics! The world will scarcely credit the truth when they are told that fourteen children, five old women, one hundred taylors, and six common councilmen, were actually drowned in the inundation of tears that flowed from the galleries, lattices, and boxes, to increase the briny pond in the pit. The water was three feet deep, and the people that were obliged to stand upon the benches, were in that position up to their ankles in tears! . . .

'. . . Nero himself never performed the scene of madness, of grief, of joy, of woe, of distress, of sorrow, and of pity, so well as Mrs S—!

'May the curses of an insulted nation pursue the gentlemen of the college, the gentlemen of the bar, and the peers and peeresses, whose wisdom and discernment have been so highly extolled, that hissed her on the second night. True it is Mr Garrick never could make anything of her, and pronounced her below mediocrity; – true it is, the London audience once did not like her; but what of that? Rise up, bright goddess of the sock and buskin, and soar to unknown regions of immortal praise, for

Envy will Merit as its shade pursue.'

There was a good deal more of this sarcastic journalese, and, as it appeared anonymously, several claimants both in Dublin and London hoped to be considered as the author. But although unimportant in itself, the abusive article was indicative of a section of organized feeling, and worse, indeed, was to happen before long.

Mrs Siddons had been engaged by Daly for a stipulated number of performances in Dublin. She was to play there for twelve nights, and after the charges of the house had been deducted she was to have half the receipts. The charges were estimated at £60. At the end of her short season she wished to perform for the benefit of the Marshalsea prison. For one reason or another she found it impossible to fit in this engagement before she left for Cork, and she sent a contribution to the governors of the Marshalsea. The present was acknowledged in the Press. The sequel to this trivial incident was to have grave consequences in the following year.

In the intervals of acting, however, Sarah enjoyed the full advantages of Irish life. Her brother had already made for himself a great reputation and had been admitted into exclusive and influential circles. Before her arrival Jephson the playwright, then attached to the Lord-Lieutenant, had given a dinner-party at which Lord Inchiquin, proposing the toast, 'The matchless Siddons', had rather theatrically taken from his finger a ring set in diamonds, and had sent it round the table to Kemble for his inspection and criticism. The ring proved to be a miniature of Sarah. Her approaching visit was, in the highest circles, clearly awaited with intense anticipation.

John Philip Kemble had pursued the course of his own star with more than reasonable success. He had tried his hand at writing plays, some of which had been produced, dreary enough though they now seem, in the provinces. He had written a tragedy, *Belisarius*, a comedy, *Oh! It's Impossible*, and had adapted Massinger's *New Way to Pay Old Debts*. The Dublin seasons had been his first important engagement, and on the strength of these he was contracted for the next three years to Drury Lane. He was an exceedingly handsome man; as a player as serious as his sister, though more solemn, more pompous, more didactic and even heavier in the hand; although this weight was certainly relieved by a curious and peculiar sense of humour which combined conviviality and pedantry with extraordinary results.

*   *   *

Soon after the opening of the winter season at Drury Lane, the Royal family attended a command performance of *Isabella*. The party, which consisted of Their Majesties, the Prince of Wales, and the Princesses Royal and Augusta, was embedded in a profusion of elaborate upholstery. The front of their box with its elliptical sweep had been advanced in order not to deprive the pittites from the pleasure of beholding so much splendour as well as from the wish not to obstruct their view. The King, in a plain quaker-coloured suit with gold buttons,

Mrs Siddons rehearsing in the Green Room with her father
and Henderson

From a drawing by Thomas Rowlandson
in the Victoria and Albert Museum

and the Queen, in white satin and splendid diamonds, sat beneath a state canopy almost rivalling in grandeur the silken awnings of Cleopatra. Its dome of crimson velvet was adorned with an elegant cornice and mouldings, carved and gilt with burnished gold, and hangings of more crimson velvet were draped about them with the aid of innumerable valances, cords, knots and tassels.

The two princesses, to the right of their parents, wore blue and white and rose and white figured silks, and were protected by a canopy of blue satin; while the Prince of Wales, under his canopy of blue velvet trimmed with silver, in violent contrast with the sober figure of his father, wore a dark blue suit of Geneva velvet heavily trimmed with gold lace. Mrs Siddons clearly could not have been attended in greater state.

That she had, during her first London season, totally neglected Shakespeare, may have contributed slightly to her disadvantage. For one thing it had the effect of arousing the hostility of certain enemies who were not slow in declaring that she dared not risk the attempt for fear of not succeeding. She confounded these whispered hopes by appearing on 3rd November 1783, shortly after the opening of the season, as Isabella in *Measure for Measure*. It was a part which, played by her, proved something of a revolution. Not since her failure as Portia had she attempted a character as passionless, as moral, as intellectual and as chaste. She turned the interpretation into a brilliant success. She was lofty; she was the triumph of morality over humanity; she became identified with Uncompromising Principle. The play was just such a one to appeal to the King and Queen. Back they came to Drury Lane for the next performance of *Measure for Measure*. The intense emotion aroused by hearing Mrs Siddons in Isabella's tremendous moralizing –

> *But man, proud man,*
> *Dress'd in a little brief authority,*
> *Most ignorant of what he's most assur'd,*
> *His glassy essence, like an angry ape,*
> *Plays such fantastic tricks before high heaven*
> *As make the angels weep –*

can be best imagined. Its effect must have been overwhelming.

*   *   *

During the same month there occurred the momentous meeting with Dr Johnson. The kindly officiousness of Miss Monckton had again much to do with the acquaintanceship, for she had badgered the infirm lexicographer to go to the theatre and see the great actress for himself. But Johnson was then bearing the burden of his overwhelming physical afflictions. Palsy, dropsy and gout added to blindness and deafness the disabilities under which Mrs Siddons found him when, unable to visit the theatre, he invited her to tea at Bolt Court escorted by their mutual friend William Windham. There was at first no chair to offer her; the room being, possibly, littered with books. The Doctor's excuse was gallant and prompt: 'Madam, you who so often occasion a want of seats to other people will the more easily excuse the want of one yourself.' A chair was finally procured; Mrs Siddons sat down, and Johnson was soon deep in the subject of English drama. Sarah stressed the importance in her opinion of a part being 'in nature', and said that she thought Queen Katharine in *Henry VIII* the most natural of all; an observation calculated to please the Doctor, whose preference for the character was well known. She was anxious to play the part before long at Drury Lane, and to arrange that he should have a seat in one of the wings to protect him from the curiosity of the public; but he never lived to see the project carried out.

It was during this visit that Dr Johnson uttered his classic pronouncement on the celebrated Mrs Pritchard, the virtuous and homely predecessor against whose formidable reputation Mrs Siddons had to contend, for there were many who still remembered her. To Sarah's inquiry the answer was deliberate and awful. 'Madam, Pritchard in common life was a vulgar idiot; she would talk of her *gownd* and she never read any part in a play in which she acted except her own.' Mrs Siddons was scandalized: she could hardly believe her ears; but she later verified the statement. Pritchard indeed, for all her great reputation, had, it seemed, openly and shamelessly confessed to having never read the whole of *Macbeth*, in which, as the Lady,

[82]

she so fascinated her audience. But Johnson then passed on to other great players. To Garrick, of whose career he was still jealous: 'His most enviable qualities were his social talents.' He discussed Mrs Porter's rage and Mrs Clive's sprightliness, and afterwards, as a corollary to Sarah's visit, the Doctor in a letter to Mrs Thrale expressed himself unusually gratified with his new acquaintance. She had, he found, behaved with modesty and propriety, having left behind her no ground for censure. On the contrary, he added: 'Neither praise nor money, the two powerful corrupters of mankind, seem to have depraved her.' It is hardly to be supposed that Mrs Siddons's character was to be corrupted by receiving £10 a week; and as for praise she resisted it with lofty scorn. She mistrusted public idolatry, and during her first season she had feared, with every new part she created, to lose popularity. Her immense ambition was always tempered by diffidence. She visited Dr Johnson several times again before he died, and his invariable custom was to conduct her to the head of the stairs, kiss her hand, bow with great courtesy and say: 'Dear Madam, I am your most humble servant.'

EIGHT

THE next undertaking at Drury Lane gave the public an interest which had been eagerly anticipated. A revival of *The Gamester*, which had not been seen for four years, was staged with John Philip Kemble and Mrs Siddons as the hero and heroine.

The Gamester was an old and established favourite. It still reads passably as a prose play, and the situations, though exasperating, were then apparently considered telling. In a period when tragedy dealt chiefly with the passions of individuals in exalted situations, it was no doubt refreshing to sympathize with the very real troubles of a Mrs Beverley whose husband – a feeble gambling creature – gets into the hands of a thorough-going villain with deep-laid schemes to ruin him and obtain his wife. He makes dishonourable proposals to Mrs Beverley. The fury of indignation with which these advances were received by Mrs Siddons could not have been exceeded had she dealt with them in actual life. 'Wou'd that these eyes had Heaven's own lightning! that with a look, thus I might blast thee!' were her withering words, as, dilating, one may imagine, very perceptibly, her already rather exaggerated nostrils, she made the utmost use of her magnificent eyes and flexible features.

Throughout the play runs the amiable and sentimental character of Jarvis, the old and devoted retainer; anxious, though dismissed, to be useful in the hour of adversity. To the age that fell a victim to deep play the moral of the piece was like a cold plunge. Gaming was the vice of the century, and Moore tried to redeem it by appealing to the softer emotions. *The Gamester* received a brilliant Press and had a tremendous reception. The audience responded to Mrs Beverley's mood of gentle sacrifice by a storm of weeping, led by the Prince of Wales and the Duke of Cumberland, both present, enthusiastic, and, it was noticed, full of 'tears and acclamations'.

Moral though *The Gamester*'s purpose, it was not patronized by the Throne. Their Majesties waited until something worthier and more lofty could be countenanced at Buckingham House. But the public were delighted, horrified and stirred to the depths at the heartrending realities of the playing. One veteran, indeed, was so shaken by the effects on himself and the overwrought audience that he was reduced to seeing the play through the glass panel of the box door, and so assisted without distressing himself by hearing. Palmer, in the thankless part of Stukeley, was actually assailed with cries of horror and indignation by the audience at certain stages in the piece, and Macready has left an account of Mrs Siddons when he played Beverley to her Mrs Beverley twenty-nine years later. As she stooped above him after he had taken the poison: 'Her glaring eyes were fixed in stony blankness on his face; the powers of life seemed suspended in her; her sister and Lewson gently raised her, and slowly led her unresisting from the body, her gaze never for an instant averted from it; when they reached the prison door she stopped, as if awakened from a trance, with a shriek of agony that would have pierced the hardest heart, and, rushing from them, flung herself as if for union with death on the prostrate form before her.' Mrs Clement Parsons mentioned[1] that it was the custom of Mrs Siddons to instruct an inexperienced Jarvis to hold her very tightly at the moment when she flung herself upon Beverley; her tremendous physical strength being aroused by her imaginative energy. So strong was her power now that she was beginning to hypnotize the imagination of her colleagues. Her effect upon Brereton has been mentioned: it was now the turn of Young to react. During the next winter he played Beverley with Sarah at Edinburgh. Earlier in the agonizing prison-scene, when she turned from her prostrate husband to Jarvis, seizing his arm, and hotly and

[1] *The Incomparable Siddons.*

passionately exclaiming: "'Tis false, old man! – they had no quarrel – there was no cause for quarrel!' there was in her voice such a revelation of suffering that Young was physically paralysed. His throat contracted, his heart swelled, and his muscles refused to obey him. The prompter repeated his lines for him several times to no purpose; and then Mrs Siddons touched him on the shoulder, saying in a low voice: 'Mr Young – *recollect yourself.*' Perhaps it occurred to her to remember the time when she too had quailed before Garrick in all his horror as Richard III.

Fortunately, however, a play like *The Gamester*, ennobled though it may have been by the art of the Kembles, was not strong meat enough for the combined intelligence of the sister and brother. They needed to appear together in Shakespearian characters in order definitely to exercise their unusual powers. On 10th December they played in *King John* to a command performance: Kemble as John, and Sarah as Constance; a part which she explored and developed as richly as she was later to develop Queen Katharine and Lady Macbeth. She has left her own analysis of Constance in her personal notes of the character, who, though only appearing during two acts of the play, throws a shadow of such grandeur across the other more permanent personages as to make them appear even more ignoble in her absence.

In Mrs Siddons's opinion it was necessary that the artist who was to play Constance should be in many ways richly gifted by nature. This certainly had been the case with her great predecessor, Mrs Cibber, whose masterpiece Constance had been. But even then the principal work remained to be performed by the actress herself, in order to surmount the great mental and physical difficulties that arose in the development of the play. Of these she noted, the greatest of the mental tests was 'that of imperiously holding the mind reined-in to the immediate perception of those calamitous circumstances which take place during the course of her sadly eventful history'.

As the disasters to which she alluded take place while Constance is off stage, the reasons for this severe concentration of mind are obvious and pertinent. So much so that Mrs Siddons always kept open the door of her dressing-room throughout the entire play so as not to miss a fragment of the

[86]

disastrous events that were developing upon the stage. Finally, having strung herself up to the highest pitch of emotional strain she would place herself, holding Arthur by the hand, where she could hear the roll of the triumphal march on the reconciliation of France and England, and the ratification of the marriage; '. . . because the sickening sounds of that march would usually cause the bitter tears of rage, disappointment, betrayed confidence, baffled ambition, and above all, the agonizing feelings of maternal affection to gush into my eyes. . . .' So, charged with the violent nitre of her affliction, she was able, when the curtain rose upon the third act, to explode it in her passionate and bitter reproaches:

> *Gone to be married! Gone to swear a peace!*
> *False blood to false blood joined! – Gone to be friends!*

King John was not so great a success as *The Gamester*. During the whole of the winter season it was played only four times; and even then it became usual for some spectators to leave the theatre after Constance's exit, without waiting for the play to end. Even the rising popularity of Kemble, whose début as Hamlet had been made earlier in the season, and whose performance had won golden opinions, was not able to retain the interest of the fashionable and superficial world. They left before the afterpieces, the comic relief of the evenings; for there were many who felt too shattered after Mrs Siddons had done with them to assist at the levity inspired by farce, and it was not long before serious complaints from disgruntled comedians began to be heard.

In *King John* it was felt that Sarah did not occupy the stage enough. While she was there, it is true, robed in black satin, and with dishevelled hair, she commanded the entire house; but her next plunge was to satisfy everybody by the great scope and range of its undertaking. *Douglas* was being performed at Covent Garden with Mrs Crawford as Lady Randolph and Henderson as Norval. Mrs Siddons resolved to beat the old lady at her own game.

Mrs Crawford was the principal theatrical veteran who had struggled to uphold a great reputation in the face of the newcomer's triumphant progress. Her professional life had lasted

[87]

nearly forty years. As a young widow in Dublin she had married the captivating Spranger Barry, and as Mrs Barry her career of celebrity had begun. Garrick had invited them both to Drury Lane at very high terms, and between them they were known to have been earning £1,500 a year some time after 1766.

But Barry had died in 1777, and his widow had made the mistake of marrying once more. Crawford, her third husband, was unkind to her, and she entered a lean period. She fell back from her prominent position and accepted lesser parts. She depended more upon her popularity and less upon her work, and not until the rise of Sarah Siddons did she take much trouble. Then, goaded by her new rival at Drury Lane, she returned to Covent Garden. It was her last chance to recapture her public, though she was nothing now but a gaunt and aged harridan. In November, as her last throw, she staked her star part, Lady Randolph. Mrs Siddons accepted the challenge, and also played Lady Randolph in the following month for her benefit to a packed and cheering house. True, one or two faithful voices, those of loyal old playgoers, were raised in Mrs Crawford's favour, but to no purpose. They knew, though they dared not own, that there was nothing left of the great tragedian of the mid-century. Even her famous screams had turned to screeches. The defeat this time was final.

Douglas: A Tragedy, was the bombshell which had been hurled into Presbyterian Scotland in 1756 by one of its Ministers, the Rev. John Home. It had been greeted by salvoes of indignant protest from the combined forces of the Scottish Church at a time when the drama was considered as an invention of the Devil. Pamphlets condemning the only Caledonian dramatic work of merit had flooded the presses, and arguments by enraged divines had been put forward, urging 'that this thrice accursed tragedy called *Douglas* ought to be publicly burnt at the hands of the Hangman'. The play was denounced as the work of Satan in spite of the opinions of an academic group, and indeed, of the whole of enlightened Edinburgh: it was held to encourage suicide. Its champions included Lord Monboddo, David Hume and Dr Blair. Home had been forced to resign his living, and had accompanied his play to London, where *Douglas* was enthusiastically received at Covent Garden, the first Lady Randolph being Peg Woffington, and Young

[88]

Norval, Spranger Barry, resplendent in a suit of white puckered satin. Home's reputation had been sealed, and the Prince of Wales had presented him with a pension in place of his lost stipend.

Thereafter, until the middle of the nineteenth century, *Douglas* became a stock favourite in the tragic repertory. The play is a good one. It deals with mistaken identities. Douglas, Lady Randolph's long-lost son by a former secret marriage, having been concealed at birth, turns up as a youth, and has secret meetings with his mother. Lord Randolph, believing Douglas to be his wife's lover, has him murdered, and Lady Randolph commits suicide from grief. The situations which occur in the play, improbable though they are in detail, need not be discussed at the moment. The action itself is simple, and the language poetic. Mrs Siddons's interpretation of the woman whose past – like Lady Dedlock's – is wrapped in silence, conveyed the impression that her secret was never out of her consciousness. Here it was that she differed from Mrs Crawford, who, for instance, on being told how her infant son had been discovered by a shepherd, betrayed herself by giving vent to a piercing scream:

Was he alive?

Mrs Siddons, who was only happy when recreating a part in a manner original to her own ideas, and who was quite prepared if necessary to abandon any existing convention when a better interpretation occurred to her, delivered the important line in quite a different style. Certain, from the context, that Lady Randolph remains unconvinced of the shepherd's good faith, she breathed the words in a hurried, incredulous murmur, giving them little importance in her disbelief, only to turn upon the old man with a burst of exasperation and pain:

Inhuman that thou art!
How could'st thou kill what waves and tempest spared?

As Lady Randolph she wore a black dress and train, and made a slight concession to period by using an amount of white upon the bosom which was evidently frilled out into a ruff. This innovation, commented Boaden, 'was much, in those easy times, when nobody thought of risking the laughable in the correct.'

The Kembles had a strong sense of historical accuracy in stage setting and in costume, and Mrs Siddons persisted in risking the laughable to the uttermost extent in her passion for exactitude. Her innovations took time; she developed them gradually but she feared no ridicule when she felt her sense of propriety to be justified. Those easy times indeed made few demands upon the imagination. Spranger Barry as Romeo had worn the rich clothes of a Georgian gentleman in 1760; Garrick had played Macbeth in a tie-wig and an English general's uniform; while Henderson, as Cato, was rigged out like a county magistrate. So that when Mrs Siddons, not only made the attempt to clothe a part according to period, but eventually decided that the piled-up monstrosities of hairdressing were superfluous, and the elaborations of dress and trimming un-suited to tragedy, she rebelled against the fashions, wore her hair close to the head – a method which delighted Reynolds – and took as her model in style the severest classic standards. 'She now saw,' wrote Boaden, 'that tragedy was debased by the flutter of light materials, and that the head, and all its powerful action from the shoulder, should never be encumbered by the monstrous inventions of the hairdresser and the milliner. . . .'

She was coming under the direct influence of classical antiquity. She was moved by the simplicity of Greek statuary, and developed a style latent in her own character of austere and noble repose. Her notes upon the painting of *The Tragic Muse*, which belongs to this period, are completely in accordance with the characteristics of this development. She was passing through a phase which, it cannot be denied, was slightly pompous, and she took upon herself much of the credit for the success of the portrait. When she went to Reynolds for the first sitting, he made her a flowery speech and, taking her hand, led her to the platform with a graceful exhortation: 'Ascend your undisputed throne, and graciously bestow upon me some good idea of the Tragic Muse.' She did ascend the throne and, in her own words, 'instantly seated myself in the attitude in which the Tragic Muse now appears. This idea satisfied him so well, that without one moment's hesitation he determined not to alter it.'

[90]

Reynolds worked at white heat throughout the creation of the painting which Lawrence afterwards described as 'indisputably the finest female portrait in existence'. After the last sitting he was uncertain whether the pallor in the face was not excessive. But Mrs Siddons was insistent that he should leave it as it was; so bloodless, and, as she thought, 'so deeply accordant with the concentrated musings of pale melancholy'. It was not long before he agreed that she was right; and he sealed his satisfaction by the celebrated tribute that he paid in inscribing his name in gold lettering upon the border of her robe that he might not lose the opportunity of going down to posterity upon the hem of her garment. The original painting is in California, but a replica hangs in the Dulwich Gallery, a brown and cracking blister. The engravings give a finer impression than the large portrait itself. But here is the first instance in which may be traced the beginnings of severer influences upon the form of the actress. The 'flutter of light materials' is entirely absent from the thoughtful and abstracted figure, flanked by the shadowy forms of Crime and Remorse, and arrested apparently by a transient flash of inspiration. The hair, too, is nearer the natural shape of the head. Gone is the elaborate demi-cannon; the plastic curls stiffened with pomatum. The rust-red powder only remains. William Hazlitt, writing in the *London Magazine* for 1823, having walked through the Dulwich Gallery, dismissed the finest female portrait in existence with his inimitable acumen. He had the temerity to say that it was in a bastard style of art. 'Sir Joshua had an importunate theory of improving upon Nature. He might improve upon indifferent nature,' he continued, 'but when he had got the finest, he thought to improve upon that too, and only spoiled it.' He was not alone in criticizing *The Tragic Muse*. He found it bore very little resemblance to Mrs Siddons; Miss Seward was also critical of the painting, of which the defects and incongruities of situation amazed her. She deplored the heavy theatrical throne upon the clouds, and was shocked at the inclusion of pearls, gold lace and the imperial diadem 'upon an allegorical figure, which sorrow and high-souled resolve must be supposed to have incapacitated for the studied labours of the toilette'.

* * *

By now Mrs Siddons's reputation had spread all over the country, and people undertook long journeys in trying circumstances to have an opportunity of seeing her.

In the summer of 1784 she went up to Edinburgh for an engagement at the Theatre Royal. The business arrangements, negotiated chiefly by William with Jackson, the manager and lessee, proved advantageous to the pair but disappointing to the manager. Before the commencement of the engagement, the terms had been settled, when a person of influence in Edinburgh suddenly opened a subscription fund in connexion with the visit of Mrs Siddons. The amount raised was £200, but whether this was destined as a personal tribute to the actress or as an aid to the manager on account of his heavy expenses was not clear. Unfortunately, as soon as the existence of the fund was revealed, the Siddonses went back on their contract, and, in view of the additional sum of money, they clamoured for better terms. Jackson, after an unseemly wrangle – he was never a popular manager – became fearful of losing Mrs Siddons altogether, and eventually the whole of the subscription fund passed over to William's safe keeping. The legendary improvidence of actors was being soundly refuted by his wife's businesslike methods. Garrick had had the same characteristic, an unpopular one in the theatre and among the public, who expected that a player should live extravagantly, and that an actress, supported no doubt by the lavish generosity of an infatuated member of the peerage, should give as good value as she received by her luxurious living and ostentatious behaviour. Sarah Siddons had to provide for her husband and for her family: she would allow nothing to stand in her way when it came to business.

She gave twelve performances in Edinburgh, and received nearly £1,000. Ten were performances in the ordinary terms of the contract, one was for the benefit of a local charity, and her own benefit came at the end. Her presence created a furore. The theatre was besieged by crowds exceeding its seating capacity by fourfold. She played in *Macbeth* and in *Douglas*, delightful to local sensibilities, and she was received by the academic portion of the capital with infinite honour.

The Scottish audience at first were alarmingly unresponsive. They sat stolidly through *Venice Preserved* without betraying any signs of the emotion that she had come to expect as an accompaniment to her impassioned scenes. 'Stupid people, stupid people,' she muttered in disgust. And then she made one prodigious effort to surpass herself and stir her dour spectators into some show of feeling. It was exhausting. She did so because she relied upon the accustomed bursts of applause to refresh herself, and to relax between her repeated expenditure of energy in action. The result of her effort brought its gratifying reward. A single occupant of the gallery showed his approval. 'That's no bad!' he called, in an encouraging manner. The solitary gesture shook the house. With roars of laughter vibrating through the theatre the ice was shivered. From that moment Edinburgh laid itself at the feet of Mrs Siddons. Unprecedented scenes attended her appearances, and exaggerated gestures attached themselves to her performances. During a representation of *The Fatal Marriage*, the heiress, Miss Gordon of Gight, was so overwrought with hysteria that she was carried out of her box in convulsions, echoing in shriek after shriek Isabella's agonized cry: 'Oh! Biron, my Biron!' And when, later in the year, the same lady married Captain Jack Byron, to become eventually the mother of the poet, the circumstance must have been recalled by many who had been in the theatre from which she made so dramatic an exit, as being curiously prophetic.

Among the welcoming arms and friendly voices that received Mrs Siddons in Scotland none impressed her more than the circle of cultured men who considered themselves privileged to make her acquaintance. These included Robert Blair, David Hume, James 'Minstrel' Beattie and Henry Mackenzie, 'The Man of Feeling'. She was snowed under with presents, offerings and tributes of admiration, most of them anonymous and many of them superfluous. A source of gratification, however, was the presentation of a magnificent silver urn bearing the inscription 'A Reward to Merit'.

NINE

AFTER Edinburgh came Ireland, where this time Sarah was engaged to play in Dublin for twenty nights at £50 a night. She also played in Belfast, Cork and Limerick, repeating from a financial point of view, the enormous successes of the preceding year. In between her various engagements she was invited to country houses, and, in general, fêted by the cream of Irish society. She also renewed an old friendship. The Miss Boyle of Cheltenham days, her earliest admirer, had now become Mrs O'Neill, and she at once invited Mrs Siddons to stay with her at Shanes Castle, her home on Lough Neagh. Here Mrs Siddons was vastly impressed by all that she saw. The sumptuous style of living reminded her of an entertainment in the *Arabian Nights*. The party, 'a numerous throng of lords and ladies', appears to have passed the entire visit in touring the estate in an immense cavalcade. Six to eight carriages seem not to have been enough to accommodate the company, for the rest rode gaily behind. As for the meals, Mrs Siddons had never seen anything to compare with the magnificence with which they were served, and she was particularly impressed with some great silver flagons on the sideboards containing claret. In the passage outside the dining-room musicians played throughout dinner, after which, in true Arabian luxury, the guests wandered into the conservatory and for their dessert helped themselves to the exotic fruits which grew there. One of the guests at Shanes Castle was Lord Edward Fitzgerald, '. . . the most amiable honourable, though misguided youth I ever knew,' wrote Mrs Siddons, romantically touched. She was subsequently invited by the young patriot's mother, the Dowager Duchess of Leinster, to her house near Dublin, from which she drove in comfort to rehearsals during the latter part of the season. Entertainments upon so large a scale were found by Mrs Siddons to be truly delightful interludes to the endurance of her work and the vexations of professional life, for meanwhile, in the theatre, Daly had not shown himself to be above petty jealousies. He had played Faulconbridge in *King John*, and she herself, as Constance, very naturally had the final word in matters affecting her great scenes. In that with Austria she suggested that Faulconbridge should stand beside the King. The Kings were seated at opposing ends of the front of the stage, and Daly sulked at having to occupy an inconspicuous position where, she wrote, 'he absurdly fancied that he was of less consequence'. Part of Daly's revenge was to increase his venomous campaign against her private character. Half-way through the season an opportunity occurred for revenge to display itself in full measure. Mrs Siddons fell ill. She took to her bed with a high fever and remained there for a fortnight. During her absence incalculable mischief was let loose. Malicious reports were circulated that her illness was feigned, notwithstanding the fact that she immediately acted again upon her recovery. A few days after her return she was rehearsing Belvidera and was present when West Digges, playing Pierre, collapsed upon the stage with a paralytic stroke which completely disabled him. Digges, a worthless old reprobate was a favourite with his public, so that his affliction immediately made him an object of popular concern. It was decided that he should be given a benefit, and Mrs Siddons was asked to play for him. Her season was almost at an end, and in a very few days she was to leave for an engagement at Cork. She had only one night to spare, and, after considering the matter, she said that she thought she was bound in honour to play for the benefit of the Marshalsea prisoners, a promise that had gone unfulfilled in the preceding year. Daly, who acted as go-between, returned to Digges with the message, which purported to be a blank refusal. He had hardly reached the infirm actor when word came after him, saying that Mrs Siddons had reconsidered the matter and would play for him. Digges was apparently grateful, replied by note and they fixed a date – the last night of the season – for the benefit. But the story leaked out, and the anti-Siddons faction exaggerated it. She had, it seemed, not only hard-heartedly refused to play for an infirm colleague, but, having changed her mind, only agreed to do so if he would pay her £50, insisting that this part of the transaction should be kept secret. Her own version of the circumstances of the benefit was different. She complained of the indefatigable labour and cruel annoyances which she and her husband had undergone in scraping up a collection of actors from outlying districts to form a company that would go through *Venice Preserved.* 'Oh! to be sure it was a scene of disgust and confusion,' she lamented. 'I acted Belvidera, without having ever previously seen the face of one of the actors. Poor Mr Digges was most materially benefited by this most ludicrous performance; and I put my disgust into my pocket, since money passed into his.'

Although there is no doubt that there was lacking a certain spirit of enthusiasm in this act of charity, the accusation that Mrs Siddons accepted £50 from the old man was obviously wild and certainly unfounded. When taking money at all for her services of assistance to fellow actors she ordinarily accepted £30.

When the benefit was over Mrs Siddons left for Cork. But she had counted without Mr Daly. The Press campaign which had begun the year before was openly continued with renewed fervour, and the public were urged to boycott her and hoot her from the stage on account of the inhumanity with which she had treated poor Mr Digges. More than this, a letter to the papers was printed in which the writer inquired whether she had ever been known to perform a kind action? The question was fortunately controvertible. She had recently played, out of ten nights at York, three times for nothing: once for the benefit of Aickin, again for Lee Lewes, and once for a charitable institution. Lee Lewes, who was also in Cork, felt himself bound to publish this testimony in the papers.

The unhappy episode was, however, not all. There had been in Dublin, coinciding with that of Digges, another benefit muddle; this time on account of Mr Brereton. Brereton, whose

An Idea for a Head of Mrs Siddons as the Tragic Muse

Drawing by Sir Thomas Lawrence
in the possession of Mrs Fitzroy Newdegate

career Mrs Siddons may be said in some ways to have established, had this year again accompanied her to Ireland. He had been engaged without a fixed salary, but she had undertaken to play gratis for his benefit. He was not in poor circumstances as he was drawing a good salary at Drury Lane which relieved him from the compassion usually accorded to indigent actors, when, in the middle of the season at Dublin, he fell ill. He, therefore, was unable to play for Mrs Siddons's benefit, and she then saw no reason why she should be expected to play for him for nothing. Instead of the customary £30 she agreed to perform for him for the sum of £20. But she, too, then fell ill, and, what with one thing and another, what with the limitation of available nights and her slow recovery, Brereton's benefit never materialized. His unstable mental condition perhaps led him to over-emphasize his injuries, and the next thing that happened was the circulation of a rumour that she had refused altogether to play for him. A correspondent signed 'Laertes', but believed to be Kemble, rushed into print in defence of the victim of the attack and reminded the public that only a few months earlier Mrs Siddons had played for Brereton's benefit, on which occasion he must have pocketed nearly two hundred pounds.

*   *   *

In the midst of the violent partisanship that divided the adorers of 'the matchless' from the detractors of 'stingy' Siddons, the heroine of the agitation returned to England. During her prolonged absence calumny had been active on the other side of the Irish Sea. This, too, had an unfortunate origin. Sarah possessed a mysterious sister, Anne, with the soul of an adventuress and a talent for associating herself with notorious persons and inconvenient activities. This discreditable character, a large and squinting woman, had been conducting herself in an unseemly manner. She had married a Mr Curtis, a bigamist, had parted from him, and now employed herself in various ways. She would, in fact, never keep quiet. She read lectures at Dr Graham's Temple of Hymen – 'at which decency would have blushed' – and in other ways associated herself with the inventor of the Celestial Bed. But when this occupation turned out to be a pecuniary failure, she applied to her family for money. She now traded upon her relationship to Mrs Siddons, and, in order to enforce her demands, attempted a kind of moral blackmail upon the respectability of her celebrated sister: *Poems on Miscellaneous Subjects by Ann Curtis, sister of Mrs Siddons*, had appeared in 1783, dedicated to the Duchess of Devonshire. The tiresome creature ended by making appeals to the public, and finally hit upon a diabolical plan. She drew attention to herself by swallowing poison in the precincts of Westminster Abbey. She did not die; it is doubtful whether she cared to try the experiment; but the event certainly earned immediate notoriety. A storm broke right over Sarah's unsuspecting head. 'The mighty Mrs Siddons' was attacked by an anonymous journalist to whom *The Secret History of the Green Room* darkly referred in the following passage: 'a person employed in a newspaper, whose writings have been justly described to be "every line a libel, and every word a lie", because, perhaps, Mrs Siddons would not comply with his extortions, or soothe his viperous tongue by the hospitalities of her table, set every engine in motion against her. . . .' In addition to these attacks upon her character, the public were treated to an account of her uncharitable behaviour towards Messrs Digges and Brereton, and the agreeable paragraphist concluded his campaign by stating that Mrs Siddons was so beside herself with arrogance that she never read the reviews of her playing, and was impervious either to panegyric or censure.

Beneath all this malevolence not much detection is needed to discover the author. The hand of Mr Pratt may be safely assumed to have been hard at work scribbling away, in his most genteel manner, with his pen dipped in venom. This was the snake which had been nurtured in the bosoms of Mrs Siddons and the Bath set for the last few years. It had been an age before she had found him out. And although Miss Seward had already begun to detect his baseness, and wrote of him in the severest terms, Mr Whalley positively refused to do so for a long time.

Pratt, who had been *persona grata* in the Siddons household, had taken to borrowing money from the family. They had lent him substantial sums; William had produced £500, and the last straw had come with the loan by Sarah of £10 from her small quarterly allowance, which sum she felt she could ill afford. This she had no scruples in asking to be repaid. Pratt ignored the request, and when much later he did write to her, it was merely to commend to her notice his latest tragedy. Mrs Siddons felt put upon and disliked being treated as a convenience. She replied that she had had to make a rule against reading plays for fear of giving offence to authors whose works she had not time to read, and she advised Mr Pratt to submit his tragedy to the managers. But during this time he had been insinuating himself into the good graces of Miss Frances Kemble. He pretended to her hand, sat upon her doorstep, and abused Mrs Siddons in her apparently none too loyal ear. He threatened to publish a poem called 'Gratitude' in which he figured as the ladder up which Mrs Siddons had ascended to celebrity and which she was now kicking away. Sarah's version of the story was that, finding 'Pratty' to be conducting a sentimental campaign with her sister, she continued to invite him to her house until the episode of the letter to which she took exception. Pratt, she noticed, was anxious not altogether to lose touch with her, and desirous that the first step towards a reconciliation should come from her. 'But,' she manfully wrote, 'I will die first.' Humility and Mrs Siddons were not synonymous. She did express a readiness to serve him all the same; but the offence had sunk deeply into 'Pratty's' small nature, and in revenge at being forbidden the house he determined to expose her 'avarice'.

Miss Frances Kemble had after all not lacked a certain measure of success. She was a beautiful woman, and George Steevens, of the Shakespearian Commentary, was her declared admirer, comparing her in no uncertain terms with Mrs Siddons. His insistence that she had a mind 'in every way stronger and more cultivated than her sister's' had led her to fancy her chances as an actress, and herself as a personality; and though Steevens seems not to have actually wished to marry her – d'Israeli's opinion of him was that he was 'guilty of arch deception and malicious ingenuity' – he was evidently in love, and employed his powers and his high reputation in fighting for her success. His rather extravagant claims on her behalf were substantiated by her performance of Harriet in *The Guardian*, in which delicate part, said Boaden, she succeeded 'beyond the warmest expectations of her friends'. It did not take much to corrupt the loyalty of the lesser Kembles. Mrs Siddons had done her utmost to help them by every means within her power, and now envy was to be her reward. 'Alas,' she once told Samuel Rogers, 'after I became celebrated none of my sisters ever loved me as they did before.'

*   *   *

In the meantime moral indignation was filling the breasts of the London public. The papers printed wild and unreliable statements about Mrs Siddons and her avarice; and 'Laertes', 'Theatricus', and a crowd of correspondents ventilated their opinions according to their inclinations. She therefore found, when she settled into her new house in Gower Street for the winter, that a battle was raging on every side with herself as the cause of the dispute.

Explanations and recriminations succeeded one another daily in the Press during September and October. Mr Digges was dug up again, and his son wrote to the *Morning Herald*. The inference of his letter was to the effect that Mrs Siddons *had* accepted £50 from his necessitous father. Old Digges was still in Ireland and, although hard pressed to give a frank statement, remained stonily silent. Several people tried to get some sort of declaration from him, and he eventually wrote to the editor of the *Morning Chronicle*. His letter contained the admission 'I did not pay Mrs Siddons for acting for my benefit'. But as he shortly afterwards died, and as his letter was delayed by contrary winds, it was not received until late in October, before which time the climax to the affair was long over. Meanwhile, William Siddons had been busily denying the accusations, also in a letter to the Press. In this he challenged Brereton to come to the rescue. Brereton had been nourishing his grievance as well, but he too, at last felt obliged to come forward with his testimony. He did acknowledge that Mrs Siddons had agreed to perform at his benefit, 'for a less sum than for any other performer, but her illness prevented it; and that she would have played for me after that had not the night been appointed after she played three times in the same week – and that the week after her illness – and I am very willing you shall publish this letter, if you think it will be of the least service to Mrs Siddons, to whom I am proud to owe

[100]

many obligations of friendship.' This communication appeared in print on the morning of 5th October. It was considered coldly expressed. That night Mrs Siddons was to make her first appearance of the season as Mrs Beverley. But when the curtain rose discovering her, she was greeted with hostile cries of 'Off! Off!' Hissing and hooting broke out in various parts of the house, and her voice, when she attempted to speak, was inaudible. She tried again to address the outraged audience, standing with great dignity and self-possession until a moment of silence should come. But she was prevented from excusing herself. An unknown champion jumped up in the pit and called out: 'For Heaven's sake, madam, do not degrade yourself by an apology, for there is nothing necessary to be said.' When he had done, the uproar broke out again, and she was finally led away by Kemble. Once off the stage she fainted in his arms, but even then the spirit that had carried her through the disagreeable scene was still high. 'On my recovery,' she wrote in her memoranda, 'I was thankful that my persecutors had not had the gratification of beholding this weakness.'

The distressing evening wore on, and behind the scenes Sheridan, Kemble and William pleaded with Mrs Siddons. She, for her part, was so disgusted that she wished never to appear again before the inconstant audiences of London. But she thought of her children, away now at school in the country, and she made the effort for their sakes to face the pandemonium once more. She went back on the stage and waited with great self-command for the curtain to rise. The temper of the audience had suddenly changed. The curtain rose upon a crowd that was as hushed as though it were in a cathedral, giving Mrs Siddons the opportunity to clear herself. She courageously spoke to them in tactful words.

'Ladies and Gentlemen,' she said, 'the kind and flattering partiality which I have uniformly experienced in this place, would make the present interruption distressing to me indeed, were I, in the slightest degree, conscious of having deserved your censure. I feel no such consciousness. The stories which have been circulated against me are calumnies; when they shall be proved to be true, my aspersors will be justified. But, till then, my respect for the public leads me to be confident that I shall be protected from unmerited insult.'

Her straightforward method of dealing with the situation was very well received. James Boaden, a young man then, was in the pit, and got as near as he could to examine every detail of her behaviour. There was, he observed, a male dignity in her understanding that raised her above the helplessness of most women in such a situation, and there can be no doubt that the audience respected the courage with which she faced their hostility. Brereton was acting Lewson in the play that very evening, but curiously enough, although his letter had appeared in the paper the same morning, he neither came forward nor was called upon to do so to give his version of the business. Aickin, however, was present, and had in fact come to Drury Lane especially to testify to her having played for him gratis some weeks before.

The worst of the trouble was fortunately crushed after this aggressive night, although a small but determined faction, judged to be one-eighth of the audience, deliberately greeted her with abuse for some time to come. The rest made honourable amends for the past with the waving of handkerchiefs, beating of hands and sticks, and loud and repeated huzzas.

On the whole Mrs Siddons had come through the humiliating ordeal with a head unbowed albeit a little bloody. Her manner for some time afterwards was thought to be visibly damped, and she had, indeed, half a mind to retire for good into the country, as far from London as possible, and live on the few thousand pounds that she had saved. She was luckily prevented from indulging in this rash act by being warned of 'the exultation of her enemies', who would most certainly have made the most of her flight, and she remained to face them. It cannot have been easy. Rumours of the meanness of 'Lady Sarah Save-all' swept through the purlieus of Long Acre and were credited in St James's Square. Print-sellers sold cartoons depicting Melpomene grasping at money bags which hung upon a tree a little beyond her reach, while from under her draperies protruded more bags stuffed with bills of exchange and overflowing with gold. She was reported never to attend performances by other actors; she was said never to applaud them. It would be easy to account for this. The fact is that she very frequently was seen at the play on her free evenings, and that, in order to maintain a strict impartiality with regard to her colleagues, she, knowing the intrigues of the green-room, refrained from any demonstration that would lead to jealousy. Then imagination produced a really effective story. Mrs Siddons, it was said, had actually been seen in St Martin's Church, lingering behind the departing congregation to avoid having to contribute to the collection at the door. No doubt if there were any foundation for the absurd little slander, the explanation would be that she had remained on her knees a little longer than the rest in order to avoid the disagreeable experience of being surrounded and stared at when she left the building.

The taste of the cup of humiliation was acrid to her, but she swallowed it bravely. In a letter to Lord Hardwicke on 30th October she thanked him for his congratulations, supposing he had heard of the attacks made upon her by her enemies, 'of which no Prime Minister had ever more. . . .'

She fell ill from worry and distress at her continued persecutions, and must have dreaded to open a newspaper during the early part of the autumn. Minor facetiæ at her expense were repeatedly to be read, and '*Consols, Stocks, Siddons, Teas*, have all fallen within these last few months, and are likely to be still lower in the public esteem,' was only one example of the hundreds of defamatory paragraphs. She shrank more and more into the depth of her reserve; a remote, sibylline figure clothed in her own mysterious and rather cold thoughts. She read and she studied, and in her solitary state of mind she took to comparing herself with figures of the past. Lord Hardwicke had lent her the memoirs of Pericles, and here she found a similarity between the patriot and herself. Pericles caught her imagination and held it strongly, for she had felt herself in his situation, as she wrote to Lord Hardwicke, 'having been the favourite of the Mob one year – and the *next degraded* by them – it remains only that I *may* like him be reinstated, when Malice is cold and Candour takes its turn.'

*   *   *

The very unlucky combination of recent events had arisen no doubt partly from deliberate and organized hostility, but the clouds of smoke must somewhere have originated in a flame, however small. It was clearly impossible to attack Mrs Siddons from a moral standpoint. Her nature was neither light nor amorous. She was an affectionate wife and a primitive and devoted mother, and the law of self-preservation was the only one that she admitted. She could be tender, passionate where her heart was stirred; but adamant where exterior forces interfered with the interest of her dependants. She even supplied her inconvenient sister Anne with £20 a year on condition that she should relinquish her shady pursuits and retire to a distance of not less than 150 miles from London. The *ci-devant* Mrs Curtis then married a publican called Hutton, and took to writing five-volume novels. Thus, eventually known as 'Anne of Swansea', lived and died the black sheep in the Kemble family.

Looking over the correspondence of the period, it is difficult to understand exactly why Mrs Siddons came to be accused so unjustly of hardness. Letters exist which are a flat denial to these accusations. One to Lord Sydney, written in the preceding year, pleads eloquently, although inflatedly, for the family of a condemned man: 'My lord, a Distracted Mother and her numerous Progeny, have sent me what my heart knows not how to *resist*, and yet trembles to undertake. How shall I presume my Lord to address, or how remain deaf to the cries of the Widow, and the disgrace of her desolate children? The unhappy creatures have fixed upon me, the humblest instrument perhaps they cou'd have chosen, to stand between Disgrace and Death – I dare not think what I am doing when I enclose the discription of thier sore calamity, in the trembling hope of Royal Clemency, when aided by your Lordship's kind interposition.'

'If anything on earth cou'd embolden me to take so unwarranted a freedom, where silent and respectful *distance* only, wou'd become me, it is that even I, the most lowly of my most gracious Sovriegn's subjects, may, by the very presumption which afflicts me, be the means of carrying to the foot of the Throne, proper objects of that never failing Mercy which it is the glory of his nature to exert whenever there is a possibility, which God-like disposition makes it no less the *Delight* than the *Duty* of his subjects to love and honour him. To neglect the remotest *chance* of saving the life of a fellow creature, whose family have laid before me the narrative of their Sorrows, wou'd forever embitter my own existence, I hope therefore, your Lordship will pardon the trouble I have presum'd to give you, and permit me the honour of subscribing myself, with the utmost respect,

Your Lordship's

Most obedient humble servant,

SARAH SIDDONS'

There were constant appeals to friends at Westminster. Lord Liverpool and William Windham were from time to time implored by her to assist deserving cases whose 'voice of modest misery' she hoped might be heard among the 'stunning tumult of politicks'. Mrs Siddons, though weak in orthography and erratic in punctuation, was never at a loss when it came to expressing herself in writing.

*   *   *

In spite of enemies and difficulties, work progressed. On 3rd November she undertook the part of Margaret of Anjou in Franklin's version of La Harpe's *Earl of Warwick*. It was an attempt that once more assailed a great reputation, for the creator of the character had been Mrs Yates, who, when rehearsing, had so ably concealed her appreciation of the part that she had actually allowed the men in the play to suppose themselves the important characters. In secret she had then mastered Margaret and when her moment arrived she had utterly eclipsed both Edward IV and Warwick by the consequence she had given to the Queen and by her brilliant interpretation.

Although the play was replete with historical inaccuracies the character of Margaret was pretty much what one would have been led to expect from a superficial reading of history books. Mrs Siddons was admirable. She appeared to increase her stature to that of a giantess, as on her entry she stood in the archway, seeming entirely to fill it. She walked, we read, 'as though she trod upon her enemies'. This entirely new creation was different from either the silent, pathetic mourner or from the tempestuous wife or mistress of other plays with which she had come to be associated. In the *Earl of Warwick* she was clever, sneering and sarcastic, withering her adversaries with

[105]

words. In her, dignity now assumed monumental proportions, and Margaret of Anjou was the precursor of a long succession of regal parts. Pride, spirit and vengeance were dominant throughout the tragedy, veneered by the superb usage of pointed raillery.

In a play such as this Mrs Siddons received the greatest scope for her individual powers. Boaden thought, for instance, that she was never at her best in very modern tragedies. She seemed chiefly to realize herself when pitting her energies against some established reputation; shattering a prevailing tradition by her original conceptions, or, when she thought a previous interpretation justified, weighing its merits against her own opinion and acting as her judgement informed her. She was seldom wrong. But she was considered by some judicious critics to be playing too frequently, and one of them uttered the conviction that if she hoped to be followed by crowds '. . . she should never perform more than once a week, or twelve times in a season'.

During this year, as in every succeeding year for that matter, she was in enormous demand with portrait painters. Gainsborough's brushes had for ever transfixed her – for the ultimate benefit of the nation – in black plumes and sable furs, composedly gazing down the vista of her endless ironical nose, and Reynolds, Romney, Hamilton, Cosway, Stothard, Beechey, Stuart and an innumerable list of others were from now onwards reproducing her extraordinarily mobile features. Many years earlier, Lawrence, as a boy of ten, had rapidly made one of his brilliant and precocious sketches of the woman whose countenance dominated his imagination so completely in after life. Actually, in the spring of 1785, Mrs Siddons wrote to Lord Hardwicke that she could not sit to Collins for the portrait that he wished to commission as she was then simultaneously under the hands of three painters, which beside her work kept her constantly occupied. The wonder is that she was able to do so much.

She went through life using the intelligence with which she had been fortunately equipped. It was characteristic of her that no idea was too simple or came too late for her to disregard. From the Egyptian statues at Lansdowne House it struck her how she might convey increased intensity of feeling. From them she imitated the attitude of rigid muscular tension, with arms pressed tightly down the sides, and clenched hands, being firmly convinced of the emotional quality of the pose. Again, almost at the end of her life, *Guy Mannering* appeared; and, as she was then giving her Readings from Shakespeare, she obtained a new idea of the witches in *Macbeth* from studying Meg Merrilees. She immediately substituted the new and better version for her original interpretation. It was perhaps this professional sincerity, working deliberately through everything that she did, that so pleased and astonished old Kitty Clive when she came up from Cliveden to inspect the famous tragic actress. Egged on, no doubt by the provocative comments of Horace Walpole, 'Think!' she said, when she was asked what she thought of Mrs Siddons's performance, 'Think! I think it's all truth and daylight.'

Zara, Hill's version of Voltaire's *Zaïre*, in which Mrs Siddons played the title-part, was revived on 7th November, and much was expected from her. It was thought that this character, one of the great accomplishments of the late Mrs Cibber, would renew its fire under Sarah's inspiration. No such performance was forthcoming. She was found to be frigid in a part that remained cold and declamatory. It was succeeded on 2nd December by Cumberland's *Carmelite*, in which she played Matilda, the Lady of St Vallori. Cumberland had not strayed far from the path trodden by Home in *Douglas*, and Matilda, like Lady Randolph, has a secret sorrow, and a son whom she rears with the object of avenging his father, who is believed to be dead. Considering the tedium of the endless, inflated speeches; the atmosphere of thunder and lightning, Norman knights and insoluble mystery that pervades the drama it is surprising that anybody ever went to see it at all. Certainly, in this unimpressive piece Mrs Siddons produced little effect. The next attempt by the enterprising management of Drury Lane was Massinger's *Maid of Honour* – Mrs Siddons as Camiola. The responsibility for this revival lay chiefly upon the shoulders of Kemble, whose antiquarian tastes were now beginning to have free rein. The *Maid of Honour* had a slight success. It was in an incomparably better class than either of the two preceding plays, and Mrs Siddons did what she could with the part. Kemble pruned away the coarser allusions, for, to quote

Boaden, 'the grossness of the author's age has tainted her [Camiola's] reproof to Fulgentio with a little too much muscular preference in the person of a lover'.

The last two months of 1784 were not noteworthy, in so far as they concerned Mrs Siddons, for theatrical or artistic successes at Drury Lane. Christmas found her sadly depressed. There were reports abroad that William was unkind to her, but these it seems originated with their old servant who drank more than was necessary, and who had been spreading slanderous reports. John Taylor, too, described dropping in one morning and finding Mrs Siddons occupied in destroying old letters, written, she told him, by a dead poet. As he helped her to burn them, a newspaper-cutting fell from one of the letters. He read it. It contained an anonymous attack upon her character apparently by the deceased, who had then sprung forward publicly to defend her. He had told her, too, that Mr Siddons kept a mistress at Chelsea. So poor Sarah sat heavily, with a load of thoughts darkening her heart, and threw her letters one by one into the fire. Taylor, secretly thinking that she should have been a queen, so dignified was she in her sentiments, so noble in her bearing, left her, in consternation.

TEN

WHEN it had been suggested to Mrs Siddons that she should play Medea and Lady Macbeth, her answer had been 'No', for she did not look upon them as female characters. It was a sweeping statement, most typical of her intolerant nature. She had in fact played the Lady in the provinces, and the overwhelming effect of the part when she had studied it at the age of twenty had made an impression upon her that was never to be removed. The fact that she reconsidered her opinion is another example of her artistic integrity. She would otherwise not have agreed to compromise on such a point. She was in her thirtieth year, and gradually approaching a maturity that had never been forced. During her first three seasons at Drury Lane she had been remarkable for an indefinable quality, a certain pathos or tenderness that was elusive and extremely moving. There was a look that in certain situations would be seen in her eyes – they appeared to revolve in her head – which had an almost painful effect; yet it was so exquisite that it seemed to tear the hearts of her spectators. This pathos was giving way to a quality other than might have been expected. Power had arrived – mature, grand and irresistible. Human yielded to inhuman, and genius was emerging that could create dæmonic giantesses – characters that in their essentials were indeed not female.

Early in the year of 1785, when the fever that raged round the Westminster Scrutiny was at its height and all eyes were riveted on the House of Commons and the precarious situation of Fox, Mrs Siddons was engaged in rehearsing the part of Lady Macbeth. She had something in store for the town that would detach its interest from the voters in Westminster; she was about to endow a legendary character with such inconceivable reality that future generations would unconsciously apprehend in her physical appearance and mental presentation the Lady that Mrs Siddons had revealed to their forefathers. 'When I read Lady Macbeth's part,' wrote Byron years later, 'I have Mrs Siddons before me; and imagination even supplies her voice, whose tones were superhuman, and power over the heart supernatural.'

Lady Macbeth, in fact, was minted by Mrs Siddons; and the notes she gave to Campbell contain an explicit statement of her conception of the character. They are pedantic, capricious, intelligent and original. For with the exception of Shakespeare the parts that she played were seldom worthy of her; and when presented with a character whose spiritual problems she had to contend with to an unusual degree, the exertion called out all her emotional and intellectual superiority. As Constance she had been epitomized by Campbell in a single line: 'Her very body seemed to think'. As Lady Macbeth she went a stage further. Her body not only seemed to think: it became. It revealed something transcending all baser feelings, and entered the world of sublime evil. Ambition she could understand well enough, and ambition pursued beyond human limits she was able to imagine and to transform into something lofty, horrifying and inescapable. In the loneliness of the figure there was, to her, something as detached and as impersonal as a cataclysm.

She had one or two unusual ideas about the Lady, it is true, For instance she rather fantastically imagined her to be small, fair and blue-eyed; a fragile creature uniting physical charm with abnormal strength of mind and vitality. Only such a woman – and Mrs Siddons lived in an age when fragile women were fashionable – could have gained complete ascendancy over so honourable a man as Macbeth: 'to seduce him,' she wrote, 'to brave all the dangers of the present and all the terrors of a future world; and we are constrained, even whilst we abhor his crimes, to pity the infatuated victim of such a thraldom.'

Her conception, submitted though it may have been to certain vagaries, was arrived at by the hold which the character had taken on her imagination. She realized that she must relinquish experience and allow judgement alone to guide her along a path that was unknown and difficult but strangely exciting to her intellectual apprehension. When she agreed to play the part she knew, too, that she would be confronted by the ghost of Mrs Pritchard, who, whatever Dr Johnson may have thought her – and even he had called her 'the inspired idiot' – had been the greatest Lady Macbeth within living memory. Mrs Pritchard, moreover, had established certain traditions in utterance and action, and Mrs Siddons's opinion of traditions for their own sake was negligible. It was therefore with a good deal of trepidation that she decided to perform.

*   *   *

She played Lady Macbeth on the evening of her second benefit, 2nd February. The occasion was as fearful as that of her first appearance three years earlier; and as she sat, controlled and silent in her dressing-room, desperately taking stock of herself, she was disturbed by Sheridan, who insisted upon coming in to see her. His entry was a violation. Sheridan had, at the eleventh hour, lost his head: Mrs Pritchard and Tradition had been too much for him. He came to implore Mrs Siddons to reconsider her decision, having heard that she meant to set down the candle on her entry in the sleep-walking scene. She argued that to her mind this course was imperative since she needed free hands to go through the movements of washing them. He retorted that Mrs Pritchard had always carried the candle throughout the scene, and that the public would think the alteration unjustified and presumptuous. Mrs Siddons had not yet lost her respect for Sheridan's judgement. She was anxious to defer to his wishes. But it was at that hour, too late for her to consider a change. She had, besides, observed the habits of somnambulists at first hand; her mind was made up. She decided to go through with her intention.

She walked on to the stage reading the letter so skilfully and reflectively that the audience were immediately under the impression that it was a continuation of something begun

[111]

elsewhere. 'They met me in the day of success,' she was reading,
'. . . They made themselves' – and here she paused – 'air'.
The wonder and the speculation in her voice was a new treatment; but when she came to 'Glamis thou art, and Cawdor—'
she paused again, and with a violent determination continued:
'and shalt be what thou art promised.' The audience, already
spellbound, were electrified by the energy with which she
uttered the words 'shalt be'. She had scored her first two points
against Mrs Pritchard and Tradition. As to this public opinion
was more or less unanimous, although Lord Harcourt, a great
friend and benefactor to Sarah, permitted himself impartial
criticism. He considered that, although she had much more
expression of countenance, she lacked Mrs Pritchard's dignity
and the melodious compass of her voice, and he found also that
her 'Are you a man?' compared unfavourably with that of the
earlier actress.

In the violent light that she turned upon the character of
Lady Macbeth, Mrs Siddons proved herself at heart a Victorian. She caught wherever possible at every straw that might
save her heroine from spiritual perdition. Wherever a gleam of
human feeling could be read into the text she amplified it to
the best of her power without distorting the interpretation.
In the desperate allusion to maternal tenderness –

> *I have given suck, and know*
> *How tender 'tis to love the babe that milks me.*
> *I would, while it was smiling in my face,*
> *Have pluck'd my nipple from its boneless gums,*
> *And dash'd the brains out – had I but so sworn*
> *As you have done to this –*

she explained the unnatural sentiment as the result of ambition,
for she wrote in her notes: 'The very use of such a tender
allusion in the midst of her dreadful language, persuades one
unequivocally that she has really felt the maternal yearnings of
a mother towards her babe, and that she considered this action
the most enormous that ever required the strength of human
nerves for its perpetration.' Again, in the superb scene between
the accomplices, she was insistent upon emphasizing the
Lady's one moment of weakness:

And uttering this there was pride in her tones, and tenderness.

It was some time before she was satisfied with the manner in which her answer to Macbeth's 'If we should fail?' was to be given. Mrs Pritchard, of blessed memory, had instituted a quailing tone of incredulity into her reply, '*We fail?*' as who should say, Can you actually suppose such a possibility? Mrs Siddons experimented; and after two variants embodying contempt and indignation, neither of which satisfied her, she came to rest upon a characteristic reading. She adopted a tone of fatality and resignation. To 'If we should fail?' she answered, 'We fail. But screw your courage to the sticking-place and we'll *not* fail.' The reading was conclusive, and in its determination it obviously closed the argument. 'It's effect was sublime,' wrote Mrs Jameson in her *Characteristics of Women*. She was convinced that it was the correct interpretation.

Mrs Siddons had a theory that Lady Macbeth was directly responsible for the second murder in the play. She linked up the idea by quoting Macbeth's 'Thou know'st that Banquo and his Fleance live' with her reply, 'But in them Nature's Copy's not Eterne' – a direct suggestion to his unexpressed wish. So, bearing this in mind, she concluded it not unreasonable to suppose that the Lady also sees the ghost of Banquo in his second apparition.

The horrible banquet therefore showed Lady Macbeth at her grimmest. She conceived that she should play right through the scene with the Lords, 'dying with fear,' as she wrote, 'yet assuming the utmost composure . . . entertaining her wondering guests with frightful smiles, with over-acted attention, and with fitful graciousness; painfully, yet incessantly, labouring to divert their attention from her husband.' The peak was achieved with her dismissal of the guests. The limit of endurance, strain and resistance being almost reached, and the Lady having completed her mission, she said:

> *I pray you speak not; he grows worse and worse;*
> *Question enrages him; at once good night;*
> *Stand not upon the order of your going,*
> *But go at once.*

T.A.—8   [113]

Her reward was a thundering salutation of applause. A most valuable eye witness, who annotated her actions in his copy of the text, wrote that here she 'descends in great eagerness; voice almost choked with anxiety to prevent their questioning; alarm, hurry, rapid and convulsive as if afraid Macbeth should tell of the murder of Duncan.' In his introductory note he makes the following observation: 'Of Lady Macbeth there is not a great deal in this play, but the wonderful genius of Mrs Siddons makes it the whole.' This eye witness was Professor G. J. Bell, who in 1809 collected in three volumes a mass of material labelled *Siddons*, and whose discrimination as a critical theatre-goer places him as a reliable source of information. His estimate of Sarah was, one cannot help feeling, correct.

She fulfilled the ideal; she very probably was the Lady Macbeth of all time, and the actress whom Shakespeare could only hope to hear in Heaven. The changes of expression that passed across her face, her gestures and her movements while she was listening to Macbeth, reached such perfection that the fascinated audience entirely forgot to attend to him and were riveted upon her. She proved that she could be as convincing to spectators through her own dark and monstrous presentation of the character as she would have been were she able to have played the version of her imagination: that of the fair and fragile charmer whose ascendancy would have been due to different causes, and who would have demanded a totally different interpretation. Instead of which the blood-lit Megæra, her tremendous shadow falling across the path of an irresolute consort, stood, flail in hand, at his back, speeding him on his way to destruction. If she had had her way the part might have been lit by a gleam of tender sentiment. But she adapted herself to her own physical and mental calibre. So, as the attentive eye of Dr Bell noted, she created the greatest female figure in English Drama. She forgot that she was acting; her eyes never for one instant admitted the existence of a spectator, but were the continual registers of her various passions. Her words, according to Dr Bell, so accompanied her thoughts that they seemed scarcely necessary.

She entered suddenly in the sleep-walking scene, dressed in white, rather rapidly went to the table, and setting down the candle, settled the question of Mrs Pritchard for good. Then

with restless gestures she began to rub her hands in air, seeming
at intervals to scoop up water with the one and pour it over the
other. Her great eyes were blank and glazed as they fixed into
space or glared straight at the house, and yet she moved freely
about in the obscurity, miraculously avoiding obstacles, sometimes stepping backwards as if feeling for the candle, yet bound
in the depths of sleep. Her 'Out damned spot' was said in
hollow, tortured tones, and then she appeared to be listening
eagerly, '*One! Two!*' followed by a strange unnatural whisper,
'Why then 'tis time to do 't.' Later she became seized with
melancholy. '*The thane of Fife had a wife:* where is she now?'
'*What*' – peevishly – '*Will these hands ne'er* be clean?' And then
with eagerness, 'No more o' that, my lord, *no more o' that*: you
mar all *with this* starting.' In the final phase of the scene she
indicated mental collapse. The sigh that shuddered round the
house shook her frame convulsively, and in the succeeding
groans a hint of imbecility was distinctly perceptible. 'It was a
dreadful homily yon, sirs,' says the Ettrick Shepherd, 'and wha'
that saw't would ever ask whether tragedy o' the stage was
moral, purging the soul as she did, wi' pity and wi' terror?'

It has been suggested that she kills herself. The fact is unimportant. The dramatic value is enhanced by our ignorance of
the manner in which she dies. Her work is at an end as the evil
genius that has moulded the destiny of a man and then destroyed him. She has nothing further to do than to disappear.
Like Hedda Gabler, who too is in a sense a sterile Lady
Macbeth, her exit is rightly timed; but it is an exit not through
frustration but through completion.

*   *   *

Sheridan was the first to seek out Mrs Siddons in her dressing-
room and to offer her his congratulations. 'Mr Sheridan . . .
most ingenuously congratulated me on my obstinacy' was the
modest way in which she expressed it. But she had only half an
ear for compliments. She was still under the influence of her
recent impersonation, and the words were chasing one another
through her head. She waited until Sheridan had left, and
mechanically began to undress before the mirror. She took off
her mantle, repeating, 'Here's the smell of the blood still!' This
remark considerably alarmed her dresser, who saw her mistress

[115]

apparently trying to remove a stain from her hands. 'Dear me, ma'am,' she exclaimed, 'how very hysterical you are to-night. I protest and vow, ma'am, it was not blood, but rose-pink and water, for I saw the property-man mix it up with my own eyes.' Which circumstance caused Mrs Siddons so much diversion that she forgot the doubts and anxieties of the whole evening.

A very impressive assembly had met at Drury Lane to honour Mrs Siddons at her benefit. Part of the pit had as usual been converted into boxes, and these in their turn exposed a mass of plumed and pomatumed heads, above bosoms encrusted with diamonds. A Siddons benefit had all the social lustre of a first night. Reynolds was in his accustomed place in the orchestra, doting upon his Muse of Tragedy; and if the production itself was simpler than later generations of playgoers have come to expect, it had the merit of throwing the genius of the dominant figure into stark relief. The costumes were barely worth mentioning. Smith, too conscious of gentlemanly qualities, was unhappily cast as Macbeth, and his solemn attempts to adapt himself to social conditions in the Dark Ages were merely dismal. He immediately collapsed beneath the ascendancy of Mrs Siddons and remained more or less of a cypher for the rest of the performance. She herself was enveloped mysteriously in a cloud of white, although, to judge from contemporary prints, she still preserved the general style of formal dress. Not until some years later came the shroud-like garment and bandaged chin, more familiar, and far more suitable; and Harlow's portrait with the tightly swathed headbands is clearly the eventual costume that she adopted early in the next century.

But, even in this triumphant moment, hostility had not entirely ceased. George Steevens 'ever prepared', in the words of Mrs Thrale, now become Mrs Piozzi, 'to injure those he cannot hate', was not going to allow such a moment to pass without comment. He preserved his animosity in a letter to the *Public Advertiser* in which her parsimonious habits were reverted to. In a reference to the banqueting scene, '. . . the soul of Mrs Siddons,' he wrote, '(Mrs Siddons, whose dinners and suppers are proverbially numerous), expanded on this occasion. She spoke her joy on seeing so many guests with an earnestness little short of rapture. Her address appeared so like reality that all her hearers about her seized the wooden fowls. . . .'

*   *   *

On 8th March *Othello* was produced at Drury Lane with Kemble as the Moor, and Mrs Siddons as Desdemona. Surprisingly enough, considering the gentle sweetness of the part, she made it a great success. She threw off her formidable aspect, softened, became persuasively winning, and Boaden even declared that she appeared to lose some of her height. It was agreed that by her Desdemona she added to her reputation and popularity, and the Press were unanimously enthusiastic. 'In this wonderful transition from Lady Macbeth to the bride of Othello,' wrote one critic, 'Mrs Siddons had shown her genius to be a star of the first magnitude, that could reach and adorn the most distant and opposite points in the horizon of tragic excellence.'

She was thankful for her reinstatement into public favour, but the traces of suffering still overshadowed her thoughts and her correspondence. In March she wrote to the Whalleys, then abroad, a letter long overdue but flowing with warmth and affection. 'I have been very unhappy; now 'tis over I will venture to tell you so. . . . I have been charged with almost everything bad, except incontinence; and it is attributed to me as thinking a woman may be guilty of every crime in the catalogue of crimes, provided she retain her chastity. God help them and forgive them; they know but little of me. I dare say you will wonder that a favourite should stand her ground so long; and in truth so do I. . . . But it is over, and I am happy. Good God! What would I give to see you both, but for an hour! . . . Suffice it to say that I have acted Lady Macbeth, and Desdemona, and several other things this season, with the most unbounded approbation; and you have no idea how the innocence and playful simplicity of the latter have laid hold on the hearts of the people. I am very much flattered by this, as nobody has ever done anything with that character before. My brother is charming in *Othello*. . . .

'Next week I shall see your daughter and the rest. Sarah is an elegant creature and Maria is as beautiful as a Seraphim.' Mrs Siddons was just off to see her girls at Ashton, and although

Whalley had no daughter, his niece, Fanny Sage, was an orphan more or less adopted by him, and she may very possibly have been educated at Ashton too. In spite of the success of Desdemona the first performance was attended by a distressing incident. In the death-scene Mrs Siddons was made to lie on a bed which was damp. The result was that she had an attack of rheumatic fever which disabled her for a few weeks.

Her next play was *Elfrida*. Its author, The Rev. William Mason, who was eccentric, had taken a strong aversion to Mrs Siddons, whom he did not know, but when she eventually met him at Nuneham, where 'he was petted and coaxed by Lord Harcourt . . . like a spoilt child,' she discovered that he disliked her because he could not bear her to be compared with his old friend Mrs Pritchard. The guests indeed only referred to Mrs Siddons before him as 'The Lady'. She reached Nuneham at tea-time, and found the eccentric clergyman wrapped up in a Spanish cloak, sulking. At supper they were neighbours, and during the next morning the pair were discovered, to the delight of the party, practising a duet together. The friendship resulted in an invitation to stay with him in Yorkshire, and all prejudices were forgotten. *Elfrida* was, as may be gathered from its name, a dull play. It was only performed twice, and not asked for again. The setting of its action is in the grounds of Harewood House.

*　　　*　　　*

Although it is not suggested that Mrs Siddons, in the flush of tremendous triumphs, lost her head and began to think herself infallible, there is certainly some indication that she now felt equal to any part. She actually dared to challenge Mrs Jordan, and decided to play Rosalind. The mistake was great: she exposed herself to ridicule; and even though she had played Rosalind in the provinces, the day when she had first enchanted Bate by her performance was long past, and with it had departed that exquisite youthfulness and golden immaturity. Even now she charmed by her tenderness, but she fell into the error of attempting a quaint gaiety. She was also constrained, through what Miss Seward described as 'the scrupulous prudery of decency', to appear in a strange androgynous garment resembling that of neither sex, but uniting the

[118]

characteristics of both. Her matronly hesitations about dressing up as a boy resulted in a most astonishing compromise. She wore hussar boots surmounted by what seemed to be a gardener's apron in front, and a petticoat behind, thus giving herself the most equivocal appearance. And then, in order to emphasize sprightliness, her delivery took on 'a frittering refinement' – according to the *Morning Post* – punctuated by an odd sinking of the voice which rendered part of her words inaudible. Her attempts at archness were unsuccessful; 'Not because she did not properly conceive it,' wrote Charles Young, 'but how could such a countenance be arch?' But it was Colman who produced the most blasting description of Mrs Siddons in the character of Rosalind. He called her 'a frisking Gog'.

Meanwhile the engaging Mrs Jordan, her rival, having romped her way up from Yorkshire into the affections of the London public, got well away with the part in which she became celebrated, and which she played to perfection, and Rosalind, in so far as concerned Mrs Siddons, discreetly retired after two nights. Miss Burney had seen *As You Like It*, and thought Sarah's performance beautiful but 'too large for that Shepherd's dress'. She became far more tolerant in her opinions about Mrs Siddons, although she thought her talent quite wasted in comedy. Joanna Baillie, on the other hand, thought that but for unfair discouragement she would indeed have made a fine comic actress. But she was not to be discouraged; she continued to try comedy parts with the best will in the world, convinced that she could succeed in them. And when in the next year she played Lady Townly, she was not found to be airy enough, and her smiles were exquisitely hit off as 'glorious condescensions'.

Her sense of humour was present and active but too individual to be put across the footlights. It was rather slow. In her quiet way she was often extremely entertaining, and could tell a story to a small group of friends, or read scenes from comedy, in a most amusing way. Mrs Piozzi described her as an inimitable Sir Anthony Absolute when she performed this character to some friends after carefully shutting the parlour door; and she was renowned for her lugubrious and droll rendering of the popular ballad, 'Billy Taylor'. She was, indeed, always at her best in intimacy, and the fact that she suffered throughout her life from shyness accounts for the dread that always seized her before she walked on the stage. Her timidity in public was overwhelming. It was a glaring example of the universal modern complaint: an inferiority complex. For Mrs Siddons once told Samuel Rogers that her silent and haughty attitude in public was due to the fact that she had a character to support and was afraid of losing importance.

The season that had begun in tears and ended in triumph was over. She had performed on seventy-one nights. Of her new characters, Lady Macbeth, which had been seen thirteen times during the spring, was unquestionably supreme. Her salary had been increased during the autumn to more than double its original amount. She now received a little over twenty-three guineas a week. Kemble's salary had been correspondingly raised. From a paltry five guineas a week he had now been promoted to ten.

ELEVEN

WHIT Monday, the twenty-third of May, saw the opening of a short season at Manchester in which Mrs Siddons played for six nights. She opened with *Isabella* and the next evening played *Jane Shore*. Mrs Robinson,[1] who was locally known as 'the Manchester Siddons', watched Sarah's triumphs with a wry face, attributing her successes to 'the folly of whim, novelty, and fashion'. To see her best parts snatched from under her nose and the whole theatre inaccessible from the rush to adore her rival can have been anything but stimulating to this rather depressed and none too charitable lady. It was she who had been so malicious about Dora Jordan. The tables were, however, turned upon her a few nights later at Leeds where, while she was on the stage, Mrs Jordan's mother, sitting in the wings, as possessive as a tigress, seized the manager by his coat and, hiding her eyes with her apron, implored him to let her know when 'that horrid fright' had done acting and speaking, for she could not look at her.

With these and a thousand other spiteful cabals the managers had to deal. They were always thankful when they had Mrs Siddons with them. For she, if even accused of a cold reserve, was at least above the smallness of humours. And though she insisted on a good business deal, she kept her word, never let down her manager, never pretended illness, or, if really ill,

[1] Mrs Mary Robinson, actress, authoress, and mistress of the Prince of Wales. Celebrated as 'Perdita'.

got up to play at the earliest opportunity. Sometimes she arrived at a provincial town without knowing what play in her repertory was to be given on the first night. Nothing disturbed her serenity. If her dresses had by chance not arrived she would inquire what was to be played that evening, and was always ready to agree to the manager's plans without fuss or comment. Above intrigue and above mischief-making, she was a model whom few attempted to copy.

Tate Wilkinson gives a typical account of one of her provincial tours under his management in the 1780's. She was playing at York during the Assizes at the end of July, and the season was brilliant. Her performances excited the greatest sensation of his entire theatrical experience, and only failed to be remunerative owing to the enormous expenses incurred in journeying about Yorkshire. York simply went mad about her; all the boxes had been sold six months in advance, and on 4th August she played to the largest receipts she had ever drawn in any place, London excepted. But if Tate lost money by his enterprise, Mrs Siddons's experience proved the contrary. Her Yorkshire venture brought her in, all told, very nearly £1,100 for seventeen nights, excluding material tributes from distinguished patrons at her benefit. At Hull, for four performances, she raked in nearly £450 – while her manager's profit worked out at £128.

From Hull she returned to York, where, during the Race Week, she played Euphrasia, Elwina and Calista. The last night was performed to such commotion in the gallery that throughout the play not a word was audible. She played for Stephen Kemble's benefit on the following Monday, and then whirled away with the company to Leeds, where, in spite of its well-known Methodism – too rigid, according to Macklin to appreciate the passions of either Shylock or Richard – Euphrasia, Zara, Isabella and Belvidera rampaged or mourned across the stage from 30th August to 5th September, to appreciative audiences and the disgust of Wakefield, whose citizens took umbrage from the fact that the company had not planned to visit them. They followed up their discontent in a letter to a Leeds newspaper in which the ladies and gentlemen of the town and neighbourhood of Wakefield were grateful to Mr Wilkinson for the 'animated exertions' he had so often *professed* in their interest, as well as his indulging them with a performance by Mrs Siddons; returned him hearty thanks for his signal kindness and begged leave to assure him that 'his leaving Leeds to open his theatre here so much earlier in the season than usual, will be held as a distinguishing characteristic of his disinterested (though unmerited) attention to them, and will, on every future opportunity, be returned with a due sense of the obligation it has impressed upon every frequenter or well-wisher to the Theatre.'

Mrs Siddons was booked for an engagement at Liverpool after the Leeds season, which ended on a Tuesday; but, notwithstanding the pertness of the letter, she and Wilkinson planned to squeeze in one performance at Wakefield on the Wednesday before appearing two days later at Liverpool, ninety miles away. Her energy was incredible; Wilkinson, exhausted but resigned. Receipts at Wakefield amounted to £67 6s 6d. He had to convey his company there and maintain it during the day, returning to Leeds that evening. His expenses totalled £62 14s 11d, and his profit was £4 11s 7d. There was little to be gained by producing Mrs Siddons except immense fatigue and corresponding prestige. It is indeed even doubtful whether his great Siddons season was a practical success, for York took so long to recover from the effects of her visit that the *ton* refused to patronize the theatre, and fashionable neglect produced a slump in theatre popularity. The desperate manager declared that things continued in this state for a whole year after her departure. Even Mrs Jordan failed to revive the despondency of the public, so oppressive was the pall of tragedy which fell upon Leeds. Only for Mrs Siddons was the Yorkshire tour a happy memory. She sent a message to Tate through a friend saying that she never mentioned his name but, 'I wish to be regaling with him over a pinch of his most excellent Irish *snuff*, which I have never had a snift of, but in idea, since I left York.' She was an habitual snuff-taker, and the accounts of Messrs Fribourg & Treyer show that they supplied her weekly with a quarter of an ounce.

*   *   *

She returned to London in the autumn to find a lull in the enthusiasm for tragedy. The truth was that the public, suffering

[123]

from a surfeit of tears and what had seemed to be an inexhaustible capacity for hysterics, had turned its attention to the lighter of the dramatic muses. This taste was preferred by King, the so-called acting manager of Drury Lane, and King did his best to encourage the fashion. Sheridan's volatile fancy was also more in favour of comedy, though his attention was now becoming more and more deeply immersed in politics, and on the turn of the tide in rushed Mrs Jordan, who had bounced her way into popularity with a spring, a smile and a giggle. Mrs Jordan had it all her own way. She became the darling of the public, with her careless buoyancy and her artless enchantment. She was, it is true, not made for polite comedy, a domain exclusively occupied by the fashionable Miss Farren; but in romps, hoydens, tomboys and pert country misses Dora Jordan was idolized by packed and overflowing houses.

Poor Mrs Siddons was hard put to it to know how to hold her own. She did her utmost to provide some sort of counterattraction to the rage of the moment, but the fresh material to hand was so poor in quality that she had little chance. She began the season at Drury Lane with Desdemona, and the next night played Lady Randolph to a command performance. On 20th October *Braganza* was revived, in which she played the Duchess, but the piece inspired little enthusiasm on the part of the public. Then came a revival of Garrick's pageant, *The Jubilee*, in which she was borne along upon a triumphal car as the Tragic Muse. Some time during this year – according to an existing engraving dated 1785 – she played the Princess Katharine in *Henry V*, although the performance is not mentioned by Genest.

She was soon expecting the birth of another child, but this did not prevent her from working as energetically as usual. On 26th November she played the part of Mrs Lovemore in *The Way to Keep Him*, Murphy's comedy on the efforts of a forlorn wife to regain the affections of her husband, Lovemore. In the hands of Mrs Siddons she became serious and tragic – too heavy for the light design. The Press was not slow in predicting her imminent fall from the pre-eminence which she had reached, and she quietly retired from public view, allowing the honours to fall upon Miss Farren until her confinement should be over. George, her second son, 'healthy and lovely as an angel', she told Whalley, was born on 27th December. The few months that had immediately preceded his birth had been attended by royal interest and solicitude. Queen Charlotte had twice invited the expectant mother to Buckingham House, and at Nuneham, when the whole of the Royal Family had arrived apparently without warning and had stayed the night, causing no small stir though little inconvenience to Lord and Lady Harcourt, they twice sent for Mrs Siddons, who was on a visit there and, in her own words, overpowered her with their condescension and goodness. 'And the other day,' she wrote to Whalley, 'Her Majesty very graciously sent me a box of powders, which she thought might be of use to me, and which she said I need not be afraid of, as she always took them herself when in my situation.'

*   *   *

That autumn Henderson had died at the early age of forty, robbing the theatre of his very considerable and accomplished talents. It was Henderson and Mrs Siddons whom George III had had in mind when he said that, were he monarch of the theatre, his two favourites should act upon the same stage. Mrs Siddons was quick to remember the ugly, thick-set man for whom she had great professional regard, who had been instrumental in obtaining her first introduction to Palmer of Bath, and who in Taylor's opinion had been the best general actor since Garrick's time. Hearing that Henderson's family was in distress, she tactfully conveyed her offer to play for their benefit should this be undertaken. The widow and children accepted the offer, and on 26th February 1786, she performed *Belvidera* at Covent Garden, which, besides being Henderson's theatre, held a greater seating capacity than Drury Lane, and was therefore capable of larger receipts. The pit was let at box prices and the benefit was successful.

But novelties from the tragedy point of view were either not forthcoming or were total failures. In her extremity Mrs Siddons was reduced to playing Malvina in *The Captives*, a piece below consideration, and on 25th March Elwina in Hannah More's sickly composition *Percy*, for which she had been so praised at Bath. Horace Walpole perversely found some merit in her passionate scenes in this indifferent play, but thought

[125]

her voice hollow and deficient in cool declamation. For her benefit, early in March, when she played Hermione in *The Distressed Mother*, she had lacked the formality demanded by Augustan poetry, and in depicting stormy heroism had apparently given way to rant. Boaden thought that as Andromache she would have been better cast, adding that her affections always seemed to need the inspiration of some duty. Andromache, however, was played by Frances Kemble, whose stage aspirations were not yet extinguished, and the performance was made memorable by Mrs Siddons's brilliant 'Why, Pyrrhus!' in a tone of arrested surprise, as she disengaged her train from her attendant.

*   *   *

In spite of a depressing season, she was at least in one respect able to set her mind at ease. She had for some time past secretly determined to put by enough money to form a small capital upon which to retire into the country at no very distant date. On 1st October, she was able to announce to the Whalleys that she had at last saved ten thousand pounds, the sum she had set her heart upon obtaining. The prospect of a quiet life filled by her children and her friends made her heart glow with tender feelings, and when she thought of the plans that she had made with the Whalleys to settle down snugly near Langford, the idea filled her with enchantment. Her cottage was to be crowned with the laurels of that divine friendship and the peace for which she longed. But the Whalleys were still abroad and unable to share except by letter in her warmhearted hopes. 'Your last was indeed a very scrambling letter,' she wrote. '. . . I beseech you not to give me descriptions of the country, for I am totally uninterested in such accounts, and I grudge the room they take up in some of your letters, which might be so much more satisfactorily filled up with the most trifling accounts of your dear selves: all that relates to you is interesting, but I don't care sixpence about situation, vegetation, or any of the ations.' Which shows what a sensible and matter-of-fact woman she was. She was not above occasional frivolity, and she told the Whalleys that her baby was so like a certain Royal Personage that 'I'm rather afraid he'll bring me to disgrace.' He bore a curious resemblance to the Prince of

Wales, but as the Prince was at that moment devoting himself to Mrs Fitzherbert, causing the whole world to be in an uproar about it, Mrs Siddons's reputation continued to be as high as it had been before the birth of the compromising child.

*   *   *

During the last few years she had become an extremely busy woman. She had appointments, engagements and work from morning until night. The whole world wanted to see her, to touch her, to stare at her and to hear her talk in those celebrated sepulchral tones. It is not surprising that she had no time at all for the simple enjoyments for which she craved. She found herself unable to keep in touch with many old friends. She saw less of Mrs Inchbald for a time, but a warm feeling still subsisted between the two households, and the letters that passed between them continued to be in the old affectionate strain. Mrs Inchbald was associated with Covent Garden, and the future that was to unite the Kembles with the second of the great national theatres was also to strengthen the bond between them and their old friend.

Mrs Siddons's second benefit was given on 15th May when she played opposite her brother's Hamlet. She was not an ideal Ophelia. She was too grandly designed for that fragile part. Her head-dress was lowered in order to lessen her height, and she was thought inferior to Mrs Cibber. But yet in the mad scene, when she touched the arm of Gertrude, Mrs Hopkins, playing the Queen, was astounded into forgetting her own lines. Boaden thought it 'the truest piece of delineation that was ever made from a "ruined piece of nature."'

*   *   *

'I can think of nothing in London,' lamented Mrs Piozzi[1] on leaving the delights of Italy in 1786, 'that is to make me amends; excepting a muffin in the morning and Mrs Siddons at night.' And certainly the season that winter, opened at Drury Lane without any novelty. Dodsley's *Cleone* was the only new production before Christmas, and in this play there was no scope for Mrs Siddons's talents. But the following January for her benefit she played Imogen in *Cymbeline*. It was a marvel of

[1] *Thraliana*, II, 683.

delicacy; strong yet gentle, and energetic yet dignified. Mrs Jordan, who had in the preceding year gathered fresh laurels in the same part, was completely put out of countenance. She could not compete with the high and noble qualities of her rival. In the scenes as Fidele the dress chosen by Mrs Siddons was scarcely less prudish than her peculiar costume as Rosalind. It was designed by her friend Hamilton the painter, and her own request was that he should 'make her a slight sketch for a boy's dress, to conceal the person as much as possible.' The benefit concluded with *Comus*, with Sarah as the Lady, in which chaste part she had little to do but to stand or sit and recite. The grave Miltonic periods, shorn of action, produced an effect of heaviness, and one cannot resist thinking that she would have been heard to greater advantage in the rhetorical part of Comus himself.

On 15th March she played Hortensia in *The Count of Narbonne*, by Miss Seward's favourite author, Jephson. The Gothic revival that was to swamp the stage for the next two decades with various aspects of pseudo-mediævalism was now in full swing, and *The Castle of Otranto* and *The Mysteries of Udolpho* were suggesting themselves as themes for endless variations by a succession of romantically inclined playwrights. Neither Campbell nor Boaden can find much to say for *The Count of Narbonne*, which was a rehash of Walpole's romance. Hortensia showed melancholy dignity and maternal solicitude and left no mark as a character.

The 29th March was the occasion of Kemble's benefit, on which was given Murphy's *All in the Wrong*. Mrs Siddons, still pursuing the will-o'-the-wisp of comedy, appeared in the dashing and, to her, utterly ill-suited part of Lady Restless. She spoke her lines cleverly but failed miserably in her action. She darted about the stage in the manner of a flighty woman, and tried to add frivolity to her restlessness, but that 'the laughter excited was not of the hearty kind,' was the polite comment of her admirer Boaden. The last novelty of the season was Jephson's *Julia, or The Italian Lover*, with Sarah as Julia. Jephson had written the play expressly for her; as doubtful a compliment, perhaps, as an actress can receive unless she can be sure of the author's merit. But there was a dearth of new material, and in comparison with the derivative work of

Maria Siddons

*From the engraving by George Clint after Sir Thomas Lawrence
in the British Museum*

amateurs like Whalley, Pratt and Greatheed, who were constantly thrusting unplayable MSS under her nose, Mrs Siddons had to make the best of that of Jephson, who had at least a certain reputation and following. But in *Julia* the honours, and, indeed, most of the exertion of the acting, went to Kemble, whose Italian lover was Latin in his ardour. Colman had written an epilogue to the play, which, although originally intended for Miss Farren, was offered to Mrs Siddons for recitation. Epilogues, after the custom of the times, were usually facetious and frequently ribald commentaries, with special admonishments to the ladies, on the plot of the play. In a tragedy, the levity of an epilogue was misplaced and harsh, and Mrs Siddons saw no reason why she should reduce the effects of her death-throes to the point of absurdity by scrambling to her feet after the fall of the curtain and coming forward with a comic recitation by no matter whom. So she refused Colman's contribution to *Julia*, and created a situation that in itself was delicate, for Colman, besides being the best writer of epilogues of his time, had a high position in the theatre as a playwright, critic and manager. He was hurt and offended, and when it was hinted to him that his epilogue contained some coarse allusions he was seriously angry. Still, the season came to an end with no further incident.

The summer now for the first time found Mrs Siddons indolent and exhausted. She was, in fact, far from being well, and decided to spend the summer quietly in the country. She went to Nuneham, where she was always welcome and happy. She enjoyed the ease and the agreeable life. In later summers she sometimes rented the Rectory House, which Mrs Piozzi, the former Mrs Thrale, called 'Sweet Siddons's fairy Habitation,' a charming cottage that stood upon a hill scattered over with fragrant flowers, and from which in the distance a prospect of Oxford could be seen, with its pinnacles shimmering in the heat haze beyond the gleaming curves of Isis. Lord Harcourt's grounds included a rich wood on a neighbouring slope, that masked out some offending flat country. All around the landscape was undulating and, in Mrs Piozzi's words, so aristocratic that she began to feel quite a democrat.

The relations between Mrs Piozzi and Mrs Siddons, although not secure enough for the cementing of real friendship, were

cultivated by the one and reciprocated by the other on a level
of social expediency and intellectual interest. They knew the
same people, mixed in the same world, shared the same tastes,
visited at the same houses. For all this the intimacy was shallow.
Mrs Siddons, slow, reserved, attached, sincere, was no match
for Mrs Piozzi's mischievous quirks, shrewd judgement and
devastating wit. Yet the clever, stabbing account of the state of
affairs at Nuneham Rectory which is given in *Thraliana* for
August 1791, unkind and disloyal though it is, must be valued
for its intimate view of the Siddons' family circle, *en déshabillé*.
According to Mrs Piozzi, whose husband was touring in Wales
with a friend, 'my scheme was to reside with dear Mrs Siddons
at Nuneham till they returned : but she miscarried, & to increase
her Illness came a Storm worthy of hotter Climates, which killed
a woman within our view, & fired ten Shocks of a neighbouring
Farmer's Corn under the very Windows. Our young girls Cecilia
and Miss Siddons fell into Fits, the Baby Boy George not 5 years
old was from Home, gone o' merry-making with our servants to
some village not far off – the Mother became a real picture of
Despair, supposing him to be killed by the Lightning : & I had
to comfort & support them all : but my Task was too Great
& gave me a Pain in my Bowels that might have had bad
Consequences. Meantime I had many petty vexations : the
Eating & Drinking at Mrs Siddons's was insupportably ill
dress'd, diry, & scanty : my little favourite spaniel Phillis went
proud ; & as I had received a charge from Mr Piozzi to let
her have no Dog she distress'd me in that small House beyond
all telling : My Maid was discontented with her place of
Residence, ill Lodged I believe she was sure enough, & worse
fed : so the plagues increased upon me, while the pleasure
faded away. At our first coming I liked Nuneham vastly ; the
view from our cottage window was enchanting, Mrs Siddons
sat spinning under a Great Tree at the Door, . . . but her
illness laid an Extinguisher on every comfort, & that settled
Despair of Recovery with which Nervous Patients are particularly afflicted, preying on *her* spirits, stole mine imperceptibly
away : I long'd to see My Travellers again. . . .'[1]

There were plenty of country houses at which the Siddonses
were welcome. The Whalleys had returned from their long

[1] *Thraliana*, II, 814.

visit to the Continent, and when they were not living with Mrs Siddons in London, were dividing their time between Bath and their so-called cottage in the Mendips. From its description Mendip Lodge appears to have begun life as a cottage, continued as a *ferme ornée*, the latest fashion in modest architecture, and been so extended and expanded that it finally reached the proportions of a Gothic mansion. One of Mr Whalley's cherished ideas was that the cottage should be hallowed by a personal gift from each of his dearest friends, who were in return to receive a special shrub or arbour dedicated to themselves. The place was a sylvan wilderness of sanctified arbours, creepers, grottoes and hermitages. Miss Seward, on being invited to contribute as a beloved friend, bluntly excused herself on the ground that she knew nothing about taste or furniture, and that, even if she did, Lichfield was too unrefined to produce it, but begged to be forgiven her inelegance and hoped her dear Edwy would purchase a suitable trifle and send her the bill. When she eventually visited the cottage, she found a special grotto dedicated to Mrs Siddons with a charming poetical inscription which she, unfortunately for the muse of Mr Whalley, did not transmit to posterity in her correspondence. Whalley was harder than ever at work upon his literary compositions. Heedless of rebuffs he continued to write quantities of affected verse. And the year before in Florence he had made the acquaintance of another aspirant to literary fame. Little Bertie Greatheed, now a young man, was contributing to Mrs Piozzi's *Florence Miscellany*, and seriously thinking of submitting a tragedy to Mrs Siddons in the humble hope that she might play the lead.

With August there came a command to read to the Royal Family at Windsor. The occasion is memorable, as it is described at length by Miss Burney as being that of the first interview between herself and Mrs Siddons. Sarah had for a long time been anxious to make the acquaintance of the most celebrated novelist of the moment; and the author of *Evelina*, conscious of this fact, yet dreading it on account of her peculiar whims relating to publicity, had been equally reluctant to comply. They had met before, but always at assemblies or receptions, and had had no private talk. It happened that when on this occasion Miss Burney, as Woman of the Bedchamber, was deputed by the Queen to receive and entertain the Preceptress in English Reading, there was no means of escape. Consequently, when she welcomed the actress in the gallery of Royal Lodge, and conveyed her to the tea-room, Miss Burney surveyed her guest with mixed feelings in which a sense of justice struggled against prejudice but was eventually overcome.

If Miss Burney had expected brilliance, wit and subtlety, she was disappointed. She found that she was expected to entertain a veritable tragedy queen, 'sublime, elevated and solemn'. She admitted that her demeanour was truly noble and commanding, but found her manner quiet and stiff, her voice deep and dragging and her conversation – alas, for Miss Burney's hopes! – was 'formal, sententious, calm and dry'. The delicacy and subtlety which were so prominent on the stage were, away from it, entirely wanting, and her conversation fulfilled in no way the promise of her stage perfections. It was altogether a sad disappointment, and Mrs Siddons even made the incomparable blunder of violating Miss Burney's sensibilities by telling her that 'there was no part she had ever so much wished to act as Cecilia.' The truth is that Mrs Siddons had little small-talk. She might and could converse seriously and intelligently with intimates, but she had nothing but commonplaces to serve to strangers, who, judging from that august and dominating exterior, had little suspicion of the shyness that quelled the springs of amiability which she was unable to express.

Yet this is not to suggest that, to her more intimate friends at least, she was averse to the exchange of gossip. Mrs Piozzi alludes to Mrs Siddons as having sized up Miss Burney shrewdly enough, concluding that for all her apparent influence at Court, she was not in the Royal Confidence, since the Queen 'was not one of those who let the Maids comb secrets out of her Head, & that she certainly had no immediate & personal partiality for Fanny Burney.' In fact Mrs Piozzi could often rely on Mrs Siddons for tit-bits of Court Gossip received from Lady Harcourt. There were times of relaxation from etiquette, and thus the Court ladies were given to entertaining their friends – Mrs Siddons among them – with displays of mimicry shocking yet entrancing to Mrs Piozzi: 'Take snuff like the Queen, & draw the white hand across the dirty nose . . . very impudent.'[1]

1 *Thraliana*, II, 821.

TWELVE

THE system of theatre queues, a politeness which had not yet crossed the Channel, was still unknown in Mrs Siddons's time. On popular evenings, her nights in particular, a crowd numbering anything from five hundred to a thousand persons packed itself indiscriminately before the entrance about one hour before the performance was due to begin. When the doors eventually opened, there was a rush towards them and a brutal stampede. The men, using their elbows and fists to excellent purpose, ploughed their way through screaming women and weaker men, and pick-pockets took full advantage of the profitable situation. There was no attempt at crowd control. Officials stood about warning the public to take care of their pockets and a desultory effort was made to preserve the peace. But once the doors were rushed the populace took their places by right of possession. In the gallery seats were often seized and not paid for, and on particularly rowdy evenings the performance was made intolerable for the respectable occupants of the pit; for some unknown reason both at Drury Lane and Covent Garden, it was quite impossible to hear what was being said upon the stage beyond the seventh row unless absolute silence prevailed in the auditorium. The spectators in the gallery, however, used the slightest excuse for showing signs of displeasure. Their behaviour was often unbridled. When they were bored they began to sing and whistle; when they felt intolerant they yelled catcalls; and when they were seriously annoyed they hooted, hissed and stamped. For that matter there was something to be said for these diversions. In both of the patent theatres were parts of the gallery from which a view of the stage was quite unobtainable, and when for some reason or other hearing was interrupted as well, the occupants felt entitled to amuse themselves.

The boxes presented an equally disturbing scene. Late arrivals kept coming in, too often on 'free passes', and banging the doors; and among the uninterrupted chatter loud voices calling for 'Mrs So and So's places', were constantly to be heard. Then the men occupied the front seats, perching themselves on the parapets of the boxes with their backs to the audience, and carrying on animated conversations with their neighbours. Only the people in the pit behaved sedately. The quiet middle classes, having paid for their seats, went to the play intending to hear every word.

Later in the evening the audiences poured out of the patent theatres spilling themselves across the Piazza of Covent Garden. On snowy nights the scene was one of utter confusion. The distressed crowds rushed for shelter through a forest of coaches, chairs, linkmen and thieves. Every moment people were in danger of falling down on the uncertain ground, a morass of slush and puddles. Coaches and chaises were called for at any price, and sometimes as much as half a guinea was offered for a lift to the City or to Grosvenor Square. Indeed, for visitors coming up to London on a yearly jaunt, it was unwise to stay in lodgings at any distance from the West End, for transport was precarious and inconvenient. There was, for instance, Mr Warburton's hotel in Gray's Inn Lane; comfortable and agreeable to stay at, but so far from the theatres that, when Tate Wilkinson stopped there, he had the greatest difficulty in persuading a coachman to drive him home on a winter's night from the Pantheon, or the Haymarket, or even Drury Lane, on account of the ill-lighted streets in the neighbourhood of Holborn and the shady characters that infested them.

*   *   *

The winter season provided Mrs Siddons with five new characters. For her benefit which took place on 21st January

[134]

1788, she played Cordelia to her brother's Lear. It was a part which, had they adhered to the original text, might have increased her list of triumphs; but the Kembles insisted upon a version which had been popular throughout the whole century, in which the conceit of Nahum Tate had caused him so to mangle the story that the Fool was banished, and a 'love-interest' introduced between Edgar and Cordelia. There was also a great deal more of Cordelia, and the lines she had to speak were mostly those of the innovator.

Mrs Siddons admitted that she had played the part mostly on Kemble's account – that is to say, chiefly to reinforce his Lear. But, if this is the case, the occasion should have been made his benefit and not hers. History does not know what she would have made of the real Cordelia; it only admits and regrets that on this occasion she was quite subordinated by her brother's magnificent acting. That she was gently impressive with filial tenderness there is little doubt, but only one notice is discoverable of the Kembles in *King Lear*. In its gushing praise it pays more attention to the titled audience than to details of acting. It concludes: 'The repetitions of this enchanting play, however frequent, are not likely to tire; on each of them, hitherto, there have been so many *new perfections*.'

*   *   *

For Kemble's benefit – 'certainly not for her own,' commented the sage Campbell – on 13th March, the brother and sister appeared in Garrick's version of *The Taming of the Shrew*, called *Katharine and Petruchio*. There was nothing shrewish in Mrs Siddons's nature, and although she was naturally able to rise to certain heights in whatever she undertook to play, the choice was not a happy one. So far the season had once again yielded nothing profitable. But during the past autumn she had had to face the difficulty of accepting to play a character that she felt was unworthy of being taken seriously. The problem that confronted her was more personal than objective, since its author, Bertie Greatheed, was the son of her former benefactress. He had, no doubt preserving a romantic memory of his childhood, written a tragedy for Mrs Siddons with which he now presented her in the hopes that she would play the leading part. She, again and again, using all her tact, had tried to point out where the character fell short of natural qualities, but the author cheerfully took it away and altered his text, and as cheerfully returned it to her. The trouble with Greatheed was that he had a passable talent for versification and not the least idea of how to write a play. 'It certainly has some beautiful poetry,' Mrs Siddons wrote patiently to Whalley, 'but it strikes me that the plot is very lame, and the characters very, very ill-sustained in general, but more particularly the lady, for whom the author had me in his eye. This woman is one of those monsters (I think them) of perfection, who is an angel before her time, and is so entirely resigned to the will of heaven, that (to a very mortal like myself) she appears to be the most provoking piece of still life one ever had the misfortune to meet. . . . I am in a very distressed situation, for unless he makes her a totally different character, I cannot possibly have anything to do with her.' She hoped by this letter that Whalley would induce Greatheed to drop the matter altogether. But as Whalley was friendly with him, and as the young man had received encouragement from various quarters, this course was the last that he was prepared to adopt; and Mrs Siddons with a heavy heart found herself committed to appear as the insipid Dianora in *The Regent* on 20th March. The play was a tragedy in blank verse, and its epilogue had been written by Mrs Piozzi, who had encouraged the young man's literary en-deavours when, as a member of 'Gli Oziosi' in Florence, and a Della Cruscan in embryo, he had made her acquaintance. Miss Seward did not mince matters after reading *The Regent*. 'To be sure it is a strange composition,' was her verdict. '. . . The author has conceived his characters strongly – but his metaphors and similes are an odd set of unresembling resem-blances.'

It was on the whole not surprising that after the second night of the play, Mrs Siddons was taken ill.[1] So far as she was concerned her honour was vindicated, and Mr Greatheed had the consolation of believing that but for this accident his tragedy might have lasted a considerable time. As things turned out it ran for nine nights. It received little or no encouragement from the critics, one of whom described it as

1 In the *Thraliana* Mrs Piozzi declares that Mrs Siddons miscarried at this time, and that this helped to stop the run of the play.

'catching at finery'; but 'A Lover of Real Excellence,' wrote enthusiastically to the *General Evening Post* testifying to the fact that on its second night *The Regent* had been received with unbounded applause, and distinguishing the author with every sort of compliment.

Tremendous though she could be when simulating passion on the stage, bringing with it the conviction of reality, the parts which most suited Mrs Siddons were those in which she was brought to a state of desperation by adverse circumstances, or raised to superhuman achievements by the consequences of independent action. In Great Tragedy she had one limitation. She was no siren; and she could not easily beguile. Her Cleopatra, in *All for Love*, which took place on 5th May, her second benefit, must have lacked above all the wantonness of Dryden's Egyptian, though she had the pride, the dazzling beauty, the power to subjugate, and the technical mastery over the luxuriant cataract of poetry. It is not that the translation of sensuality was beyond her powers. But its expression trespassed beyond her sense of propriety.

After spending the summer at Guy's Cliffe with the Greatheeds, and after a short season in Scotland, she returned to London and in due course received a summons to Windsor. With May had come the first mild warning of a succession of shocks that were soon to fill the country with alarm and perplexity. At Windsor Mrs Siddons thought that the King behaved in a very odd manner. He took her aside, in his friendly way, and presented her with a blank sheet of paper at the bottom of which he had signed his name. She could make nothing of it at all. It was not to be supposed for one moment that his exemplary private conduct was faltering under the stress of admiration for his favourite actress; she thought too highly of him for that. So she acted quickly and deliberately: she took the paper straight to Queen Charlotte. The first attack of lunacy had overtaken George III and plunged the Court into a state of chaos.

*   *   *

Of the three proprietors of Drury Lane, Forde had been the first to resign his share, and the option to purchase it had gone to the stage manager, King. King, however, was insolvent. His heavy gambling debts prevented him from accepting the offer, which was seized by Sheridan, who then refused his stage manager any participation in the share though on a good security. So that during the summer schism had rent Drury Lane, and when the autumn season reopened the theatre was being managed under entirely new conditions.

The patentees of the theatre had not been liberal with the powers they had allotted to King. His hands were tied throughout his occupation of the post. His activities were so limited that they were practically confined to stage-managing and acting. To Mrs Siddons's disadvantage his preference lay in the direction of Comedy, but here he also preferred Miss Farren to Mrs Jordan. The practical reason for this choice was obvious. It was mainly owing to the support given to Miss Farren by Lord Derby and his party with its consequent influence. The proprietors were dissatisfied. They decided to give King enough rope to hang himself with, and set about sounding Kemble as his possible successor. King complained bitterly and openly of his equivocal position, but the summer had passed and the recess had been dawdled away in a great deal of talk and no action. King then resigned his post and wrote to the papers. They attacked him in return, deplored his loss as an actor but made no concealment of his incompetence as a manager. This gave him his opportunity for lodging a complaint on the undefined powers of the manager of Drury Lane. 'Should anyone,' he wrote in an open letter to the Press, 'ask me what *was* my post at Drury Lane, and, if I was not manager, who was? I should be forced to answer . . . *I don't know . . . I can't tell* – I can only once more positively assert that I was *not manager*; for I had not the power by any agreement, nor indeed had I the wish, to approve, or reject, any new dramatic work; the liberty of engaging, encouraging, or discharging any one performer – nor sufficient authority to command the cleaning of a coat, or adding, by way of decoration, a yard of copper lace; both of which, it must be allowed, were often much wanted.'

Shortly after the publication of this statement, which had its calculated effect on the public, came the announcement that Kemble was to succeed King as manager. He was instantly pounced upon by King's friends as having accepted a trust under humiliating conditions. He cleared himself in the public's eyes by stating openly that 'no humiliation degraded his services to those who did him the honour to employ him; and that the power entrusted to him was perfectly satisfactory to his own feelings, and entirely adequate to the liberal encouragement of poets, of performers, and to the conduct of the whole business of the theatre'. And there the matter ended.

For the Kembles, however, it was only a beginning. The new arrangement, besides immensely strengthening the position of Mrs Siddons, consolidated the family influence in the theatre in manner without precedent. Kemble's qualities as a manager were unquestionable. He based his system upon that of Garrick with sound principles of steady team-work. His rules were strict, regular and well-balanced, but he still, like his predecessor, King, depended entirely upon the authority of Sheridan.

*   *   *

Sheridan's habits were flinging him down a slope that terminated in a pit of irregularity, drunkenness, irresponsibility and debt. Although he was now the chief proprietor of Drury Lane, although his decisions were hallowed by the glamour of his brilliant literary and political reputation, he had no methods in business, and he possessed a talent for procrastination in an unexampled degree. The centre of his interests was now at Westminster rather than in Long Acre, and although at the theatre nothing could be done without his consent, he was hardly ever to be seen there, much less was he accessible. His room at Drury Lane was in a state of constant siege. Authors, actors, and all kinds of petitioners were kept semi-permanently waiting for appointments that never materialized and favours that were never granted. Sheridan might come, or he might not. When he did appear he was always in a hurry, rushing in, usually drunk, only to find fault, and was gone again in a flash, leaving behind him a trail of amiable excuses, and taking away a host of brilliant notions. He was, in fact, always on the way to his club, or his home, or the House of Commons, and would be seen wrapped in his worn greatcoat, threading his way through side-streets to Westminster with his eyes fixed upon the pavements in a state of abstraction. There is little wonder that the entire staff of Drury Lane were in a state of exasperation.

Most of their salaries were overdue, and the treasury was in a state of chronic vacuity. But the moment the suppliants saw their proprietor they found something in the expression on his florid face, and a look in the full and luminous eyes, that made them forget the reason why they had come. Sheridan had charm.

He had even once tried it upon Mrs Siddons; for, one evening, as she drove away from the theatre through the surging crowds of Drury Lane, he jumped into her carriage. Her words to him on that occasion were few and frigid. 'Mr Sheridan,' she had said, 'I trust that you will behave with all propriety: if you do not, I shall immediately let down the glass, and desire the servant to show you out.' The chief proprietor of Drury Lane, subdued by the atmosphere of reproof, behaved as circumspectly as he could until the carriage reached her house, when, as she told Samuel Rogers, 'Only think! the provoking wretch bolted out in the greatest haste, and slunk away, as if anxious to escape unseen.'

*   *   *

Kemble had not long married Brereton's widow, who had begun life as Miss Priscilla Hopkins, known to her family as 'Pop', the daughter of the prompter at Drury Lane. Her pretty face with its peevish expression was a familiar sight to audiences, before whom she usually appeared in the insipid part of a polite young lady in Comedy, when her thin voice generally left an impression of complete indifference. Kemble's motive in marrying Mrs Brereton was certainly obscure. For one thing he had been expected to marry Mrs Inchbald, now a widow, and it was thought that his good looks, charming manners and cultured mind would have enabled him to find a wife considerably above his station. There had been rumours attaching his name to that of more than one young lady of good birth. A daughter of Lord North's was at one time supposed to have been engaged to him, and he was said to have been bought off by her outraged father. But there was no accounting for Kemble's choice of Mrs Brereton. He was not in love with her, and he had little to gain from marrying her beside a slight strengthening of his position at Drury Lane, for the prompter had considerable influence within the theatre. But one day, behind the scenes, he told her with an affable

[140]

chuck under the chin that she would soon hear of something to her advantage; and as this, with a fortnight in which to think it over, was his only intimation, the young woman consulted with her mother. That oracle interpreted it as an offer. The end of the fortnight brought with it a wedding so characteristic of John Philip Kemble and his grandiloquent, if casual methods in private life that the fact that the marriage proved a success is greatly to the credit of both parties concerned.

The wedding took place in the winter of 1787. The Bannisters, friends of both families, were there, and Mrs Bannister found that Kemble had actually made no plans for his wedding dinner: he supposed they would dine at home. The new Mrs Kemble had to play that night at Drury Lane, and Mrs Bannister thereupon invited the party to an early dinner at her own house. Kemble failed to arrive. The guests were in a state of consternation, the bride ready to leave for the theatre at any moment. Presently John Philip arrived in the most deliberate and imposing of his humours, spent the rest of the evening with the Hopkins family, and after the play collected his bride, who by this time must have been looking even more peevish than usual, and finally took her home. Mrs Kemble was from the outset intended to realize that a most unusual favour had been conferred upon her.

But Kemble's idiosyncrasies were limited to his private life. His work in the theatre was in every way salutary. He had a certain amount of uncertain scholarship, a decided leaning to antiquarianism, and a distinct and very useful knowledge of period in costume, decoration and staging which had been sadly lacking in the theatre until his time. He discarded several superannuated players, and his company, when properly weeded out, included Mrs Siddons, Mrs Jordan, Miss Farren, Miss Pope, both Palmers, Moody, Bensley, Dodd, Suett and Barrymore.

The resemblance between the new manager and his sister was of an outer rather than an inner nature. 'Anthony Pasquin' had had his little joke when describing them together on the stage, reacting to praise,

> . . . in the very same tones
> The same Ahs, the same Ohs, the same starts, the same groans.

[141]

Indeed, their general style of solemn and alarming grandeur, their consequential manner of uttering the simplest sentence, and the overwhelming impression of stately importance that they made indiscriminately upon shopkeepers and dukes were merely the Kemble hall-marks. The rest of the family possessed these characteristics in a lesser degree. They were as inherited as their unmistakable features. But the gulf which separated Mrs Siddons from her brothers and sisters was not one of mere degree or even of quality. On its far side she stood alone, spiritually different in her transcendental powers. Kemble remained with both feet on the ground: a first-class actor with a good brain, and an excellent capacity for hard work. Dr Johnson had once asked him whether he was one of those enthusiasts who believe themselves transfigured into the character they impersonate; and he had confessed that he had never felt so strong a persuasion himself. So sincerely did he recognize the truth of the admission that on another occasion he told Croker that although he was invariably overcome by his sister's pathos in a certain play, he always struggled against any inclination to be swayed from the study of his own part by the manner in which she affected his feelings. The difference between Mrs Siddons and her eldest brother was simple. His art, while he was not an artist, was studied. Hers was natural: she was a born artist. Even the scholarship of the new manager was doubted in some quarters. The animosity of Gifford struck out at him in 'The Baviad' with a stinging shaft:

> *Others, like Kemble, on black letters pore,*
> *And what they do not understand, adore.*

Northcote defined the difference between the pair as an example of the inferior person reminding him of the superior. In seeing Kemble it was possible to be reminded of Mrs Siddons, but she never put him in mind of her brother; her personality was too great.

Although his love of mediævalism had the greatest influence upon Kemble's stage management at Dury Lane, the indirect results of this mania were disastrous in the succeeding century. His close attention to accuracy in text, due to the magnificent library of dramatic first editions that he was then beginning to collect, led automatically to meticulousness in the details of production. In his staging of historical plays he was exact in every detail from period ironwork to the heraldic quarterings on the banners. The natural effect of this impressive elaboration was deteriorating to the standards of acting. Audiences, hypnotized by the appearance of plumed crusaders in suits of finely chased armour – where before Kemble's time they would have used their imagination in transposing Georgian generals into the flower of chivalry – began to pay more and more attention to scenic effects, and correspondingly less to the work of the actors. And from this stage in the history of the national theatres began the rise of public demand for display and the decline of public judgement of the powers of the player. And yet it was the solemn and scholarly Kemble, who once, catching sight of a pedagogic old figure straining towards him with an ear-trumpet to catch his words in a most pathetic part of *All for Love*, broke down upon the stage in an uncontrollable fit of laughter. He had a strong sense of the ridiculous. Mrs Siddons had the same; she too sometimes laughed in tragic moments when she thought of some of Mrs Piozzi's absurd jokes.

The summers were now often spent with Mrs Piozzi at her house, Brynbella, in Wales, and when Sarah felt in low spirits, as she frequently did she paid a visit to Streatham. Happily for posterity Mrs Piozzi was confiding, in her notebook *Thraliana*, a series of indiscretions whose preservation had been encouraged by Dr Johnson. She was astounded at her charming friend's cultivated mind. 'She is a fine creature Body and Soul and has a very distinguished superiority over other Mortals. Poor pretty Siddons,' she wrote, 'a warm heart and a Cold Husband are sad things to contend with, but she'll get through.' She remembered her own experience with Mr Thrale. With all her sportive tendencies and inconsiderate behaviour Mrs Piozzi had a certain perception. She guessed that Sarah was unhappy, and had come to the conclusion that she was by no means beloved by the members of her family: her parents, her husband, her brothers or her son, Harry. 'They all like to get what they can out of her; but all the affection flows from her to them, not from them to her. I guess not the reason, but five thousand are better liked by their families.' This is an extraordinary assertion, but it is repeatedly renewed by Mrs Piozzi

[143]

in these private notes. Her observant eye had detected the cause of the apparent enigma in so far as it concerned the relations of Mrs Siddons with William Siddons. When placing her eighth among the beauties of England and Italy, she defined her as belonging to a type 'unlikely to fix a man's fondness' half so effectually as many women with fewer pretentions to good looks. No doubt the air of remoteness which often enshrouded her in daily life, with its chilling appearance and effect of reserve, had something to do with this lack of power over her husband, and a frigidity of temperament must have existed to have caused his eventual loss of interest.

With regard to her other relatives, however, their abuse of her affection seems to have originated in her own strongly possessive instincts to advance them and their interests at all costs. Such benefits as theirs, deriving from her own strong sense of nepotism, placed them under obligations too heavy to be accepted as part of the pattern of Sarah's intentions, with graceful acknowledgements of her superiority. Matriarchal, all-embracing, she occupied, like a spreading tree, the foreground of the Kemble territory, crowding its humbler members in under the protection of her powerful boughs – glad as they doubtless felt of this patronage, the density of the foliage had its drawbacks; it irked them sorely. 'Dear! charming! excellent! admirable Mrs Siddons remains indeed,' wrote Mrs Piozzi, 'but ever on the wing – to serve some brother, or save some sister, or satisfy cravings from her own hungry family'.[1] Hungry they were, though she seems to have felt herself fortunate in the affections of her children – she devoted to them as much time as she was able to spare, and George would enchant her when he said his prayers with her at night, praying for everybody, including his little footstool called Jackanapes. And when his mother, worn out with work, lay down to rest, she felt comforted to see him run to stroke her back, plastering her sofa with his little prints to amuse her. And even when he banged his drum beside her she endured the torment as a noisy proof of devotion.

But in the spring of 1788 a death occurred in the Siddons family. Elizabeth Ann, their youngest girl, died at the age of six. Until the present time the existence of this child has been

[1] *Thraliana*, II, 938.

Mrs Siddons

*From the portrait by Thomas Gainsborough
by Courtesy of the Trustees of the National Gallery*

a matter for conjecture, since evidence was lacking, beyond occasional references to her name, that she was in fact a member of the family. Mrs Clement Parsons, indeed, devoted an ingenious appendix to her book[1] in the hope of finding an answer to such mysterious and tantalizing allusions as those made by Mrs Siddons in her correspondence with her friends: 'Your little Eliza is as fair as wax, with very blue eyes, and the sweetest tuneful little voice you ever heard,' or 'I want sadly to find a genteel, accomplished woman to superintend my three girls under my own roof.'

The mystery is at last explained, and I am indebted to Mr Rupert Siddons for kindly showing me his transcript of the entries made by Mrs Siddons on the flyleaf of the Bible presented to her in 1819 by Cambridge University, in which she has recorded, among the births, marriages and deaths of her family, the name of

> Eliza Ann. Bath, 2 June, 1782. Died April 16, 1788. Was buried at Marylebone Church at 5 in the evening.

[1] *The Incomparable Siddons.* (See also *Thraliana*, II, 714, for supporting evidence.)

THIRTEEN

WITH the autumn of 1788 Kemble's influence was immediately perceptible. His production on 26th November of *King Henry VIII*, which had not been given for the past fifty years, proved that his judgement was worthy of the revival. Henry was played by Palmer, Wolsey by Bensley, Cromwell by Kemble and the Queen by Mrs Siddons who, as Katharine of Aragon, completely eclipsed every tradition of the part. Her entry in Act I, Scene 2, was a marvel of grace. When, at the cry of 'Room for the Queen!' she came into the council chamber, knelt on her cushion before the King and proceeded to make her petition, her poise and dignity immediately revealed complete mastery of the character. The friendless figure was shorn of the unnecessary pathos which so easily might have accompanied the interpretation and, played by Mrs Siddons, was a figure of courage, generosity and grandeur. Boaden insisted that her majestic energy exceeded the eloquence of Lord Thurlow at the impeachment of Warren Hastings.

In the trial scene, where she commanded the situation, her duel with Wolsey must have been a prolonged intellectual excitement. All her intelligence was roused into reading between the lines when the text was bare. It was either her idea or that of Kemble to wave aside Campeius as he jumped to his feet at her 'Lord Cardinal', for then, pointing past him to Wolsey, she continued imperatively, 'To *you*, I speak'. The effect of the reading was extremely dramatic. At this, it was

said, 'Her form seemed to expand, and her eye to burn with a
fire beyond human.' In the first act her words to Buckingham's
Surveyor were withering in their calm solemnity.

> *If I know you well,*
> *You were the Duke's surveyor, and lost your office*
> *On the complaint o' the tenants. Take good heed*
> *. . . I say, take heed!*

The effect of this speech was so blasting to the nerves of the
acting surveyor one year when she was at Edinburgh that he
came off the stage saying as he sweated with agitation, 'That
woman plays as if the thing were in earnest. She looked on me
so through and through with her black eyes that I would not
for the world meet her on the stage again.'

It was a part which increased in interest as the years went
by, and her age and appearance adapted themselves to more
matronly characters. When she played Queen Katharine for
her youngest brother's benefit in 1816, four years after her
retirement it was noticed that she still retained her old fire,
and that the sparks flew as she uttered the famous remonstrance
to Wolsey. Her eye was still the same, and her brows so
flexible as still to give perfect expression to every feeling. Each
note of her harmonious voice was heard throughout the theatre,
and though she had perceptibly aged and was by then enor-
mously stout, she was still great enough to produce tremendous
effects. 'This extraordinary woman,' wrote one observer, 'like
a cartoon of Raphael, preserves the truth of drawing and depth
of composition which first distinguished those wonderful
productions – though in her, as in the cartoon, the colouring
may have sensibly given way.'

The last scene of Act IV, in which Katharine makes her final
appearance, was very remarkable for the gradual and consistent
disintegration of body and spirit. The dowager Queen, dying at
Kimbolton, was played by Mrs Siddons with all the natural
truth of sickness and decay. As she sat back in her chair, en-
feebled and obviously failing, she was seen to be fighting a
tendency to irritability, constantly restless, making the fretful
movement of an invalid, and showing a continual desire to
change her place. From time to time as her pillows slipped she

would have them shifted, and her hands plucked at her coverings with impotent gestures. Now and then leaning forward with both hands on her knees to relieve the strain from her back, perpetually fidgeting and morbidly peevish, she went through the innumerable exhausted phases of life at the end of its tether. Yet she never forgot the underlying grace of the character she was playing, and her parting request was exquisitely made:

> *When I am dead,*
> *Let me be used with honour. Strew me over*
> *With maiden flowers, that the world may know*
> *I was a chaste wife unto my grave!*
> *Although unqueen'd, inter me like a queen;*
> *And pay respect to that which I have been.*

Mrs Siddons that winter was the one shaft of light that pierced the dense fog of politics. Party feeling was tactfully ignored on two evenings of the week; those upon which she appeared at Drury Lane.

*   *   *

Her superb performance as Queen Katharine might alone have justified Mrs Siddons's fewer appearances this season. For one thing her health was far from good; it was beginning to reflect the strain from years of overwork upon a constitution that, though powerful, was not invulnerable, and although little was left for her to conquer she had still to reserve her strength in order to keep what she had won. She was no nearer the realization of her ambition: retirement and repose. The demands of her family had increased, were increasing, and showed no signs of early diminishment: they were insatiable. Harry was growing up, the girls had been sent to school at Calais. But the public, still marvelling at the great theatrical event of the autumn, was hardly prepared for a second treat during the same season. On 7th February 1789, *Coriolanus* was given at Drury Lane, with Kemble as the hero, and Mrs Siddons as Volumnia. The part suited her admirably; it realized her inherent love of the heroic. It is true that at the age of thirty-three she looked a little young to be the mother of

Coriolanus; indeed she seemed by common consent to look more like his sister, for she made no attempt by artificial means to modify her youthful appearance. But in the end this did nothing to detract from the impression she produced. Kemble's adaptation of *Coriolanus* was not purely Shakespearian in its text. He had compromised with the original by grafting on to it some of Thomson's poetical decorations; but even this version was an improvement on the massacres of Nahum Tate which had somehow satisfied the public between 1682 and the first half of the eighteenth century.

Yet on the whole Volumnia retained her original characteristics, and almost all the words spoken by Mrs Siddons were memorable in one way or another. But her finest accomplishment in the play was a piece of miming that brought the entire house to its feet in the wildest delight. Young, the actor, gave one account of it to Campbell, while a fuller and better description occurs in the memoirs of his son. It was the scene of Coriolanus's triumphal entry in a procession of pageantry devised by Kemble's riotous imagination. When Volumnia came down the stage, towering above all the rest, she walked alone, her head erect, and pressing both hands upon her breast to control somehow the passion of pride that swept across her, and surrounded with a radiance which Mrs Piozzi declared to be unequalled in her grand, heroic scenes. With every step that she took she seemed to lurch deliberately out of time with the music, and drunk with the triumph of the moment, until, according to Young, 'her action lost all grace, and, yet, became so true to nature, so picturesque, and so descriptive, that pit and gallery sprang to their feet, electrified by the transcendent execution of the conception.' Other actresses than she might have been ashamed to exhibit so much exuberance and vigour, but she knew that the representation was demanded by truth.

The Law of Lombardy, by Jephson, appeared on 18th February in which Mrs Siddons played the Princess. Whatever Miss Seward may have had to say in its favour the play was not one in which Sarah shone. She played it for her benefit, capping the performance by Garrick's farce *Lethe*, in which she was the Fine Lady who uttered without the least conviction a series of malapropisms which were intended to be humorous but only resulted in vulgarity.

A month later there was a still more lamentable novelty, since it turned out to be both pretentious and vapid. A Mr St John, brother to Lord Bolingbroke, who might have known better, had written a tragedy called, *Mary Queen of Scots*, and this he inflicted on Mrs Siddons with the same importunity that distinguished Bertie Greatheed. So poor was the play that Mrs Fawcett, who was cast for Queen Elizabeth, was on the point of resigning her part, and only accepted it when she was told that she was to act under Mrs Siddons, who astonishingly concluded the evening with an epilogue introducing the names of contemporary boxers. But the season was still to see her play one more interesting character, when she acted Juliet for her second benefit on 11th May. Her performance is not likely to have been more than an attempt at proving herself equal to any field of Tragedy. It was not repeated, for it was obviously unsuitable as a choice. Her features by this time were far too full of character and strength to give any semblance of adolescent passion. The general impression was that her playing was natural; but Mrs Piozzi, who was present, found it the opposite. She thought Mrs Siddons as Juliet was artificial, '. . . but she is a great performer; the parting scene with old Nurse was the cleverest thing I ever saw, so pretty, so babyish so charming.' Illness and sorrow certainly had reduced her figure to childlike slenderness, and she looked in the part as graceful, light and airy as could be wished. Miss Weston thought that she had never seen a finer or more captivating performance.

During that spring the country had surpassed itself in demonstrations of national exuberance, for by an apparent miracle the King had recovered his health and his sanity. The excitement came to a head on 23 April with a state procession to St Paul's along streets festooned with laurel, hung with purple and gold through which swarmed crowds wearing charming emblems of their loyalty. Above them in the houses, where the windows had been removed, sat rows of ladies in full dress displaying loyal insignia, and looking for all the world as though they were at the theatre. In the evening there were illuminations, fireworks and transparencies, and Mrs Siddons contributed to national rejoicings in a rather regrettable way. Dressed in the allegorical draperies of Britannia she recited an ode before the members of Brooks's: an effusion specially composed for the occasion by Mr Merry, the Della Cruscan poet; and she repeated the ill-advised recitation at the conclusion of her benefit. A few days later she left for a tour in Yorkshire.

Conditions at Drury Lane had been steadily approaching a state of crisis in which salaries were so overdue that the leading performers were now extremely in arrears. Mrs Jordan was taking advantage of her popularity to be ill whenever it suited her and refused to appear with Mrs Siddons in a farce because as it was remarked in the Press, '*she* will not fill the house and let Mrs Siddons run away with the reputation of it'. Certainly reputation appeared to be all that accrued to the performers. The worst part of the situation was that nobody knew what Sheridan did with the funds. The receipts were good, the money was received, and yet the treasury was always empty. In the provinces Mrs Siddons was always sure of being paid, and although the engagements and the constant journeys were exhausting she was less nervous before the performances than when she was in London.

So during the summer she toured in the south of England, and in the latter part of July she went to Weymouth, which was just then enjoying a period of celebrity owing to the visit of the Royal Family. Miss Burney was in attendance at the time, and one morning as she walked along the sands with Mrs Gwyn, they overtook a majestic figure who bowed to them gravely. It was Mrs Siddons, who was enjoying the sea air with her husband and child. She took advantage of the Weymouth visit to give a few performances, and one evening in August was to play Lady Townly in *The Provoked Husband* before the Royal Family. But Their Majesties had been sightseeing that day. They had gone over by sea to Lulworth Castle, and a contrary wind prevented their punctual return. A messenger was therefore sent to the theatre begging the farce to be put on first as they hoped to be back by eight o'clock. The audience waited in great patience and cheerfulness. It was the year of the King's recovery, and nothing could put them out of humour. But it was ten o'clock before the royal party eventually landed, and even then they could not come at once, for they sent home for their wigs before appearing at the theatre. Miss Burney noticed with satisfaction that they were greeted with the most loyal cheers and huzzas from every part of the house, even from the gallery from which they were invisible; and as for Lady Townly, she found her exquisite.

*   *   *

At the end of the summer Mrs Siddons took a strong line with regard to the disastrous policy of Sheridan, for instead of finding herself in a firmer position at Drury Lane through her brother's influence, she had discovered his utter helplessness where financial matters were concerned – a state in which he was as dependent as his predecessor upon the whim of the chief proprietor. So she went on strike. She refused to accept any further engagements until her salary should be forthcoming, and stayed pertinaciously away from Drury Lane for a whole year. If her abstention from the theatre was designed to bring Sheridan to his senses, for a time at least it had the opposite effect. He felt that he could manage perfectly well without the services of Mrs Siddons, and that now his strong company of comedy players, Mrs Jordan, Miss Farren, Palmer, Moody, Parsons and Wewitzer, would shine more brightly than ever in her absence. But by the autumn of 1790 he had realized his mistake. The theatre could not do without her: the public missed her; and his tactful approaches, with solemn under-takings of punctual payment, were eventually made to her. She did allow herself to be persuaded, but even then she only struggled through seven performances during the early part of the next year. She was ill, listless and indifferent to work, and by the end of 1791 she had gone to Harrogate to try a cure for what Campbell mysteriously called a 'very serious state of ailment'.[1] Its symptoms appear to have been unpleasant enough, though hardly worse than the cures prescribed by her doctors. Mrs Piozzi commented tartly upon their inadequacy. 'The Physicians have mistaken her case, & have under a silly notion of scorbutic humours – dosed that poor Dear with mercurial Medicines till they have torn the fine vessels to pieces, and shattered all the nerves that her profession had not

[1] Her nervous system had been bad for most of this year. On 2nd June 1790 she was writing to Bedina Wynne, 'Doctors differ you know and it seems they are very much at odds about poor me, for Sir Lucas Pepys says my complaint is *nerves* and nerves only – and that acrimony has nothing to do with it'. *Thraliana*, II, 769n.

ruined before'. It was not, in fact, until a year or two later that the truth about this strange ailment was discovered. 'Her complaint turns out to be the P— given by her Husband, what a world it is!'

But not only health was depressing her; Press hostility had lately broken out again under the revengeful inspiration of Pratt, for Miss Seward wrote to Penelope Sophia Weston in terms of fine indignation: 'You speak, and beautifully do you speak, of indignities and gross insults committed upon the abilities of the Glorious Siddons in several of the public prints. . . . It is past conjecture that P. is the source and master-spring of all the blasphemy against Siddonian excellence. Mr Siddons, as you know, traced to him the first malicious paragraphs that appeared against his wife; Mr W— knows this, amongst other countless instances of his dark ingratitude – and yet it seems he corresponds with him. Alas! how does this weakness abase the dignity of Mr W's character!' Whalley's support of Pratt had not diminished with time, for throughout his life he seemed perpetually bent upon foolish behaviour.

*   *   *

In spite of a few trivial alterations Drury Lane Theatre had stood for a hundred years. It was now condemned as unsound, pulled down during the summer, and for two years the company was moved to the Opera House in the Haymarket on the site of which now stands Her Majesty's. Meanwhile Sheridan, with his usual grand ideas, had placed the rebuilding of Drury Lane in the hands of Henry Holland, who was to design the theatre to proportions verging on colossal. Kemble, who was allowed some influence in the matter, encouraged these plans in support of his own lavish taste, with the result that by the spring of 1794 a monster playhouse, only half completed, was opened to the public as the Grand National Theatre.

The unwieldy building was vast and disproportionate. Holland had aimed at loftiness wherever possible, and a lightness consistent with the size. The final result was that the frontage to the boxes – of which there were four tiers – and their partitions, were far too low. On the stage itself were eight private boxes, and on either side of the pit eight slips so inconveniently placed that on wet nights the hats and coats of the dripping proletariat were very disturbing to the more privileged spectators. Altogether the boxes held 1,828 persons; the pit 800, the two-shilling gallery 675, and the upper gallery 308. In its total capacity the Grand National Theatre held accommodation for 3,611 persons, and a full house was worth £826 6s a night. Nothing in size had been seen like it before. Its interior magnificence had run away with all the available money from the funds set apart for construction, so that the exterior had not even been completed. In fact it never was completed; although from time to time the subject was, like an after-dinner entertainment, allowed to appear, provide a source of lively discussion among the management at a dull moment, invariably to be discreetly withdrawn until a later season.

*　　　*　　　*

'Mrs Siddons is come home; handsome, celebrated, enriched, adored. Everybody worships that admirable creature except her own family – to *them* she is no Heroine – tho' content to make herself Valet de Chambre.' [1]

Like many of Mrs Piozzi's confidential remarks these lines bear the ring of truth – shrewd observer that she was, critical though she frequently allowed herself to be, she had after her fashion, a capricious loyalty and felt profoundly shocked by the state of affairs in the Siddons family.

During the interval in the Haymarket Sarah had rejoined the company, and had acted with it on twenty-two occasions. In spite of her lowered vitality she was more than ever admired, and was as thin, as elegant and as expressive as she had ever been known to be. Her voice had lost some of its strength, though it had a sweeter, more pathetic tone, but she was very far from happy. Her husband was making her suffer by petty tyrannies. It was as though he were bent on making her pay for her superiority of mind and body and she was resentful and bitter. 'Indignant melancholy sits on her fine face,' wrote her impulsive hostess, during the summer; and, 'How shall I do to endure the sight of her husband?' But Mrs Piozzi had to make the best of William, for, after a visit to the Twisses at

1 *Thraliana*, II, 867.

[154]

Catton, near Norwich, where the Siddons girls were left with their aunt and cousins, Sarah and William stopped again with Mrs Piozzi at her Welsh home, Brynbella, on their way to Ireland in a stormy October. She was engaged there for a season, and was to wear herself to pieces in order to supply the demands of her family. A visit to Poland had for a moment been contemplated at the invitation of King Stanislas Poniatowski, but was considered too much of a hazard. Actually, the Irish expedition was a success, for a cheerful letter came to Brynbella saying: 'I have reap'd my laurels plenteously . . . but I count the minutes till I return to my poor girls whose tender reproaches for staying so long, (silly children for whose sake do I encounter these fatigues and inconveniences?) almost destroy me sometimes . . .' There was, too, to be an addition to the silly children, for by the end of April definite plans were being made. A special message was sent by Sarah to Cecilia Thrale, the youngest of Mrs Piozzi's three rather missish daughters: '. . . tell her there is no doubt but I shall present *her* with a Cecy – and not go without a *William* either, for I am sure there must be *two* I am so frightfully large and heavy'. One of the god-parents was to be Mr Whalley; the other Lady Perceval, while Mrs Piozzi had agreed to stand proxy. Between the daughters of the last-named lady and those of Mrs Siddons there was as much intimacy as between their mothers. Sometimes Sally and Maria went alone to visit their friends at Streatham, and then Mrs Siddons was in constant fear. They might do something foolish or catch cold on their delicate chests. 'They take no care of themselves,' she wrote anxiously to Mrs Piozzi, 'and I have so much to *do* and *think* of, that they *should* do, in mere kindness to your affect. S. Siddons. . . . I know not why but I could weep at every word I write to you. Adieu Adieu Adieu'. She felt crushed by responsibilities and unable to be everywhere at once. Nightmare worries surrounded her, aggravating the nervous complaint that now began to take hold of her system. Of the two new characters that she had played during the season, Queen Elizabeth, in *Richard III*, left little for her to express, and Mrs Oakley, in *The Jealous Wife*, was on the whole uncongenial. Opinions differ as to the quality of Mrs Siddons's performance, but there seems to be no doubt that she gave an extraordinarily accurate picture of a woman in the throes of jealousy, poisoning her love with suspicion and submerged rage. Her only other novelty this season had been to recite, at the conclusion of her benefit, Collins's *Ode on the Passions*.

*   *   *

Ten days before the opening of the new Playhouse Mrs Siddons wrote to Lady Harcourt in a flutter of nervous anticipation: 'Our new theatre is the most beautiful that imagination can paint. We open it with *Macbeth*, on Easter Monday. I am told that the banquet is a thing to go and see of itself. The scenes and dresses all new, and as superb and characteristic as it is possible to make them. You cannot conceive what I feel at the prospect of playing there. I daresay I shall be so nervous as scarcely to be able to make myself heard in the first scene.' Her anticipations were almost entirely justified. The theatre was larger than anything that had been seen before, and she was obliged to alter her methods of acting in proportion to the size and acoustics of the new building. She increased in austerity of style and simplicity of attitude; she moved correspondingly upon a grander scale; gave longer pauses and greater deliberation to her gestures. Her whole tendency was now, in a sense, nearer that of slow motion.

Among the novel scenery that efficiently rose and smoothly descended upon the stage of Drury Lane, Kemble had introduced a lake of real water, to the admiration of all spectators. But his production of *Macbeth* was historic because of its exclusion of Banquo's ghost, whose presence was left entirely to the audience's imagination to occupy a vacant chair. There is nothing to be said for Kemble's freakish idea in banishing a ghost whose appearance was plainly intended by the author. But the interior beauty of the new theatre was for the time being enough to fill the minds of the audience, and when the device of an iron safety-curtain was also promised for the near future, it was felt by the London public that they now possessed the finest theatre in the world.

The fashion for classicism, too, perhaps received from Mrs Siddons at this moment its chief stimulus; for the renascence that had been in progress affected England in a very different and less sophisticated spirit from that in which it left the

[156]

Continent. Paris in its iconoclastic mood had certainly sent over representative styles of taste in contemporary elegance; but these, said Mr Boaden primly, 'were received among us with unaffected disgust,' while the style of Mrs Siddons 'remains in a great degree the standard of female costume to the present hour'. French fashions, indeed, were hardly likely to meet with approval at a time when their creators were almost daily expected to land in England. William Siddons spent much of his time in studying the possibilities of such an event, and was extremely stirred at the news of the naval victory in the summer of 1794. He was in his element at Nuneham Rectory, for his wife was away on a visit, and Lord Harcourt not in residence; and it fell to himself to dispense hospitality to the neighbourhood in the character of deputy squire. From distant Oxford and Abingdon he could see the blaze of lights, and hear the ringing bells and clattering musketry, and to this stirring accompaniment he distributed forty-two pounds of candles and forty-two gallons of ale to the villagers '. . . to drink success to the wooden walls of Old England,' as he tritely observed.

Throughout that summer Mrs Siddons, intent as usual on providing for her dependants, had gone so far as to continue acting, although in an advanced state of pregnancy. Mrs Piozzi seems to have realized the inexpediency of this over-zealous demonstration of maternal zeal since to the *Thraliana*, she confided that it might be interpreted as unnecessary covetousness; the old accusations still lingered. However, on 25th July 1794, at 54 Great Marlborough Street, where they had moved four years before, Mrs Siddons gave birth to her seventh and last child, a daughter named Cecilia after Mrs Piozzi's youngest girl: 'such a lumping baby . . . I had a very safe, tho' a long, and *laborious* time, and I bless God that I have brought you [1] as perfect and healthful a Baby as ever the sun shone on. How I long for you to see the little dear fat lump. Pray don't be jealous but I really think she looks sometimes very like our dear Mr Piozzi – her eyes and her hair are as black as his . . .' [2]

This is as close to impropriety as any joke recorded by the

[1] Mrs Piozzi stood godmother to Cecilia Siddons.
[2] *Thraliana*, II, 876.

delighted mother whose humour, rather heavy, rather obvious, rarely as free as that of some of her friends, had previously on a similar occasion expressed itself on the same lines.

For the next few years she appeared in a series of plays which were on a lower level than any in her previous experience. Lessing's *Emilia Galotti*, in which she was the Countess Orsina, introduced the German School which later came into its own as an important tributary of the Gothic Revival. But for all the consequence of a prologue by Cumberland and an epilogue by Colman, which attended its appearance, *Emilia Galotti* was withdrawn after three nights. The next event was the sight of the two Kembles, in *The Roman Father*, endeavouring to make the best of depressing material. Mrs Siddons, as Horatia, demonstrated her genius in raising a play considerably above its original level, for Whitehead's tragedy was a test case of her power to create some life that was non-existent in the text; it was as though she moulded flesh upon the skeleton and infused it with poetry. But even with this accomplishment she could make nothing of Fanny Burney's extraordinary attempt at play-writing. Her *Edwy and Elgiva* was played to the un-restrained amusement of the audience, and its tragic end was concluded to roars of laughter when Mrs Siddons, as Elgiva, was removed behind a hedge to die, being later discovered, in the same scene, expiring upon a convenient couch. Besides this the authoress, now Mme d'Arblay, had chosen three bishops for her principal characters. The failure of the play was clear from the first evening. Mrs Siddons could scarcely keep a straight face during the incongruous performance, and her thoughts kept reverting to Pope's line, 'Laugh where ye must,' at every burst of laughter from the house. But to Mrs Piozzi she wrote a full account of Mme d'Arblay's admirable self-control in the face of ridicule, for ridicule it was, although 'the audience were quite angelic and only laughed where it was *impossible* to avoid it'. The next day, Mme d'Arblay, who had been present at the lamentable performance though still weak after her illness, had gone round to Kemble 'and nobly said, she had been deceived by her friends, that she saw it was a very bad thing, and withdrew it immediately. That was done like a woman of an exalted spirit, and has wonderfully rais'd her in the opinion of all who know the circumstance'.

Five more indifferent plays followed *Edwy and Elgiva*. Mrs Siddons was Palmira in *Mahomet the Imposter*, Emmeline in *Edgar and Emmeline*, a light afterpiece, Roxana in *Alexander the Great*, Almeyda in the *Queen of Granada*, and Julia in *Such Things Were*. She had gone to Edinburgh in the previous year to play for her brother Stephen, where, between his dispute with a scheming Mrs Esten over the Theatre Royal which he ran, and his endless litigation with the New Theatre, he was on the verge of bankruptcy. Mrs Piozzi had little use for the lesser members of the Kemble family. She hit off the situation with her unfailing lightness of touch in a letter to a friend. 'Charming Siddons is somewhere in the North, setting up the individuals of her family, like Ninepins, for Fortune to bowl at, and knock down again. *She* meantime secures glorious immortality in both worlds. . . .'

Charming Siddons, with the resignation of women of her period, was reaching the age when, as she thought, all personal successes might be pushed into the background and forgotten. She had not yet come to the time when she would fling discretion to the winds, make herself look very foolish, and become involved in a ridiculous entanglement. Having set her brother's affairs in order she returned again to England, but paused a day or two on the way down. Thinking over her triumphs she felt she had reason enough to be contented. She had made £800 for herself in Edinburgh, and brought £1,600 into Stephen's treasury. But 'I fancy there is little danger of anyone suffering much from the power of my charms at present, 'tis rather too late,' she wrote reflectively to one of her Scottish hostesses. 'I own 'tis not unpleasant however, to be still well-looking. Fifth of next July, alas! I am forty years old. *O, Time Time!*' Visits to the intellectual North had certain compensations in spite of exhaustion and advancing years. In Edinburgh Mrs Siddons was looked upon by the elect and by the mob as a being not far short of divine. Edinburgh audiences, from the artist's standpoint, were the purest and most correct in judgement as well as in behaviour. They were mainly composed of the legal body, which, in Macklin's words, formed 'the most sensible part of an audience, if not of the nation'. But Mrs Siddons can have had little cause to doubt her power of charming when she could earn tributes from the working classes in language that was worthy of Burns. 'Ah! weel do I ken that sweet voice, that made me greet sae sair yestreen,' was the passing compliment of a servant out marketing who recognized the deep, melodious tones.

But Scotland was not alone in its acclamation of Mrs Siddons. At their Welsh home, Plās Newydd, the show museum-pieces of the age – Lady Eleanor Butler and Miss Sarah Ponsonby – sat in their library beside themselves with curiosity, and in 'a dreadful state of envy, repining, and expiring to see ye first of human beings, and dying to receive her in ye vale of vales'. They had heard that she was on a visit to Brynbella, and wrote to their old friend, the Rev. Mr Chappelow, in order that he might transmit the invitation through Mrs Piozzi. In that engaging meditation, 'Persons one would wish to have seen,' a prominent place should be given to the occasion when Mrs Siddons, at the height of her majestic reputation, was entertained by the pistol-carrying, top-booted, swearing, cultivated romantic-hearted Ladies of Llangollen.

FOURTEEN

IT was now plain that Sheridan had not the least intention of keeping his word as to payment of salaries. Time after time he had driven up to 54, Great Marlborough Street and by sheer charm of manner had persuaded Mrs Siddons against her will to play, bringing her with him at the last moment in his coach to the theatre. By the spring of 1796 the situation was acute, and she had the melancholy experience of seeing the substantial proceeds of her last benefit engulfed in the treasury of Drury Lane, never to re-emerge. Mrs Jordan was also without payment, and Miss Farren refused to act until she received her money. It was the spring of the Ireland forgeries, and Sheridan, piling one enormity upon another, expected Mrs Siddons to play Rowena in *Vortigern*, which tragedy he hoped to pass off upon the public as a newly dis-covered Shakespearian play. A great deal of interest had been aroused by the announcement. To give Sheridan his due he half believed in the authenticity of the MS, Boaden and Steevens had their doubts, while Kemble betrayed his reputa-tion for scholarship in accepting it as a genuine discovery. Mrs Siddons rehearsed her part for a time, but she had her own misgivings; she was fortunate in managing to extricate herself from the situation while there was still time. On April 2, *Vortigern* was produced without her by Kemble before a crowded house. At his express desire the play was attended to in a silence lasting until the end of Act III. Act IV saw the end of public patience. *Vortigern* was hissed off the stage and never repeated. When young Ireland, in a boastful pamphlet, acknowledged the authorship of the fraudulent script the management of Drury Lane were confirmed in their very foolish position. Kemble was anyhow lying rather low, for he had recently been guilty of an assault upon Miss Maria Theresa de Camp, a blameless young lady who was acting with him; and having forced himself and his unwelcome attentions upon her in her dressing-room, to which her loud screams brought assistance, he was obliged to apologize publicly in the Press, a confession that was described at the time as that 'of a penitent Hackney Coachman under the threatened lash of a sharp prosecution'. The case had aroused a good deal of comment, and caused much pain to Mrs Siddons, who was always touchy upon matters of Kemble honour. So far as she was concerned she was becoming accustomed to attacks upon herself, but even she was hardly prepared for the circulation of a rumour that year that she was mad. Yet, though in possession of her right mind, she was never well for long. There was always some worry or new physical torment to keep her from old serenity. She had again been harshly satirized in *The Devil on Two Sticks*, by William Combe, who drew an exaggerated portrait of a famous and successful actress consumed by avarice. Combe, whom she had not met since the days at Wolverhampton, had recently ignored her at Nuneham, and had then gone out of his way to make himself agreeable to her. She bitterly resented the attack upon her character. She fully expected to be called proud on account of her shyness and offhand manner, as she told John Taylor, for she was, indeed, cautious by training from long necessity. But meanness, she knew, was not in her nature.

By the autumn Kemble felt himself unequal to the task of continuing as manager of Drury Lane against the handicap of Sheridan's maladministration, and he resigned the position. He was succeeded by Wroughton. Yet somehow or other Sheridan, the eternal marvel, persuaded Mrs Siddons to play for him that season, and on 22nd October she appeared with Kemble in the name parts of *Edward and Eleanora*, though she wrote sadly to a friend: 'I am, as you may observe, acting again; but how much difficulty to get my money! Sheridan is certainly the greatest phenomenon that Nature has provided

[162]

for centuries. Our theatre is going on, to the astonishment of everybody. Very few of the actors are paid, and all are vowing to withdraw themselves: yet still we go on. . . .'

After an uninteresting play by Jephson, *The Conspiracy*, had been withdrawn, Mrs Siddons appeared in a revival of Lillo's *George Barnwell; The London Merchant*. It had first appeared in 1731, and was founded upon the seventeenth-century ballad. Lillo as a dramatist had been well in advance of his time. The poignancy of grief in the lives of private people and the problems that beset them had never before been treated as subjects for serious dramatic consideration, and by the straightforward and simple manner in which he dealt with his characters and their situations, he produced tragic effects that were only comparable with those of Shakespeare. The revival of interest in Lillo was a direct preparation for the German Domestic School of Drama that was to begin with Kotzebue in the following season, and come to its logical conclusion in the nineteenth century with Sudermann and Ibsen. Side by side with neoclassicism the romantic branches of the Gothic Revival were throwing out shoots in all directions, and the rage for the diabolical in all forms had become an inexhaustible appetite. From spectral apparitions in haunted castles, and prisoners lonely and accursed in dungeons, eternal damnation and lost souls were not far removed. From the latter the cult of melancholy was now emerging, and with this spiritual state fitted in the new German tendencies. Sentimentality, *Weltschmerz*, introspection, humanitarianism and the psychological problem were to be presented under the most melodramatic circumstances.

George Barnwell was as yet only a precursor. It was chiefly revived in order that Charles Kemble, now twenty-one years old, might make his initial appearance as the hero. He played Barnwell with conspicuous success to his sister's Millwood. Mrs Siddons enjoyed acting with her younger brother, Charles, who was a far better stage lover than John Philip. She looked forward to the time when he would be playing with her in *Venice Preserved*. 'I do not like to play Belvidera to John's Jaffier so well as I shall when Charles has the part,' she wrote at a later date. 'John is too cold – too formal, and does not seem to put himself into the character: his sensibilities are not as acute as they ought to be for the part of a lover. Charles, in other characters far inferior to John, will play better in Jaffier. . . .'

In the spring of 1797 she had four new parts. She was Athenais in *The Force of Love*, Arpasia in *Tamerlane*, Dido in *The Queen of Carthage* and Agnes in *The Fatal Curiosity*. Athenais was a character in which she became very popular through her tender portrayal; and as Arpasia she entered with such strength of feeling into the performance that, on witnessing her lover's distressing death – Moneses is strangled by mutes – she clutched at her garments and fainted dead away, striking her head loudly on the boards and exhibiting her limbs in a manner that convinced the audience that the swoon was genuine and not feigned. As she remained unconscious for a considerable time the event provoked an excited rush from the boxes and the pit to inquire about her condition. The success of *George Barnwell* had fortunately inspired the management with the idea of presenting another of Lillo's plays. This time they revived *The Fatal Curiosity*. It was performed on 1st May for Mrs Siddons's benefit. Her Agnes was immediately placed in the front rank of her performances. The story was a horrible one in which an aged couple plot the murder of a young man for the sake of his jewels, ignoring that he is their own son. Mrs Siddons, showing herself old, bitter and avaricious, gave a superlative demonstration of realism. She spared neither her own feelings in portraying unattractiveness nor those of the audience. Her expression, as she sidled up to her husband to suggest the murder, was such that it made the blood of many spectators run cold as the horror crept over their flesh. At the approach of the murder, Crabb Robinson, the diarist, sitting in the pit, was so overwrought that he gave way to high-pitched laughter, and was almost ejected from the theatre until the reason for his hysterical behaviour was explained.

Besides being the evening of Mrs Siddons's benefit, the occasion coincided with a long-expected event: the marriage of Miss Farren to Lord Derby. The performance had accordingly been planned, and rather too aptly planned, to have special reference to that elegant lady's departure from a world of artificial romance over which she had presided so long as queen of fashion, to one of glamour on the assumption of a coronet. Mrs Siddons was therefore to conclude the evening by reciting an address, said to have been composed for the occasion by Mrs Piozzi, in order to compliment the new Lady Derby and her husband. It was a gala night. The address hit off the titles of the triple bill with what was intended to be special pointedness. It included such felicitous lines as 'To anticipate ill were but a *Fatal Curiosity* . . .' 'Each kindest wish waits on her *Wedding-Day* . . .' 'If 'tis not happy, why *The Deuce is in 'Em.*' As the subject of *The Wedding Day* is that of a young woman marrying an old man of position only to find that his former wife returns before nightfall, and as the late Lady Derby had only died a month or two before, the address although well meant was hardly conceived in the most tactful spirit. Tact, however, was a virtue that not even Dr Johnson had thought of attributing to Mrs Piozzi; and by her last allusion to *The Deuce is in Him*, a play which ridicules platonic love, she kept well up to her standard for indiscretion, for nobody believed that there was any nonsense about love in Miss Farren's liaison with the grotesque Earl, which had now been going on for very many years and was an accepted fact. After Mrs Siddons had delivered this appropriate tribute to her elegant colleague the season closed in so far as she was concerned. When Drury Lane reopened in the autumn she was stronger in health than she had been for some time past. She was able to perform over forty times during the winter and succeeding spring, and the first of her two new parts was that of Julia in *The Rivals*. She was still unable to obtain her money. By this time she was owed two thousand pounds which had entirely disappeared into Sheridan's pocket: 'that drowning gulf,' she bitterly called it, 'from whom no plea of right or justice can save its victims.'

* * *

The spring of 1798 was remarkable in the theatre for the presentation of the new play that had taken Germany by storm, and was to provide the subject of a raging controversy in England on the ground of its moral principles. *The Stranger, or Misanthropy and Repentance*, by Kotzebue, was produced at Drury Lane on the twenty-second of March in an English translation. Its theme was symptomatic. Exaggeratedly senti-mental, it was an attempt to treat a difficult problem in an understanding spirit, but it confused the German taste for soul-suffering, guilt and retribution with an imperfect knowledge of human character.

The Stranger, a surly misanthropist, wishing to forget the past, has buried himself in the country, where he spends his time in solitary musing, and alternately in secretly relieving deserving cases in the village. By nothing more than a theatrical miracle he has somehow managed not to meet the sad and mysterious Mrs Haller, who for the past three years has been housekeeper to Count and Countess Wintersen 'up at the Castle'. She too is known and beloved among the local poor for her kind actions. It presently appears that she is in reality a countess in disguise, who in the company of a worthless seducer has three years earlier abandoned her husband and children. It does not require much effort to identify the Stranger as the deserted husband, who is luxuriously indulging his wounded feelings in the solitude of his dwelling in the Count's park. Mrs Haller and the Stranger meet at last in Act V, during which she tries to atone for past injury by offering to present him with a signed document proving her guilt, thus placing him in a position to divorce her should he wish to re-marry. The pair are about to part for ever when their children run towards them, and in a tide of emotion they fall into one another's arms as the final curtain descends.

The moral effect was such that a large part of the British public thought that the world was coming to an end; while the rest condoned the offence by rushing to see the play again and again. Here was an adulteress not only repenting, but actually pardoned, and reconciled to her husband. Even Boaden, a hardened theatre-goer, was alarmed beyond words at 'that seduction which shocks by no external sign, but insinuates itself into the bosom entirely without defence, and in the disguise of that sensibility which is the chief grace of woman'. The hue and cry after *The Stranger* produced the most astonishing string of sententious outbursts from moralists who predicted the rapidly approaching time when not a child in the country would be patted on the head by its own father. But the best part of the situation was reserved for the humorists; and chief among these were the authors[1] of *Rejected Addresses*, who,

[1] Horace and James Smith.

[166]

in *The Stranger Travestie*, burlesqued the plot in a gay piece of doggerel:

> *Who has e'er been at Drury must needs know the Stranger,*
> *A wailing old Methodist, gloomy and wan,*
> *A husband suspicious, his wife acted Ranger.*
> *She took to her heels and left poor Hypocon.*
> *Her martial gallant swore that truth was a libel,*
> *That marriage was thraldom, elopement no sin,*
> *Quoth she, I'll remember the words of my Bible,*
> *My spouse is a stranger, and I'll take him in.*
> *With my sentimentabulus, lachrymæ roar 'em,*
> *And pathos and bathos delightful to see;*
> *And chop and change ribs à-la-mode Germanorum,*
> *And high diddle ho-diddle, pop tweedle dee.*

The Stranger, having fished the Count's son out of the river, is confronted at the castle by the grateful family, and discovers in Mrs Haller his runaway wife; so:

> *To finish my tale without roundaboutation,*
> *Young master and missee besieged their papa,*
> *They sung a quartetto in grand blubberation;*
> *The Stranger cried Oh! Mrs Haller cried Ah!*
> *Tho' pathos and sentiment largely are dealt in,*
> *I have no good moral to give in exchange,*
> *For tho' she, as a cook, might be given to melting,*
> *The Stranger's behaviour was certainly strange,*
> *With his sentimentabulus, etc. etc. . . . .*

Kemble, morose with his solemn and weighty air of importance, made history as the Stranger, dressed in sombre garments, black leather boots and a slouch hat. Mrs Siddons cried her eyes out as Mrs Haller. She wore a grey silk dress and played the part in her most charming and touching manner, though the strain of the performance always made her ill. She used all her art in refining the subtlety of the penitent wife. She stressed the fact that until the last moment Mrs Haller had been resigned to the prospect of a calm expiation of her sin, recognizing that she had no claim upon her husband beyond a modest desire that he should not hate her, but that the final embrace was due solely to an irresistible impulse and to no preconception of her being ultimately taken back as a repentant wife. The final reunion, however, was considered to be such an outrage upon English sensibilities that, with the national genius for compromise, the management defeated the author's ends by causing Mrs Haller and the Stranger to walk off stage in opposite directions after their embrace. The success of *The Stranger* was, of course, phenomenal. It was acted twenty-six times during the winter to overflowing houses and tremendous enthusiasm, and, in order to commit the adorable Mrs Haller to posterity, Mrs Siddons was painted by Sir Thomas Lawrence in this part. The portrait, now in the National Gallery, shows something beyond a facile and technically brilliant execution of Mrs Siddons at the ripe age of forty-two. Her dark eyes burn out of their liquid depth with an expression that contains more than her customary melancholy. They reveal the tragedy of success and the blank of fame upon a spirit that could bear the burden of neither; for in the flowing contours of her mouth are the correctives to success – tenderness, wisdom and generosity.

*   *   *

Lawrence had exhibited his first portrait in oil of Mrs Siddons in the summer exhibition of the Royal Academy of 1797. It showed a certain similarity in pose and general arrangement with the version in the Tate Gallery, although opinions were far from unanimous as to its resemblance. Anthony Pasquin, never favourable to her, attacked it violently: 'It is no more like her than Hebe is similar to Bellona. We have here youth, flexibility of feature, and an attempt at the formation of beauty, to denote a lady who is so proverbially stern in her countenance that it approaches to savageness.' Elsewhere the portrait was considered 'unquestionably the most exact in point of similitude that has ever appeared of that admirable actress. It seems to represent her mind as well as her features.'

The career of Thomas Lawrence had been one of astonishing precocity. Mrs Siddons could remember the day when she had walked through the graceful portico of the Bear Inn at Devizes, on her way to Bath in 1779, and had been rapidly drawn by the ten-year-old son of the landlord, a beautiful child whose easy talents for draughtsmanship and recitation were used by his father as a means of attracting the patronage of distinguished travellers. From the age of five the boy had been placed on the counter of the tap-room to entertain guests with recitations, and when later he had exhausted the intellectual capacities of local masters, he went to Bath and studied painting under Hoare. There was soon nothing left for him to learn. As a portrait-painter he took London by storm, received Court patronage, and was elected to the Royal Academy as supplemental Associate while still under age for that distinction. In 1790 he was twenty-one. In Bath and London society he had met Mrs Siddons again, and before long he was being received at her house as an intimate friend. He drew her so often that he seemed almost to be enamoured of her features. He admired her greatly. He had made drawings of her in many of her parts, and in her private character as well. In the intervals he painted her brother. For years to come the Royal Academy was regularly visited by a shower of Kemble portraits in every possible attitude and costume.

During the short time in which Lawrence was rocketing to fame, the two Siddons girls were at their school at Calais. When they emerged in 1793 Sally was eighteen and Maria fourteen. The elder of the two was immediately plunged into the movement of her mother's restless social world, and she found a natural and ready-made escort in the decorative young painter. Lawrence's presence was absolutely fatal to women. He had the disastrous faculty of appearing to be entirely absorbed in the person who for the time being occupied his attention; thus giving the unfortunate impression that his heart was entirely at the disposal of whichever woman he happened to be with. He frequently came to Great Marlborough Street, for his studio in Greek Street was not far away. He presently began to think that he was in love with Sally. Sally was not for nothing Mrs Siddons's eldest daughter. She had the same gravity and calm reasonableness; she was very gentle and very kind. But she was inexperienced for all her self-command, and she began to return the affection of her dazzling admirer. The subject evidently was not mentioned to her parents; if Mrs Siddons had any suspicions about the matter

[169]

she kept them to herself. She had always had a weakness for Lawrence, whose prospects, indeed, were brilliant but, at the time, neither reliable nor in any way substantial.

Maria, too, was growing up. She was extremely pretty; superficially far more attractive than Sally, who was considered by Mrs Piozzi to be 'just as pretty as every pretty girl of the same age'; but Maria, like her sister, was constitutionally delicate. Both girls had a dangerous tendency to lung troubles.

Once they were settled at home, Mrs Siddons was able to devote time to her daughters. They went about with a crowd of friends to the season's assemblies and to the latest sights. There were expeditions with the Thrale girls to Ranelagh; there were visits to an astronomical exhibition called the Eidouranion; and again to see the curious 'Kangarou' from newly discovered Australia. The young ladies were dressed in the height of the fashion; it was even thought a scandalous one by older people, for it came from France and was infected by Jacobinism. They wore sashes or zones worn high in imitation of Grecian models, 'self-coloured' drawers and stockings, and their heads were dressed *à la Brutus* with hair cropped short in a tousled mop in the most becoming style. The disruptive influence of the new tendencies had affected almost every house in London at that time. Weisshaupt's *Illuminati* were thought by many people to be at the bottom of the trouble; they were said to be undermining authority, law and order. Freemasons, secret societies, magnetism, and even harmless reading societies came in for a share of the blame and were looked upon with suspicion. Mrs Piozzi actually thought she detected an indescribable chill in the household at Great Marlborough Street, for although Mrs Siddons was never cold to her old friends, she was by nature careful: many people came to her house and every class of opinion was represented there at a time when politics and philosophy had invaded private life. With the indiscreet presence of Mrs Piozzi, differences of opinion might arise with the minimum of encouragement. The house was always open to the family, however, and the most frequent guests at No. 54 were the Twisses. Sally and Maria had to be dutiful nieces to their Aunt Frances, who was becoming very stout indeed; and they can have had little pleasure in the

[170]

presence of her husband, who, as he sat there stooping, with his pallid face framed in a brown Brutus wig, and planned his celebrated concordance to Shakespeare, indulged in the dis-agreeable practice of taking clouds of snuff which can have hardly been beneficial to the delicate chests of his two nieces.

FIFTEEN

B Y the autumn of 1797 the position in which Lawrence found himself had considerably altered. He made the important discovery that he had been mistaken in his choice. During his repeated visits to the Siddonses he had come to see an irresistible fascination in Maria's fragility and nervous manner. Maria, moreover, was determined to get him away from her sister. His method of disengaging himself from the one girl and transferring his attention to the other without causing ill-feeling has been considered a triumph of diplomacy. But with any girl other than Sally the manœuvre might not have been so successful. Seeing that he was acceptable to her sister, she quietly renounced her claim upon the man she had grown seriously to love and stepped into the background. Maria's courtship continued throughout the early part of winter with feverish animation. Lawrence had spoken to Mrs Siddons but had not been encouraged. He was perpetually in debt, had the entire responsibility of supporting his family and was not yet in a position to marry. Maria met him clandestinely. Notes passed to him at Greek Street through the agency of Sally Bird, their mutual friend, and there were rapid meetings to which Maria would recklessly fly, stealing out of her parents' over-heated house after dark on December evenings to talk to Lawrence in the cold of Soho. The natural result of these secret assignations was that she became very seriously ill. Her condition more than ever weakened her parents. William Siddons, having been kept in ignorance of the previous romance seemed

anxious now to humour his sick daughter in any way that
seemed to offer better health. And by January 1798, he had
consented to an engagement. Throughout its course, the
unfortunate affair proceeded with alarming velocity. Before
long Maria was confined to the drawing-room under the most
insanitary conditions, from January 1798, until March, she
was kept in an atmosphere that was never once renewed. The
windows were shut tight for three months, stuffiness being the
latest fad as a cure for disease. Lawrence came to see her
regularly; other friends were always calling to distract the
invalid; she was so well nursed by her mother and her devoted
Sally that they all felt that under the circumstances Maria's lot
might have been harder. None the less there were signs of
approaching trouble. By February she was already noticing
that Lawrence's emotional passion was subsiding. 'Nothing
can be so delightful as the *unremitting* attention of those we love,'
she wrote to her confidante, Miss Bird, 'but where shall we find
constancy enough in this wicked world to make us always
happy!' The truth was not long in revealing itself. During his
repeated visits to the sick girl Lawrence once more had assessed
his values of love and happiness. He saw Maria, to whom he
was engaged to be married, lying fretfully upon her couch in
the stuffy drawing-room, monopolizing the attention of everyone within reach. She was completely self-centred in her
neurotic condition, and only aroused from her indifference to
life by the compassion which she excited as an interesting
invalid. She was difficult, petulant, capricious and egoistic.
Lawrence began to be bored. He saw Sally, on the other hand,
a ministering angel, never far from her sick sister, keeping her
company with books and work, or singing some of the new
songs which she had composed. 'When summer's burning heats
arise,' with its note of plaintive melancholy, Maria particularly
liked, for in her close confinement she felt herself sadly out of
touch with the world. She had not even seen *The Stranger*. The
link between the girls was powerfully forged; it had not
diminished under recent strain. It became clear by degrees to
Lawrence that his first choice should have been permanent.
His attachment to Sally returned and was soon established
definitely in his heart. For a time he was moody and dejected
and unable to deal with the situation. Then he went to Mrs

Siddons and actually explained the dilemma in which he found himself. 'Violent scenes of the most painful emotion, of which the cause was inexplicable and incomprehensible,' took place between them, according to Fanny Kemble, the family memorialist. Lawrence made his confession 'in a paroxysm of self-abandoned misery . . . and ended by imploring permission to transfer his affections from one to the other sister.' Here was the moment in which Mrs Siddons should have shown strength of character and moral determination. She ought undoubtedly to have shown the door to Lawrence, and to have shut him for good out of the lives of her delicate daughters. But she did nothing of the kind. She was frightened, conventionally afraid of a scandal, terrified by Lawrence's uncontrolled state and cowed by his threats to take his own life. For the time being she was too afraid to consult with anybody. She kept the perplexing problem to herself, and from that moment onward Lawrence had the upper hand. She weakly gave him some sort of promise that she would recognize his engagement to Sally so long as the whole affair should for the moment be suppressed, even from the knowledge of her husband. It is not surprising that recent writers should have treated the episode from its psychological aspect, attributing this very weakness to a subconscious romantic affection between the older woman and the artist. Lawrence, for all his inconstancy towards the daughters, was permanently hypnotized by the beauty and personality of the mother; and in her tolerant attitude towards him might equally be interpreted a weakness due more to sentiment than to character. For an habitually strong-minded woman, Mrs Siddons was unpardonably vacillating throughout the entire course of the tragedy.

Maria, meanwhile, having wilted through the winter and spring, like a flower out of water was considered well enough by the end of May to have a change of air and scene. She was removed to Clifton, where Mrs Pennington had placed herself and her house at the disposal of the invalid. Mrs Pennington had formerly been Miss Penelope Sophia Weston of the Bath set; and since her marriage to Mr Pennington – who had hoped unsuccessfully to do for Clifton what Beau Nash had done for Bath – she lived there in Dowry Square, a well-intentioned, rather meddling, fussy creature, hardly the ideal person with whom to settle an invalid in the last stages of rapid consumption, being herself a confirmed valetudinarian. Hypochondria seems fairly to have governed her existence; her correspondence is full of the most depressing particulars. 'My nerves, from constant agitation of one sort or other, are become so excessively irritable . . .' she wrote to Mrs Piozzi. 'Faintings of such a *deadly* nature and frightful continuance come on, as no one expects me to revive from. . . . The last fit I had was so deadly, that I think nothing but the wild cries and lamentations of my husband, who, poor soul! *found me* in that condition, would have called me back. . . .'

However, to Maria she was kindness itself, and pathetically delighted to be of service to such a personage as Mrs Siddons. By July the whole family had arrived at Clifton, and had taken up their quarters quite near Mrs Pennington's house. From the windows of No 6 Prince's Buildings they could look down on the Bristol Channel, and watch the fine West Indiamen, crowding four or five at a time, richly laden, past St Vincent Rocks. And there poor Maria would lie, and be led to think she was better for the change of scene; but her cough was as bad as ever, and her pulse always over ninety. On the whole Mrs Siddons, preoccupied as she was, felt better too. She had Sally with her, but she put Cecy to a little school, because, as she said, 'her prattling hurt Maria's head'. She had time to see a few old acquaintances at Clifton, for the Whalleys were there, and her friends the Lees; while the season's most distinguished visitor was the celebrated Corsican hero, General Paoli. After a few weeks with her sick daughter, Sarah left for Cheltenham to fulfil an engagement there, leaving Maria with her hostess to drink the Clifton waters and benefit by the fine weather.

Lawrence had determined upon a violent course of action. Made desperate by his passion for Sally he definitely refused to accept the decree that he was not to meet her. In the uncontrollable state of his emotions he was ready to imagine the wildest turn of circumstance. He was, for one thing, uncertain of the true state of her feelings towards himself, and doubtful how far loyalty to her sister might have impaired her own devotion to him. On the other hand Maria, whom he loved next to Sally, was on his conscience, and he was uncertain of the extent to which he was answerable for her dangerous condition. When Mrs Siddons arrived at Birmingham, Lawrence, on the pretext of visiting his sister there, burst upon her in a desperate state. The interviews between them were emotional and excessively painful. The situation had to be kept secret from William Siddons, now an irritable and rheumatic-ridden cripple on crutches, and a meeting with Sally had to be avoided. Her mother packed her off again to Clifton to help in nursing her sister, and two days later Lawrence appeared in the same town and in a series of frantic letters began to pester Mrs Pennington. During the hysterical correspondence that followed that good lady behaved with admirable common sense. She refused to be brow-beaten by Lawrence's wild and despairing threats, agreed eventually to meet him, and, temporarily to placate him, appears to have allowed him one interview with Sally, who evidently behaved with courage and consistency. Slightly calmed, Lawrence returned to Birmingham, where, after a stormy scene with Mrs Siddons, in which she nearly fainted several times during its four-hour duration, he took himself off to London.

By September Mrs Pennington was in the thick of it. The physicians had been hopeless from the beginning, and, a fortnight after the departure of her family, Maria's condition had suddenly changed and she had grown rapidly worse. She drooped and faded daily, and her natural irritability was augmented by her disease, adding to her own suffering and to the trials of the household in Dowry Square.

When Mrs Pennington felt that she could bear the responsibility no longer, she had sent for Sally. Sally had arrived to take her share in the nursing, and had then gone down herself ten days later with asthma, so that Mrs Pennington had the two girls on her hands, increasing worry, added responsibility and very slender means. Nevertheless the amiable soul, always rather touchy, wrote to Mrs Piozzi feeling a great martyr. 'I rejoice however that it has been in my power to serve my dear Mrs Siddons and to give her this unfeigned testimony of my *true* love. I really think such a scene, as I have gone through for five weeks past, would have been *too much* for *her* health and spirits, and I always shall have the greatest satisfaction in

[176]

Mrs Siddons as Queen Katharine

*From a drawing by A. E. Chalon
in the Victoria and Albert Museum*

thinking that I have saved her so much misery, for tho' she has doubtless been very anxious and uneasy, she cannot have suffer'd as she must have done from Hour to Hour and from Day to Day *on the Spot*. We expect her here on the 24th August – unless we are under the *painful* necessity of giving her a *more speedy* summons – and it is extremely doubtful now what a Day may produce.'

The distracted mother had, after being in Birmingham, gone to play at Brighton, where, despite the alarming times – Ireland was in the throes of a rising, and the French invasion was considered imminent – frivolous life went on as usual. Mrs Siddons had never felt less like gaieties. Yet she was occasionally forced to go out. She had against her wish to meet Lady Jersey with the Prince of Wales, who was dictating taste to society from the painted alcoves of his exotic Pavilion. She was at least rewarded by the sight of the Prince's unpopular charmer wearing her hair cut to one inch in length all over her head and braided with a single row of white beads. 'But we go on dancing and singing,' she wrote back to her friend at Clifton, '. . . and I, among the rest, sometimes force a *feeble laugh*.'

On 21st September the Siddonses reached Clifton in answer to an urgent summons. Sarah had stepped into a postchaise immediately upon leaving Drury Lane after a performance of *Jane Shore*, and had driven straight down to her daughter, reaching Clifton the next evening. She had been fully prepared by the Penningtons for what she was to see, and therefore the shock on arrival was less than might have been expected.

She bore the trial with remarkable fortitude. She was a tower of strength in the chaotic household, never leaving Maria's side, and filling her with comfort and serenity by her peaceful presence. It needed all the composure and resignation that she could command to bear the sight of her daughter's sunken features and discoloured face, on which 'not one trace of even *prettiness*' remained to give evidence of Maria's former attractions, as Mrs Pennington wrote in answer to Lawrence's anxious inquiries. Maria had been carried in a sedan chair to rooms over the way that her parents had taken, her hostess being secretly relieved that 'the last sad scene' should not take place in her own house. Her intellect had gained in clearness with the disintegration of her physical powers, and she had literally become a breathing skeleton. She seemed though to gain a peculiar grace, appearing in all her actions to increase in energy, though for the last four days of her life she hardly slept, or, excepting for medicine, took nourishment of any kind.

On Friday, 5th October Mrs Siddons, who had only twice undressed since her arrival at Clifton a fortnight before, fainted on the sofa which had been placed near Maria. She was completely exhausted but was eventually prevailed upon to go to bed, and was replaced by Mrs Pennington and Sally for the vigil. Maria woke in the small hours and a great change in her had taken place. She asked to be told the truth about her state, accepted it calmly, regretted her excessive vanity and, looking at her emaciated hands, remarked that she hoped her great sufferings would be sufficient expiation.

Some hours later she summoned the energy to fulfil her last act of tremendous egoism. She extorted an assurance from Sally that she would never marry Thomas Lawrence. When Mrs Siddons had finished reading the prayers for the dying, Maria returned to the subject of her former lover and asked her mother to recover her letters to him. Then she played her trump card. In front of Mrs Siddons Maria asked Sally to confirm the promise she had made earlier in the evening, a conversation which Mrs Pennington repeated verbatim in a letter to Lawrence when all was over. Sally, taken at a disadvantage, allowed her generous heart to commit her for life. 'I did *not* promise, dear, dying Angel; but I *will* and *do*, if you require it.' 'Thank you, Sally; my dear Mother – Mrs Pennington – *bear witness*. Sally, give me your hand – you promise never to be his wife; Mother – Mrs Pennington – lay your hands on hers. You understand? Bear witness.' Then taking full advantage of the situation in which her weeping family were entirely defenceless, she pointed her finger at her sister. 'Sally, sacred, sacred be this promise. *Remember me*, and God bless you!'

Shortly after this remarkable valediction Maria expired at two o'clock on the Sunday morning. The supreme egoism which triumphed at her last moments went side by side with an exquisite transfiguration. She had charmingly taken leave of

[178]

everyone in the house, and having thanked her father for his goodness and the servants for their attention, an expression of beatific joy appeared on her moribund face, and she died breathing the names of her mother and sister. Mrs Pennington, when she examined the cold remains, noted the curious fact that she exactly resembled her mother as she might look at the age of seventy: not one trace remained of youth.

*   *   *

The newspapers had recorded the melancholy event quite a fortnight before it actually took place, and the family were prematurely inundated with letters of condolence. Maria's death had created a tremendous stir at Clifton, and the Siddonses were thankful to escape from the curiosity of the public. Three days later they deposited her remains in the Old Parish Church at Clifton, and immediately left for Bath.

Lawrence was beside himself. He had received Mrs Pennington's considerate and kindly worded letter informing him of every detail of Maria's death. She had probably hoped that by doing so his heart would be touched, and he might consequently spare Sally unnecessary persecution. She received a communication from him in reply which put an end to further correspondence. In handwriting that can best be described as an abandoned scrawl he gave vent to devilish rage:

'It is only my Hand that shakes, not my Mind.

'I have play'd deeply for her, and you think she will still escape me. I'll tell you a Secret. *It is possible she may. Mark the End.*

'You have all play'd your parts admirably! ! !

'If the scene you have so accurately describ'd is mention'd by you to *one Human Being*, I will pursue your name with execration.'

*   *   *

Mrs Pennington, over-tired and exhausted by the strain of the past two weeks, acted with sense and judgement. She sent the letter with its 'stamp of a *dark* and *desperate* character', to Mrs Siddons, advising her to take both her husband and brother into her confidence on account of Sally's protection, for 'While *he* thinks he has *only* the *timidity* of *women* to operate on

[179]

. . . there is no saying *what* he may not *attempt*,' she desperately hinted. Mrs Siddons, however, found herself in a predicament. If she confided in her brother, she knew that the story would at once be spread all over the town by his garrulous wife, whereas if, on the other hand, she were to tell William the whole truth, she was equally certain that he would not be able to resist consulting Kemble. She knew her husband well enough by now, and she realized that by confiding in him she would incur his harsh and repellent attitude of displeasure to the whole business. He was becoming a disagreeable old man. In addition to his lameness he had been speculating rashly in theatrical properties and had lately lost a great deal of money in a transaction over Sadler's Wells. His temper had not improved, and his jealousy at his wife's success had augmented. Mrs Siddons decided for the present to keep the matter to herself.

Once she was back in London she settled down for the winter, attempting to resume, as far as possible, her normal life, though inwardly bearing the scars of the recent terrible months. She returned to the theatre as Isabella in *Measure for Measure*, a part carefully chosen on account of its strictly impersonal, almost abstract qualities. Sally, although prone to violent attacks of asthma, was in the intervals encouraged to go about as much as possible to houses where she was unlikely to meet Lawrence. Notwithstanding the promise that had been wrung from her unwillingly and which she was disposed to consider as neither fair nor binding, her efforts at avoiding him, stimulated by her mother and urged by Mrs Pennington, who, at one bound had become the family adviser-in-chief, were seriously maintained. Yet she felt that she could not treat him coldly were they unexpectedly to come face to face. She was not left entirely alone to indulge in her sad thoughts, for Mrs Siddons had lately prevailed upon Tate Wilkinson to allow his daughter to come to London and spend the winter at Great Marlborough Street, and to keep Sally company while she herself was at work. From this time onward Patty Wilkinson became a permanent member of the Siddons household; almost more of a companion to the mother than to the daughter, accompanied Sarah on all her travels, and until her death never left her.

* * *

Shortly after her return to Drury Lane Mrs Siddons found
that she was committed to two new plays which had been
written by personal friends of hers. Both productions were in
the pseudo-mediæval style; the first being Boaden's *Aurelio and
Miranda*, inspired by the most audacious novel of its time,
Matthew Gregory Lewis's *The Monk*, while the second, produced early in the New Year, was a fatuous tragedy, by the
hand of Mr Whalley. In common justice to Mrs Siddons it
must be repeated that she thoroughly disliked having to appear
in bad plays, and if a bad play was written by a good friend
the situation was complicated by the intrusion of personal
relationship. Her line of professional conduct was usually too
sharply defined to allow of concessions to sentiment. But for
years past Whalley had been forcing his MSS upon her in
egregious taste, and had apparently taken no offence at her
kindly worded condemnation of them. Finally she had been
persuaded to play in his Gothic horror, *The Castle of Montval*.
It had already been condemned out of hand by many people,
but there were also some who found it by no means poor. Miss
Seward and Mrs Piozzi were warmly interested in its progress.
The latter, in her sprightly manner, wrote charmingly to Mr
Chappelow at the time: 'Remember me to kind Mr Whalley,
to whose Play I wish Success most sincerely . . . 1 now see 'tis
that has driven Siddons back to Drury Lane. She never writes
herself to anyone . . . it is *her way* never to write so one goes
merely by conjecture but I am sure tis that. Tell me if you go
to see it how far good Fortune goes before . . . and Fame flies
after with a Laurel as Prior says'. In any case, with customary
thoroughness Mrs Siddons worked her hardest to make it a
success, although the rest of the cast were so sure that it would
be a failure that they did not even trouble to learn their parts.
As it turned out, *The Castle of Montval*, although ridiculously
melodramatic, was repeated for eight nights, each time to
larger houses, until it seemed like lasting for an indefinite
period; although its rival 'Monk' Lewis's own *Castle Spectre*,
was a far better study in romantic horrors. Then, it was
deliberately killed by Sheridan, who, encouraged by the
success of *The Stranger*, and having translated another play by
Kotzebue, was now burning to see it produced with all the
splendour that he could devise. He had been working at his

version of *Pizarro* with feverish energy for many months, and the preparations that he had put in hand for its production surpassed in extravagance of design anything of the kind that had been seen before. The text, which concerned the adventures of Spanish conquistadores in Peru, and was set off to martial accompaniments among a profusion of Inca temples and sacrificial rites, had, in the bombastic sentiments uttered by the chief characters, been copiously adorned with some of the most rhetorical passages from his orations, and included flowery specimens of his own eloquence at the trial of Warren Hastings. He had, too, departed in style from his usual lightness of touch; and working from a translation, for he knew no German, had attempted to convey the rhodomontading atmosphere of the rather ponderous original. All his best actors were included in the cast. Kemble as the Peruvian, Rolla, Mrs Jordan as Cora, Charles Kemble as Alonzo, Aickin as Las Casas, Barrymore as Pizarro and Mrs Siddons as Elvira. Their patience was exemplary. In spite of Sheridan's enthusiasm for the success of *Pizarro* they were not even in possession of their complete parts by the morning of the play's production on 24th May, when the last act was distributed among the members of the company while they were actually on the stage. Sheridan well knew the value of cultivated improvisation, and the ready tension of suspense that attended it. He was not mistaken. His cast, strung up to the last moment to the highest pitch of nervous excitement, played their parts at top form.

Mrs Siddons had been far from pleased at first when she discovered that her part was that of a common camp-follower pursuing her lover into the heart of danger; but with her usual capacity for accomplishing the impossible, she somehow raised the degraded Elvira to the heights of romanticism, turning her into a fierce and elemental being of grandeur, and inspiring the character to such a degree of loftiness that Kemble himself remarked, 'My sister has made a heroine out of a soldier's trull'. Her appearance, too, was Amazonian, in a warlike outfit surmounted by a large, plumed helmet.

Sheridan attended the performances of *Pizarro* in a state of childish excitement, clapping his hands at every passage that pleased him – especially at Kemble's inflated declamations – and muttering every syllable after each player as he beat time with his fingers to the rhythmic measure of the lines. With Mrs Jordan's Cora he was disgusted, for instead of delivering her lines in the grand measured style of his intention, she spoke them, as she always did, as though they formed part of ordinary conversation. Actually she, as a naturalistic actress, supported Burke's contention that an habitual adoption of the declamatory style in the theatre was a mistake, for he saw in its continued use the danger of what he described in a letter to Murphy as 'a marked distinction between the English that is *written*, and the English that is *spoken*'. He, in fact, only conceded the use of the artificial manner here and there for purposes of eloquence, or 'when common language becomes unequal to the demands of extraordinary thoughts.' Sheridan, however, was trained to rhythmic and modulated cadence; he was accustomed to it; he expected it to be delivered by his players, and, having purposely designed his dialogue to what might be called an inner melody, it is not to be wondered at that Dora Jordan in attempting to interpret his antitheses was found wanting.

As to Mrs Siddons, he was in the state of being alternately charmed and shocked by her rendering. Her conception of Elvira was nearer to that of Kotzebue's original than to that of his own mind. Half the time she displeased him by the way in which she uttered certain passages, and then Sheridan would turn excitedly to his companions in the box, repeating the line as he had intended it should be spoken. Luckily Kemble had warned him that at first he might not be satisfied with her performance, but had assured him that she would 'fall in to it' after some time. He knew his sister well; he also knew that while he himself was technically the greatest living exponent of his art, her own instinct could be relied upon to improve her performance as her knowledge of the play developed with its progress.

Pizarro ran uninterruptedly until well on in July. It had over thirty performances on end, and was an unqualified success. During its first season it was estimated to have brought £15,000 into the theatre treasury, and when subsequently published it sold 30,000 copies among the most delighted public that had been known for years past. In the midst of the excitement, Lawrence, debarred from the sight of his 'Immortal', as he called Mrs Siddons, and prohibited from meeting Sally, gave

vent to his admiration for the family features by dashing off a
portrait of Kemble in a sublime attitude as Rolla.

*   *   *

Since the extraordinary popularity of the German School, to
the success of which Kemble had so greatly contributed, his
influence was again in the ascendant, and he was implored by
Sheridan to resume the management of Drury Lane. There
was even some talk of his entering into partnership, and buying
a fourth share in the property, particularly as he now began
to assume greater authority in the direction. All the same,
things at the theatre were so bad that they could not well be
worse on his return. Peake, the treasurer, an otherwise amiable
creature, had no control whatever over his department. The
money that should have been available was non-existent, and
there was no trace of its having ever been paid in. The wretched
actors were reduced to running accounts and were hard put
to know how to exist. Fortunately, Kemble was notoriously
punctilious, and his connexion with the theatre was hopefully
expected to be a new guarantee that business would be more
efficiently run.

He was more of an antiquary than ever now, and so intent
upon producing Shakespeare with the maximum of correct
detail, that he gave almost no attention to new talent. The
year 1800 saw no new comedy in the theatre at all. Occasionally
he felt obliged to stage a piece by some officious author; a
pushing Mrs Plowden forced her opera *Virginia* upon him, for
one thing, and he agreed to produce it. But at the end of the
evening he allowed the audience to condemn it for good. One
play was kept in hand in case of an emergency, and *A Bold
Stroke for a Wife* was always ready to be produced at a moment's
notice. It was eternally popular, always ensured a good house,
and its resurrection was a permanent joke among Kemble's
friends. Comedy was, all the same, not his strong point,
although there were times when he had found himself in the
happy circumstance of acting with Mrs Jordan, whom he
found absolutely irresistible. He was, in fact, often at a disadvantage with her, and hardly knew how he was to keep
strictly to business when she tried her blandishments on him
over points of management. According to Boaden, Kemble had

[184]

done more for her in the way of adapting, revising and altering plays than for any other actress, not excepting Mrs Siddons; and he so far forgot himself on one occasion, as to quote a passage from his favourite novelist, Sterne, which conveniently expressed his emotions regarding Dora Jordan: 'It may seem ridiculous enough to a torpid heart – I could have taken her into my arms, and cherished her, though it was in the open street, without blushing'.

For Mrs Siddons there was always the stock-in-trade of her successes upon which to fall back, such as Mrs Beverley, Euphrasia, Belvidera, and Mrs Haller, besides her Shakespearian repertory with, or without, the assistance of her brother. The main difficulty was to find good modern tragedies. They were almost unobtainable. She played in another work by Kotzebue, *Adelheid von Wulfingen*, which by the time it was translated into English by Thomson had lost most of its original interest. At the end of April *de Montfort; a Tragedy on Hatred*, was produced. Its author, Joanna Baillie, celebrated in her time as a dramatic poet, was thought by Scott to be a genius, and by Byron to be the only woman who could write a tragedy – most of them not understanding what was meant by the word. But in spite of the admiration she excited, the muse of Miss Baillie was altogether wanting for stage purposes. She had not the slightest knowledge of her craft. Her plays, eight volumes of passion in all, were generally liked, although somehow or other the passion of her characters failed to take any active part in the action of her plays. All the same, Mrs Siddons and Kemble were great admirers of Miss Baillie, and in *de Montfort* they both gave powerful performances. The character of Lady Jane suited Sarah to perfection; it might have been designed expressly for her. She is described by the Page before her entry with life-like accuracy:

> *So queenly, so commanding, and so noble . . .*
> *So stately, and so graceful is her form,*
> *I thought at first her stature was gigantic;*
> *But, on a near approach, I found in truth*
> *She scarcely does surpass the middle size.*

In staging *de Montfort* Kemble had taken immense trouble. A feature of the setting was the interior of a fourteenth-century church, painted by Capon and complete with choir, side-aisles and nave. So greatly did Mrs Siddons enjoy her part that when, after eleven nights, the play was withdrawn, she wrote to the authoress in the hope of being supplied with 'more Jane de Montforts'. Miss Baillie, however, was evidently unequal to the occasion, for only one other of her plays was successfully performed, and this, *The Family Legend*, was not produced until ten years later in Edinburgh.

SIXTEEN

THE new century had opened well for Kemble. He was at the zenith of his popularity in the most fashionable quarters, and was everywhere acclaimed, fêted and honoured. Tales of his pedantry were as common as they were original. Even the Prince of Wales was so fond of him that he took no offence at the liberty of his behaviour. When he had asked Kemble one evening at dinner to *obleege* him by accepting some snuff, his offer had been gratefully acknowledged with a pompous elocutionary rebuke: 'If you can extend your royal jaws so wide, pray another time say *oblige*—' and it is recorded that the Prince never reverted to the old pronunciation. Kemble was actually in higher favour than his sister. She had not fared so well. Her only new theatrical venture, Helena, in Godwin's *Antonio; The Soldier's Return*, was a failure, and in the midwinter she retired to have a painful operation which, though she bore it bravely, severely tried her nervous system.

After the Easter of 1801 she was rehearsing for a new play, William Sotheby's *Julian and Agnes*, in which as the heroine she was to appear in a magnificent dress of black velvet and sables. It was said at the time that she had never looked more beautiful in her life. Her acting was now heart-rending and had returned to its former tenderness of quality. Of late years, particularly since Maria's death, she had tended to become slightly monotonous and less subtle than formerly; and she was given to wearing herself out in the most overstrained paroxysms of agony. A Mrs Trench, who had seen her three years earlier, described her as seeming not to keep anything in reserve of her great dramatic effects, and that she fired these away 'as minute guns, without any discrimination'. Custom, indeed, had begun to tell on her; custom had become so confirmed that at times she was inclined to apply dramatic emphasis to the most simple objects of common life. It was one thing for her to alarm a shopkeeper by a hollow-toned inquiry over the washable quality of a roll of material; Kemble, in fact, used to do the same thing far better when buying an umbrella, with 'This likes me well! – The cost? The cost?' It was quite another thing when Mrs Siddons began to introduce blank verse into ordinary commonplaces. Her measured diction then acquired a reputation for overwhelming solemnity and lack of humour. Her pronunciation was certainly at times unique. Idiosyncrasy seemed peculiar to many of the Kembles in this respect, reducing their hearers to astonished silence. Only from time to time were babes and sucklings so bold as to imply criticism. A small boy once asked Mrs Siddons in public why she invariably spoke of the 'wynd'. She had a reason, it appeared, and a perfectly good one. She rolled it off to her precocious questioner:

> *I can find it in my mynd to call it wynd*
> *I cannot find it in my mind to call it wind.*

The explanation was no doubt satisfactory to questioner and company. It was characteristic of the Kemble emphasis on minor, and sometimes insignificant, words. There was, too, the occasion when, to universal delight, she reproached a youth for neglect in one perfectly constructed decasyllabic line: 'You brought me porter, boy, I asked for beer.' The story of the banquet in Edinburgh, at which she sat next to the Lord Provost is recorded by earlier biographers. Beef was being served, and her host was anxious to know how she liked it. Tripped up by habit, and eager to satisfy his inquiries, kind Mrs Siddons was once again caught out in a flagrant example of her failing. 'Beef cannot be too salt, for me, my Lord,' she ponderously replied. Both anecdotes are classic. There are many other instances on record; she, in any case, was the first

[188]

to be amused when they were pointed out to her. References to eating seem to have produced the best examples of her inveterate habit, for food, perhaps, caught Mrs Siddons off her guard. She enjoyed every speciality in every district. Cakes at Worcester, the Whalleys' brown bread, rich meals in great houses, ale – 'I do love ale dearly,' she was heard to say; there was space for mentioning them in most of her letters. She had at all times a very hearty appetite.

* * *

The Siddonses had latterly lost a good deal of money. Their arrangements were, as usual, under the self-appointed management of William, who, notwithstanding his unprofitable speculations, still fancied himself able to transact finance with Sheridan. Sarah, mindful of their recent losses, doubted her 'Sid's' ability to deal with the astute proprietor; on the other hand she mistrusted her own talent for business. While William completed his transactions more to his own satisfaction than to hers, she concentrated her attention on her eldest son, who was about to begin his theatrical career.

Henry, who had made his initial stage appearance long ago as one of his mother's Three Reasons for deserting the patronage of Bath, had originally been intended for the Church. Queen Charlotte had had him entered for Charterhouse, where he was educated, and his gifts seemed to indicate a clerical and somewhat scholarly career. Mrs Siddons, however, had other intentions for her eldest son. She was determined that he should adopt the theatre as his profession. He was sent to Paris, saw the great Le Kain and studied the French language. When Henry returned home his mother took him with her on her tours, and during the time that he accompanied her she watched him closely, and arrived at her own accurate, yet on the whole rather partial, conclusions. 'I think,' she had written back in a letter to Miss Coates of Glasgow, with whom they had stayed, 'when the crude materials of his composition are ripened by Time and Observation, he will be a fine creature; the more I conversed with him the more I found instinctive fondness heightened by his excellent understanding and very amiable qualities, his mind is capable of very lovely and great perception, and he only wants to get rid of his unjustifiable portion of diffidence, and to see and hear good things, to make him a fine Actor. Do not fancy this a blind partiality, for I look at those I love with the malice of a friend! . . .' In between the lines is a noticeable current of anxiety which Mrs Siddons was not altogether able to suppress. Adoring, as she did, all her children, Henry must have lacked, even in her eyes, the perfections which she loyally believed to be inherent in all descendants of the Kembles. He was useful in many ways, and, travelling with her in her husband's absence, had escorted his mother southwards from Glasgow in the warmth of the northern August, lightening considerably for her the tedium of the journey. Her departure from Glasgow had been delayed until the very last moment, as she had gone to see a ruin with her hostess, and the travellers consequently did not reach Moffat, their first stage, until well after midnight. Henry got out and thundered on the door of the inn for what seemed to his mother a good half-hour, while she waited patiently in the chaise outside. Presently a sleepy waiter appeared, who was so excessively civil to them that she was astonished, for, as she continued to her hostess, he 'must have had more temper than commonly falls to the share of man, to be so good-humour'd when we had rous'd him so unwillingly from his Bed.' Mrs Siddons was unfailingly courteous and considerate in her dealings with people in every class, provided that they were neither pretentious nor bad-mannered, although, like many people possessing these virtues, her kindness was, more often than not, abused by those who should have been the first to respect it. After leaving Moffat she had been hard pressed. She only reached Lancaster just in time to dress for the play she was to act in. Even then she was not put out. She related the incident to Miss Coates with a charmingly worded assurance: 'This was running the old gentleman (Time I mean) hard, but I had bought the pleasure of seeing Bothwell with you my dear Miss Coates very cheaply with the price of the anxieties that delay cost me, I repented me not.'

Strings had been pulled at Covent Garden on Harry's behalf by the old family friend of the Kembles and Siddonses, Mrs Inchbald, now a woman of considerable influence. In the winter of 1801 he made his début as juvenile lead in a play called *Integrity*, in which he took the part of Herman, a worthy young man who supports a decayed mother and a dependent sister. Harry's professional beginnings were not promising. Boaden called him, 'a hoarse Kemble, without his grace'. He moved awkwardly, for he had some sort of impediment in his walk, and in addition to this drawback he was entirely lacking in self-confidence. This was what his mother had indicated when she referred to his 'unjustifiable portion of diffidence'; and Harry never quite overcame it. He cherished some sort of notion that he was persecuted by Kemble, and this idea may well have been based on more than a fancied hint of avuncular disapproval in spite of the well-known family clannishness. Kemble never liked him.

Mrs Siddons had worked hard for Harry's success during the year. But while she was at Bath in the summer she found that she had done too much. Her increasing nervous malady had culminated in an outbreak of erysipelas on one side of her mouth; a most disfiguring affliction that half crazed her with irritation, and made her, besides, wretchedly self-conscious. Mrs Pennington, with her morbid interest in complaints, described her dreadful habit of scratching and tearing at her sore mouth, 'even at the moment when you are talking to her and warning her on the subject,' she told a friend . . . 'the Habit is so inveterate that nothing but tying her hands can prevent the practice'. Mrs Siddons was also now a prey to alarming nights, dreaming that all her teeth came out upon the stage. She was, in fact, very far from well; but a concerted effort was made by all her friends to notice nothing out of the ordinary, and to ignore the fact that she was for the time being frequently under the influence of drugs. So she moved back and forth between Bath and Bristol, acting much of the time, as usual taking the whole burden of her household upon her shoulders. William, though less rheumatic in his legs, now suffered acutely in his head and neck, and was thought for a time likely to die. Sally was in better health and spirits than she had been for a long time; but faithful Patty Wilkinson was confined to a darkened room on account of a violent inflammation of the eyes, and Mrs Siddons felt responsible for them all. As though she had not enough to worry her she received at Bristol an anonymous letter which cut her to the heart, and upset her for a considerable time afterwards. The writer accused her of inhumanity in reproducing realistic deaths, and understood 'that it was her custom to attend, with *unfeeling apathy, Death-Bed scenes*, in order to render the impression on her audience more strikingly shocking and affecting'; and that she had taken her latest lesson from that of her daughter, which scene she was said to represent with the nicest accuracy.

There is no wonder that the wretched mother, her nerves unstrung, was deeply distressed by the callous attack. The memory of Maria's death, continually before her, had been the cause of her perpetual efforts to obliterate the scene from her sensitive mind. With this new laceration the wound in her heart was reopened. She was, for the time being, completely undermined, both physically and mentally, by pain and worry, although, like the veteran that she was, she allowed nothing of her grief to be noticed by the world at large. Her personal friends did their best to keep her condition secret, and Mrs Piozzi, herself on the spot, wrote a very agitated though indiscreet letter to Mr and Mrs Chappelow, who, although acquainted with Mrs Siddons, were hardly to be included among her most intimate friends.

'We are all mad about dear charming Siddons, who attracts crowds to our Theatre three times a week as if she had been never seen before' – was her well-intentioned beginning. 'I have asked her what you bid me, and she commissioned me to tell you . . . that *nothing* does her any good . . . or produces any but a momentary Relief . . . that anxiety of mind increases it almost to Distraction but that she has Martyr'd herself with unavailing Remedies, and will *try no more*. Since Maria's Death it has returned upon her Terribly, and she is as lean as yourself; but very beautiful, and light and grace in her Figure . . .

'. . . We passed yesterday evening together, and she was half asleep all the while with Laudanum taken externally and internally for this horrid Torment – poor Soul!

'So now *swear* to me you *will not tell*; but say Mrs Siddons is here and acting divinely, which is the strictest Truth: and that she looks better than ever, which is the strictest Truth likewise: Confession of Illness is to her a Ruin. . . . Say not that anything ails her for Heaven's sake.'

*　　　　　*　　　　　*

Mrs Siddons, probably in the part of Andromache

*From a drawing by W. Wellings
in the Victoria and Albert Museum*

The autumn that was approaching looked unpromising at Drury Lane. Sheridan was being more than ever difficult, and from that quarter nothing encouraging was to be expected. Mrs Siddons for some time contemplated spending her winter in Dublin, where she hoped at least to replace some of the large sums that had been virtually embezzled by the proprietor, and others that had been squandered by her husband. One thing was certain: retirement, for the present, was out of the question. 'I must go on *making*, to secure the few comforts that I have been able to attain for myself and my family,' she wrote to a great friend of hers, Mrs Fitzhugh. 'It is providential for us all that I can do so much.' Somehow or other the Siddons–Sheridan tussle was eventually won by the proprietor. Sarah returned to Drury Lane for the winter and acted over forty times before a public that was encouraged and heartened by the declaration of peace that had come at last. That dove had brought with it in its beak to England the rich offering of Ceylon, yielding gold, silver, rice and rubies which, as Mrs Piozzi said, 'sweeten'd by sugar from Trinidad, would keep Great Britain in perfect good humour'.

On 25th March 1802, Mrs Siddons played a new part at Drury Lane for, as it turned out, the last time. She appeared as Hermione in *The Winter's Tale*. Her wisdom in reserving the character for so long up her sleeve cannot be doubted. Her figure was losing its remarkable slenderness, and its contours were acquiring the proportions that even her most partial admirers could not deny were 'matronly'. But with the increasing amplitude of her form there was also an increase in her appearance of the statuesque. Indeed, when she stood on the pedestal, carefully draped round her lower limbs in order to disguise her stoutness, the attention of everyone present was riveted upon the dazzling perfection of her head and shoulders; and when she came to life and embraced Perdita, 'the heart of everyone who saw her,' writes Campbell, 'must throb and glow at the recollection'. Mrs Siddons's own feelings when she thought of the statue-scene can hardly have been so agreeable. It was while she was standing on the pedestal that her draperies, fanned by the draught, once floated out over the lamps that illuminated her from behind. They had caught fire in an instant, and only the presence of mind of one of the scene-shifters, who crawled in on his hands and knees to extinguish the blaze, saved her from a most unpleasant death.

In her gratitude she rewarded him well and spent the latter part of the spring in interceding for leniency on behalf of his son, who had deserted from the army, and was to suffer 'the disgrace and hideous torture of the lash,' as she told Mrs Fitzhugh. She had gone about to parties and dinners, using her influence solely on his account, until she was half dead, adding: 'You know how pleasure, as it is called, fatigues.' The voice of modest misery was once more fortunate in its champion.

Part Three: The Parting Genius
1802-1831

'She was Tragedy personified. She was the stateliest ornament of the public mind. She was not only idol of the people, she not only hushed the tumultuous shouts of the pit in breathless expectation, and quenched the blaze of surrounding beauty in silent tears, but to the retired and lonely student, through long years of solitude, her face has shone as if an eye had appeared from heaven; her name has been as if a voice had opened the chambers of the human heart, or as if a trumpet had awakened the sleeping and the dead. To have seen Mrs Siddons was an event in everyone's life; and does she think we have forgot her?' – WILLIAM HAZLITT: *The Examiner*, 1816

'Her life was, in a manner, always withdrawn. She lived, with the tragic pall round her.' – LEIGH HUNT

THE forbearance which Kemble and his sister had so repeatedly shown in respect of Sheridan's professional irregularities came to an abrupt end with the conclusion of the summer season of 1802. They severed their connexion with Drury Lane and put an end to an association that had been called 'the greatest variety of talent ever seen combined into one dramatic company'. Kemble renounced all idea of investing in such a deplorable security as the Grand National Theatre and turned his attention to the possibilities of Covent Garden as a future professional home. In the meanwhile he talked of going abroad for a considerable time, for he could easily afford the prospect of a long holiday, and at forty-five was still young enough to take full advantage of the change. He was not rich; but he was childless. Unlike his sister he had no one besides his wife to support; he was consequently in very comfortable circumstances. On 24th June, he came forward after the curtain had fallen upon *Twelfth Night*, for the last time took leave of the public at Drury Lane, and set off abroad, leaving his negotiations with Covent Garden in the capable hands of Mrs Inchbald. Mrs Siddons had departed for Ireland a month earlier. She had as her sole companion Patty Wilkinson, and she left behind her, with a heavy heart, Sally, who was not well enough to stand the journey, and little Cecy, who was still at an inconvenient age for purposes of travel. The tour in Ireland was to be extensive and remunerative. It was intended to replace the accumulated deficits

[197]

arising from William's speculations and Sheridan's defaults. It was also intended to provide the sum required for equipping George for India and for renovating their house. Mrs Siddons saw that she was likely to be away a long time. The parting with her family was tender and tearful, for she was overwhelmed by presentiments. She had written to her friends confessing a sense of foreboding, and to Mrs Piozzi and Mrs Fitzhugh commending her children to their protection. Intuition warned her that before her return calamity would again have visited her family.

But once the journey was begun the clouds lifted and the horizon brightened. She was happy in Patty's society, and on their way to Holyhead they stopped at Stratford on Avon. They were shown over Shakespeare's house, and highly entertained by the voluble caretaker, who produced a juvenile deformity: a child with a cleft tongue whom she declared to be called William Shakespeare, a descendant of the poet; at which information Mrs Siddons drily remarked to Patty that the woman also had been presented with a double allowance of tongue. The travellers visited Conway Castle, glowing in the sunset as they arrived, and Mrs Siddons walked grandly about the ruins, sat in an embrasure, and for a long while contemplated the romantic evening scene across the shining river. Some harpers were below the castle, and when the ladies went back to their inn for dinner one of them came in and played to them, putting Sarah in mind of a Druid. The next morning they left Conway and proceeded to Holyhead.

The romantic movement had brought with it an emotional appreciation of 'scenery', the natural contours of which a few years earlier would have been thought offensive to cultured eyes. But now, mountainous country with its overwhelming sweeps and tenebrous valleys was the only possible abode of the soul; and very soon, as they were going over Penmaenmawr, the travellers stopped their carriage and walked to a bridge from which could be absorbed the full splendour of the Welsh scene. There were other sightseers within earshot, one of whom, a temperamental woman, broke out into loud rhapsodies: 'This awful scenery makes me feel as if I were only a worm,' she raved, 'or a grain of dust, on the face of the earth'. This provoked a crushing rebuke from Mrs Siddons, who, inspired

[198]

by a sublime elevation of the soul, felt such self-abasement not to be tolerated. 'I feel very differently,' was her cold remark.

The Irish season was a triumphal progress. Mrs Siddons played in Dublin through June and July, at Cork in August, and subsequently at Belfast, from whence she paid a country house a visit for a few days with Patty. It might be supposed that her earnings would now justify her return home; but with the mail that awaited her in Dublin was a letter from her husband urging the absolute necessity of her continuing to supply money for her family, and begging her to arrange a season at Liverpool on the way back. She had already planned her autumn on leaving Ireland. She had intended to go straight from Holyhead to visit Mrs Piozzi at Denbigh, and from thence to Harrogate, where she meant to rest and to take the waters for her skin disease. After this she was to have joined Miss Coates on the journey south, travelling alone with her, while Patty was to follow in her chaise with the luggage. She was looking forward to the promise of rest and relaxation. 'I wish you may find me a *tolerable* companion,' she wrote to Miss Coates, 'for my spirits are absolutely worn out with fatigue, the springs of my poor Machine have been over-strain'd, and I must have complete rest of body and mind . . .'

William's letter put an end to her pleasant arrangements. Her success in Ireland was so great that, in her own opinion, if money were the object, more was to be gained by remaining there than by playing at Liverpool; so in Ireland the bread-winner decided to stay. In spite of the popularity of her visit there were also the usual difficulties that seemed to dog her passage across the sea. The manager of the Theatre Royal was now Frederick Jones, and he was a very troublesome man to do business with. There was, besides, an echo of the unpleasant experiences of former days in the sister kingdom. During the summer Jones had proposed that she should play for a Dublin charity, a suggestion which she gladly accepted, reserving for Lady Hardwicke, as the wife of the Lord-Lieutenant, the choice of the charity. The Lying-in Hospital was mentioned as a likely and deserving institution, and there the subject seems to have been dropped. Lady Hardwicke did no more about it and treated the matter with considerable apathy; but the usual distorted account of the story got into the papers, and by early

December accusations had almost reached the high-water-mark of their activity in the days of Digges and Brereton. It was reported that Mrs Siddons had refused to play for the Lying-in Hospital, and she was obliged to clear her reputation in a letter to Jones, which she asked him to publish, vindicating her character from the charge of refusing to help 'the tenderest of all claims' – as Boaden described it. She expressed herself with dignity in words that never failed her for fluency. 'And now, Sir,' the letter concluded, 'if I may be permitted to speak of myself as a private individual, I have only to regret the sad necessity imposed upon me of vindicating my character from the imputation of a failing as unamiable, as, I trust, it is foreign to my nature. I regret that I should be constrained, from unfortunate circumstances, to endeavour to rescue myself from an obloquy which I hope I have never incurred by my conduct. I regret that the country in which I am obliged to do so should be Ireland – I have the honour to be, Sir, your obedient servant,

S. SIDDONS.'

Finally the trustees of the hospital removed all doubts by printing a declaration to the effect that Mrs Siddons had not refused to play for their institution, having, in fact, never been invited to do so.

In the midst of the trouble she lost her father. Roger Kemble, who had spent his declining years in prosperity largely at his daughter's expense, died in London on 6th December leaving his widow to survive him. Mrs Siddons had known from the beginning that she would not see him again, for in her farewell letter to Mrs Piozzi in the summer she had written: '. . . My eyes have dwelt with a foreboding tenderness, too painful, on the venerable face of my dear father, that tells me I shall look on it no more.' The loss, when it came, at a moment of difficulty, renewed her instinctive sense of combating fate. Her character was always most pronounced in the face of odds, and she reacted strongly to adversity, enjoying the knowledge of her strength in facing seen or unseen enemies. She had the courage of a lioness and the faith of a crusader. That further tragedy lay ahead of her she was still unaware. Her worries for the present were mitigated by the arrival, in February 1803, of her second son, George, now aged eighteen, who had come over to Dublin to join his mother for a fortnight before leaving for his post in the Bengal Civil Service of the East India Company, in which he had been given a writership through the influence of his godfather, the Prince of Wales. Sarah dreaded to let him go, but his happiness was great and his prospects were brilliant. He carried with him an introduction from the Prince himself, recommending him to the Governor-General of India – 'almost amounting to a command to provide for him handsomely,' says Campbell. So she concentrated all her time on George, jealously making the most of the last days that he would ever be able to devote to her. When he finally left her, avoiding a formal leave-taking in order to spare her the agony of a definite parting, he returned to England to complete the arrangements for his journey.

*   *   *

Sally, whose asthma had been severe during the whole winter, was now so much better that she was going about as usual in London, and, in spite of her mother's absence, enjoying herself immensely. To unobservant eyes, indeed even to her friends, it appeared that the wound in her heart caused by Lawrence had finally healed. They rarely met. There had been a few chance encounters; occasions when their eyes had met across crowds at the theatre, when they had bowed gravely and casually to one another; and there had been another occasion when he had brushed so close to her in Kensington Gardens, without seeing her, that she had hardly been able not to cry out. But after the interval of time that had elapsed since the death of Maria, during which his attempts at renewing intimacy with the Siddonses had gradually desisted from lack of encouragement, she had come to see the situation in a clearer light. She had told herself that she could still think of Lawrence as a friend, and tried to feel pleased when reports reached her that he was heart-whole, gay, and apparently absorbed in the charms of a Miss Betty Tickell. At the same time Sally found it hard to resist a slight feeling of hurt pride at the evident evaporation of a romance that had taken place under such extraordinary circumstances. Lawrence had even now not lost touch with her family. He had regularly visited at the Twisses' – though he had at first terrified them by his temperamental

[201]

behaviour regarding Sally – and Mrs Siddons herself had lately reopened communications with him, bridging the silence with a message of inquiry about some carmine rouge. He himself rarely missed any of her performances, and after this overture generally went round to her dressing-room at the theatre when they were ended. But Sally was never mentioned; neither was she told of the meetings with Lawrence by her mother unless she forced the admissions from her. Sally, in any case, had a new admirer now in Charles Moore, the barrister brother of General Sir John Moore. The charming and devoted young man placed himself entirely at her disposal, and no doubt would have been very happy to marry her. However, as she wrote to Sally Bird, her heart was single and constant. '. . . It never gave itself *but once* away, and I believe it *incapable* of change.'

In the summer of 1802, while her mother had been away in Ireland, Sally's time had been filled with parties and gaiety. Before she left for Bath with her father there had been a picnic given by Charlie Moore at the Temple, in delightful weather, at which they had been joined by William Siddons, Bertie Greatheed, Mrs Kemble and Dorothy Place, who was as much a friend and member of the household as Patty Wilkinson. Then there had been a party at Sadler's Wells, opposite which lived old Mr and Mrs Roger Kemble; and finally the event of Harry's wedding. It seems strange that Mrs Siddons should have missed the marriage of her eldest child; but Harry, uncouth in many ways, had chosen to ally himself, in his mother's absence, to Miss Harriott Murray, of Covent Garden. Mrs Siddons approved of the match, and decided that it was the most sensible course for him to have taken. The bride's good looks were evident. She was married in a long, dark-coloured pelisse, tied with purple bows; and she wore a white chip hat, under which was a little lace cap. Poor, unsuccessful Harry found the ceremony as trying to his self-confidence as the theatre. He went quite white and clung to the chancel rails for support. He shouted out 'I will' before the time, and produced the ring at the wrong moment, while his bride trembled like an aspen, and cried throughout the service to the weeping accompaniment of Sally and the rest of the family who acted as witnesses. After the wedding Mr and Mrs Henry Siddons were sped upon their way to Birmingham, the bride taking with her a fine coral necklace with ear-rings and bracelet to match, as a present from her father-in-law.

*   *   *

Mrs Siddons had reached middle age, leaving in her wake a succession of years incomparable in prestige and untarnished in respectability. Apart from her professional career her family had entirely absorbed her interest, and her friends had completed her existence. But during the course of her married life a subtle estrangement, due mostly to his envious disposition, had risen between herself and her once adored 'Sid'. It had happened gradually: not only her successes, but the very largeness of her character, and her grand attitude towards life in general, had tended to provoke in him a certain jealous resentment against everything that she did; developing in due course into a perpetual state of cantankerous disapproval. William, by nature, was a kind, simple-hearted, disappointed, unimaginative, fussy, small-minded mediocrity with a rather mean disposition. Had he been the real master in his household he would probably have ruled over his little flock with a moderate amount of bullying that might in his day have passed for firmness. As events had turned out he was master in name but not in reality. It seems certain that he was not hen-pecked. Sarah was a submissive wife, consulting him in most things, and handing over to him all the money that she earned. But when all was said and done, it was she who counted; she who overshadowed everything and everybody about her. William, drowned in the presence of her august personality, went for nothing and was aware of it. His attitude towards his wife was frigid and reproving; he felt his position keenly. So it happened that Mrs Siddons had had very little outlet for her emotions. The tempestuous vitality and passion that she poured out in the theatre before spellbound beholders was repressed at home, held in check by her husband's coldness, and sublimated in the stream of emotional friendships that were founded upon spiritual contact and maintained by fitful torrents of correspondence. She was now forty-seven, and had reached a time of life when the admiration of dashing young men, whom she would formerly have considered presumptuous, now aroused

[203]

in her a feeling of sentimentality and power. She began to tolerate, she even encouraged, a great deal of philandering in the name of tender friendship. The homage and flattering attentions of Thomas Lawrence, to whose suave and polished charm of manner she had so far fallen a victim that she was unable to maintain a strong line of conduct with regard to his treatment of her daughters, had opened the gate to a delightful garden in which she instinctively gathered the last flowers of enjoyment before it should finally become too late. In Bath, and more recently in Dublin, during the previous summer, she had made the acquaintance of a young couple named Galindo. The husband gave lessons in fencing; and the wife, a friend of Patty Wilkinson's and an actress, had found herself cast for parts in some of Mrs Siddons's plays. An enthusiastic friendship between Sarah and the Galindos was the immediate result. It sprang up like a hurricane and, though it lasted considerably longer, left in its wake a trail of devastation in both families which culminated with the publication in 1809, of a pamphlet by Mrs Catherine Galindo, in which she accused the irreproachable Siddons with having wrecked her home, alienated, 'with Satanic barbarity', her husband's affections, and with having caused the principal misfortunes in her life, including financial ruin, during the past seven years.

Although Mrs Siddons may be completely exonerated from the charges of Satanic barbarity and, indeed, from ruination of the Galindo household, her behaviour can best be accounted for as one of the more unexpected manifestations of human nature. It can only be described as thoroughly silly and thoroughly human. It appears the more silly on account of her own sublime magnitude in comparison with the vulgarity of the Galindos. It all began with a curricle which belonged to Mrs Galindo who, impressed by the friendship of the most celebrated woman of her time, proposed to Mrs Siddons that she should take an airing in it, and be driven about by her husband. Mrs Siddons, jaded by stifling nights at the theatre, enjoyed her airings; and Mrs Galindo, immensely flattered, placed the conveyance at her disposal for further rides. The experience turned Galindo's head and Mrs Siddons's sense of respectability. From now onward she was inseparable from the Galindo *ménage*. Revelling in the admiring companionship of

[204]

the smart young instructor, her years and her worries dropped away from her with astonishing rapidity. She even contemplated playing Hamlet, and invited him to give her lessons in fencing, in which, sourly remarked Mrs Galindo, they were to be alone and undisturbed. The friendship then developed at a furious rate. When Mrs Siddons left Dublin for her southern tour the Galindos went as well, and after the first stage of the journey was reached Mrs Galindo had the mortification of having to give up her place in the curricle to Mrs Siddons, who bowled briskly along with Mr Galindo, while she was obliged to ride in the post-chaise with Patty and the luggage. At Limerick and Cork Galindo played ducks and drakes with his wife's money to impress Mrs Siddons, who, momentarily arrested on her giddy career by an apprehension of trouble, gave a reading for Mrs Galindo's benefit – that lady complaining that on account of the great actress's popularity she now never got a part – but all the proceeds, as she bitterly alleged in her pamphlet, were spent by her husband on attentions to, or expenses centring round, Mrs Siddons while on a trip to the Lakes of Killarney. And so the story went on. Back in Dublin, Mr Galindo was everywhere with Mrs Siddons but under his own roof; and she, temporarily unbalanced by this heady wine, was doing her best to secure an engagement for his wife at Covent Garden in order to enjoy their company in London. Mrs Galindo's feelings at the time were probably subordinated to the needs of common life. She had one child, and was expecting another. Seven years later, when she published her pamphlet, she represented herself as the victim of outrageous treatment and continuous neglect. She had complained to Patty, but had only received evasive replies, and on her own showing she condoned the situation by being in constant touch with, and visiting, the cause of her distresses – Mrs Siddons.

Shortly after George's visit, which had provided an interlude in the course of the extraordinary infatuation, Patty received a letter from William Siddons containing a very disturbing account indeed of Sally's state of health. It was dated 10th March, and advised her that for the present Mrs Siddons had better not be informed how seriously ill she was. Mrs Galindo's account was that she herself was present when Patty broke the news to Mrs Siddons after her final performance in Dublin –

a reading of *Paradise Lost* for the benefit of the deserving but neglected Lying-in Hospital – and that she still resolved to go to Cork, the scene of her next engagement. The truth of the matter was that no boat could put out to sea in the furious gales that had been sweeping the coasts of Ireland for some days, that two days later Mrs Siddons received a letter from William containing a better account of Sally, and telling her to keep her Cork engagement pending further news. There she acted on 21st March, racked with anxiety for her daughter. 'Oh! why did not Mr Siddons tell me when she was first taken so ill?' she wrote distractedly to Mrs Fitzhugh, giving a convincing denial to Mrs Galindo's story. 'I should then have got clear of this engagement, and what a world of wretchedness and anxiety would have been spared to me! And yet, good God! how should I have crossed the sea? For a fortnight past it has been so dangerous that nothing but wherries have ventured to Holyhead; but, yet, I think I should have put myself into one of them, if I could have known that my poor dear girl was so ill. Oh! tell me all about her. I am almost broken-hearted, though the last accounts tell me she has been mending for several days. . . .'

The storms on the Irish Sea continued without any signs of abatement. William Siddons and Mrs Fitzhugh had addressed letters to Cork containing reassuring news, but Mrs Siddons, grown restless with impatience and desperate with anxiety, threw up her engagement with Pero, her sympathetic manager at Cork, and returned northwards, hoping that she would be able to cross over to England by the Dublin route. But here the weather conditions were as bad as in the south, and showed every intention of continuing so. She, meanwhile, was not to know that her letters home had been delayed on account of the storms, and her change of plans not been received; so that William's letters continued to be sent to Cork. In the intervening time she tortured herself with anxiety. She had received no news for days. Finally, on 2nd April she turned bitterly on Mrs Fitzhugh with an attack that must have filled her adoring friend with dismay. 'Good God! What can be the reason that intelligence must be extorted, as it were, in circumstances like mine?' was her anguished reproach. 'One would think common benevolence, setting affection quite aside, might have induced some of you to alleviate as much as possible such distress as you know I must feel. . . . I cannot account for your silence at all, for you know how to feel. I hope to sail to-night, and to reach London the third day: God knows when that will be. Oh God! What a home to return to, after all I have been doing! and what a prospect to the end of my days.' So with Patty, risking the appalling weather, she crossed that night, and posted straight for London. At Shrewsbury a letter from her husband awaited her arrival. It had been written on 24th March, ten days earlier, and prepared her for the gravest news, at the same time imploring her not to over-tire herself in rushing home. He had known as he wrote that Sally would not outlast that night. She died two hours after-wards, in the arms of Dorothy Place, of an emphysematous pressure upon the lungs, the result of her suffocating attacks of asthma.

As Mrs Siddons, bewildered with desolation and tired with travel, was mechanically reading the letter, Patty was called away to be told by a messenger outside that all was over. By the look on her face when she came back into the room Mrs Siddons knew all that there was to know. She turned quite cold, and, as there was now no need to hurry on, lay silent and motionless in her room at the Shrewsbury inn for a whole day. The return home was dignified by its surrounding grief. Never in her life did she more resemble an unhappy queen than now. At Oxford she found a letter of condolence from Kemble; and a few miles out of London, Charles, her youngest brother, came to meet her and to escort her to her sad home, and took her the next day on the first of her mournful duties: a visit to their widowed mother at Sadler's Wells.

Although Mrs Siddons behaved with composure and strength, her constitution had been severely undermined by the shock, and she spent the summer at Birch Farm at Cheltenham, taking the waters. There she was joined by Sally's friends, Charles Moore and Dorothy Place. Little Cecy was also with her, never again to be separated for long from her mother, and destined to become the rather victimized and utterly devoted support of her old age. Yet, as Mrs Siddons looked at her ewe lamb, she felt unsure that she too would not be soon taken from her; for when she wrote to Mrs Galindo on 'the inscrutable ways of Providence', in that series of letters that were eventually given to the world as an example of her devious methods of home-breaking, she was open-hearted and confiding, describing the delicate skin and tender beauty of Cecilia, so like that of Maria that it made her shudder to look at her. Like Niobe, she felt herself grasping her youngest and last daughter to her breast, fearful lest she too should be snatched away. That this impression was founded on more than a superstitious fancy there is every reason to believe. Mrs Pennington also caught sight of Cecy this year, and, describing her to a correspondent, found in the little girl something 'more lovely and more *fragile* than anything I ever beheld. Her complexion is literally *transparent*! and her *Eyes* have a *Lustre* there is no looking at!'

Kemble, who had been abroad on his prolonged holiday for nearly a year, had now returned from Spain, and went to join his sister in her retreat at Cheltenham. By her influence his 'dear Muse', Mrs Inchbald, had, during the time in which he had been away, succeeded in negotiating on his behalf the purchase of one-sixth of the property of Covent Garden. The total value of the theatre amounted to £138,000, of which sum half was owned by its admirable manager, Thomas Harris, and the rest divided between four other shareholders. Kemble's share cost him £23,000. He deposited £10,000, and the balance was to be paid off as his profits accumulated. He was to be stage-manager, having full powers of casting his plays, and sharing the profits accruing to Covent Garden from his own acting. The basis of the new arrangement was far more satisfactory from his point of view than any of his former undertakings. Harris's methods were vastly different from those of Sheridan. He was punctilious and honourable with his employees, straightforward in his dealings, and, from the professional standpoint, a man with the highest reputation for integrity. Kemble had therefore left for the Continent with the light-hearted assumption of the absentee that his business was in the best of hands, as indeed it was; while his renown – in the hands of his wife – who was his active publicity agent, was being carefully stimulated in the bosoms of the most influential families. During the winter of 1802–3 Mrs Kemble had taken especial care to draw attention to her husband's personality.

She entertained lavishly, went to a great many parties, talked volubly about him, and never missed a gathering which might be useful to them both. The winter culminated with Lord Abercorn's party and theatricals at The Priory, at which seventy people were entertained, and forty housed for the night. The Prince of Wales was there; the Devonshires, the Melbournes and the Castlereaghs were there too. But Mrs Kemble, a prominent guest, enjoyed most of all being seen by Sheridan, who appeared to be very disgusted at the distinction that was being offered to his players, and who, indeed, arrived in all the glory of a statesman, with 'a very elegant chariot, four beautiful black horses, and two footmen'. 'Pop' Kemble's propaganda was as successful as she could wish it to be. Before her husband made his initial appearance at Covent Garden in the autumn of 1803 the theatre had to be renovated in order to include accommodation for the host of influential patrons who were deserting Drury Lane in the wake of John Philip and his sister. Sixteen boxes were added to the house, and let, at a rental of £300, to some of the most powerful families in the kingdom, including the Duchesses of Northumberland and Devonshire, Lady Abercorn, Lady Holland and Lord Egremont. So that, with all these preparations in hand, it seemed as though nothing were wanting to make a complete success of Kemble's new connexion. The last place in which he might have been expected to find difficulties awaiting him was in his own family; and his disgust, when he returned, to find his sister being entirely managed by the Galindos – 'persons whom it was a disgrace to know,' as he expressed it – was as unbounded as his distress on finding that her position was becoming seriously endangered. But when it came to a stand-up fight he was afraid of his sister. He resorted to the usual tactics of the moral coward: he hid behind the screen of his 'dear Muse'. Mrs Inchbald was asked to convey his feelings on this delicate subject to Mrs Siddons, and at any price to get out of the Covent Garden engagement of Mrs Galindo – whom he took good care to insult when on a visit to Ireland during the summer. But it was no easy thing to override the will of Mrs Siddons, and Mrs Inchbald had no success with her mission. Kemble accordingly blamed Mrs Inchbald for the failure of her efforts, and she in her turn blamed him for cowardice; so that relations between the two families, cordial now for over twenty years, became seriously strained, and Mrs Inchbald declared that never again could she have the same opinion of Mrs Siddons, and never again admire her so much, for having allowed herself to be duped by such ridiculous people as the Galindos.

But the wicked flourished none the less. The very fact of opposition seemed to stimulate the attraction in Sarah's eyes, and the more she was criticized the more she saw of Mr Galindo, who had come over to London on some pretext of business during the spring, leaving his wife in Ireland with the promise of sending for her as soon as her engagement should materialize. She joined him in the autumn, and jealousy recommenced. According to her, Mrs Siddons wrote him letters in code, and posted them to coffee-houses where they were unlikely to be intercepted. She had caught him out trying to decipher one of them and, asking what it was, had been faced by her confused and blushing husband with the lame explanation that it was a puzzle that Mrs Siddons had sent him. Then, being rather at a loose end, Mr Galindo joined the Loyal London Volunteers, intending to help resist the French invasion that had been dreaded for so long, and was now becoming a certainty to all who knew anything about foreign politics. There was a great deal of recruiting, marching and drilling during the next few months. All sorts of extra regiments were raised, and before long John and Charles Kemble were also in uniform: the former in that of the Bloomsbury Volunteers, in which he was a lieutenant, and the latter a trooper in the Duke of Gloucester's Light Cavalry. Martial enthusiasm pervaded the entire country. Mr Galindo, however, had other plans in his head besides that of strutting about London in the uniform of a loyal volunteer. He decided to negotiate a deal in a theatre in Manchester, and looked about for a thousand pounds which was needed to sink in the property. He naturally had not far to look. Mrs Siddons was willing to provide the money, and, with the assistance of a friend of Galindo's, a bond was drawn up in Patty's name whereby the sum was to be repaid within the next seven years. It was drawn up in Patty's name because William Siddons was to know nothing about the loan. Needless to say, Mrs Siddons never saw her thousand pounds again; and after a year or two she saw no more of the Galindos. They vanished into Manchester, only emerging as total failures in 1809, when as a last resort Mrs Galindo published her accusing pamphlet. In this document, which sold well at five shillings a copy, she put forward every variety of argument to show why circumstances had rendered repayment of the money impossible, and Mrs Siddons was left to extricate herself as well as she might from the ruins of the one foolish adventure of her life.

EIGHTEEN

LAYING aside her griefs Mrs Siddons determined to return once more to work. She was engaged for the winter season at Covent Garden, which had now become a family stronghold, for besides John and Charles Kemble the company included her son Henry, who for the past two years had been awkwardly gracing the boards in an attempt to uphold family traditions. His mother had watched his professional début with certain misgivings, and though, as she wrote to Mrs Inchbald, she longed for him to have a successful career, she had trembled to think of his performing Hamlet under the very nose of his exemplary uncle, 'when so perfect a model has been so long contemplated.' Henry, whose heart, however, was with the Church, had certainly not imperilled his uncle's great reputation, for both John and Charles Kemble shared the honours between them. He had dragged himself laboriously through a few seasons and before long declared that he was dissatisfied with his profession. Meanwhile the Theatre Royal at Covent Garden, fresh with renovations and additions, opened towards the end of September 1803, with a performance of *Hamlet* by that so perfect a model – Mr Kemble. His new method was to share the important parts in his repertory with another actor, and for this purpose he had chosen a magnificent, though rarely sober, player, George Frederick Cooke, to alternate with him, and to provide a reply to critics who might be likely to accuse him of grasping the principal honours for himself. But Cooke, who had behind him a career of highly coloured adventure, was disposed to indulge himself in a failing that proved full of disadvantages to the management. He had been advertised for a fortnight before his appearance in *The Harper's Daughter*, when, on the first night he decided that he was 'not well enough' to play. Henry Siddons, an invaluable stop-gap, truly his father's son, was produced at a moment's notice, and went through Cooke's part, having merely studied it between the acts, and 'was hardly seen to use the book at all.' The Siddons faculty to cram a new part in record time and be word-perfect was fortunate. Cooke's escapade was unfavourably received, but even so he did not allow public censure to interfere with his self-indulgence, and later in the year he repeated the indiscretion in *Pizarro*, when he came on knowing nothing of the words and, it was said, 'soon fell backwards as mute as a turtle', excusing himself with the drunkard's ingenious method of appealing to the audience's sense of humour. 'Ladies and Gentlemen,' he announced, 'my old complaint!' Upon which Harry Siddons once more came forward in the emergency, and hastily supplied the part of Rolla for the delinquent.

On the 27th September, Mrs Siddons made her first regular appearance at Covent Garden as Isabella, still one of her most popular characters. Kemble's precaution against family logrolling was certainly justified, for on 6th October, a bumper night for them all, *Douglas* was performed with Harry Siddons in the name part, his mother as Lady Randolph and Kemble as Old Norval.

On each of these occasions there was immense applause, and Mrs Siddons played a greater number of times than she had done for years past; during her first season at her brother's theatre she appeared on over sixty occasions. Sorrow somehow physically became her, for she was again most extravagantly admired everywhere she went and whenever she appeared. The following summer the papers were full of the story of a young Irish law student, who had so persecuted her with letters and amorous declarations that she was forced to have the Bow Street runners set after him. Mrs Piozzi, was most disappointed to hear no news of the story from Mrs Siddons. Any other woman, she believed, would have been ready to boast of it. 'Dear lovely Siddons,' she wrote in *Thraliana*, 'has had an adventure of a curious Nature. A Lover so mad with Passion for a woman more than twice his Age, that she has been forced to swear the Peace against him. Comical enough! & that odious Husband of hers never coming forward to protect her: but thinking of his own Health, drinking Bath Waters. . . . How every body does hate that perverse Fellow! & how he does hate his beautiful & enchanting wife'.[1] And again, 'But she is as the man says an adorable creature . . . and puts even Buonaparte out of one's head for a while.'

Thus, for all the admiration she was receiving Mrs Siddons passed her days sadly enough. Mrs Piozzi's view of her relations with her husband is characteristically uncharitable, though as usual lively, since the estrangement of the pair was a gradual rather than a definite rift. In 1804 she had taken a cottage at Hampstead for the strong air and quiet surroundings. Her husband had joined her there on one of his visits to London, and for a while had returned to his old kindliness in his expression of pleasure at the house. 'Sally, this will cure all our ailments!' he had said as he looked contentedly out of the window at the peaceful scene. But their ailments were not all physical. They were not wholly curable by the salubrious air of Hampstead or the latest discoveries of medical science. There were moral stresses as well, and in spite of mutual differences William Siddons certainly supported his wife through a period of acute embarrassment and difficulty that autumn and winter, when she suddenly became the subject of extraordinary rumour and gossip. As early as 20th June, Farington had referred to 'Much wicked allusion abt. Lawrence and Her in public papers', rumours which he emphatically denied whenever and wherever he met them. By the end of November they had become so current that it was being openly credited that she had run away with Lawrence, and the story was widely repeated. Lord Thomond told it to Farington as a fact, adding that divorce proceedings were to be taken. Even George III attended eagerly to the Prince of Wales' own version of the affair. At all events, though no doubt with some misgivings in the family circle, William Siddons took the energetic line of inserting an announcement in *The Times* which was printed in the issue of 1st December 1804. 'Having been informed', it

1 *Thraliana*, II, 1052.

ran, 'on my recent arrival in Town, that the most wicked and injurious calumnies have been circulated of late respecting Mrs Siddons, I do hereby offer a reward of one Thousand Pounds for the first discovery and conviction of any person who has been or shall be concerned, directly or indirectly in the circulation thereof. Wm. Siddons, Upper Terrace, Hampstead, Nov. 30th, 1804.' Whoever was responsible for the reports – and in connexion with these the vindictive Mrs Galindo should not be ruled out – the object, according to Farington, was twofold: 'To drive her from the stage and from society – & to injure him in his profession.' What is, however, surprising is that any belief should have been placed in the rumour at all, when as all her friends well knew, Mrs Siddons had been confined during this time to her room in the Hampstead cottage with an acute attack of crippling rheumatism.

Even so the cleft between husband and wife was irreparable. Chief happiness now lay in the possession of her old and faithful friends. She very often stayed with Mrs Fitzhugh, the wife of the member for Tiverton, who lived at Bannisters, near Southampton: a lady whose devotion was such that she used to camp herself by the hour in Mrs Siddons's dressing-room at the theatre, and help to dress her for her plays. Then there was Mrs Damer at Strawberry Hill, and there was always Mrs Piozzi. Mrs Siddons missed the old days at Streatham, and sometimes thought that all her happiness had fled after the house was closed. All that was now left to her of her very own was her little Cecy; and even she was a great anxiety, with her frail appearance and delicate, pale skin.[1] Niobe had almost wept her eyes out with her endless griefs; those dark, flashing, sparkling and occasionally glaring eyes which, as she said, showed 'no symptoms of decay to *common observers*', were now beginning to be seriously troublesome to their owner. She was also as rheumatic as her husband which was one of the reasons why she had moved to Hampstead. But the change did her little good, and the trouble which spread from her hip to her toe and deprived her of the use of her left side, kept her in bed for weeks of agony. She tried every remedy, and all had failed.

[1] Cecilia Siddons had been referred to by Mrs Piozzi, her godmother, as 'sick and spoiled, and fretful and fragile – her mother has put her to Miss Lee for Education, but they are fearful she will not live.'—*Thraliana*, II, 992.

As a last resort she turned to the latest scientific discovery. Electricity, still in its infancy, was looked upon with suspicion by her doctors, but her surgeon advised her to try it, assuring her that it would do her no harm. She went through with the treatment, and lived to be thankful and completely cured. It can hardly have been an agreeable experience. In describing the ordeal she said that the sparks felt like burning lead being poured into her veins, and the screams she let out during the operation were so powerful and so prolonged that William at any moment expected crowds to break open the door and rush into the house in the belief that she was being murdered. But she reacted immediately to the drastic cure, and by the beginning of the winter, when her husband went back to Bath, she returned to London, though not to Great Marlborough Street which, with its distressing associations, had become too large for the diminished household, and as there was now only herself, Patty and Cecilia, she moved into Mr Nixon's lodgings in Princes Street, off Hanover Square. She was stronger in health, and in a mild way was disposed to return to the theatre, when, in the winter of 1804, the Kembles suddenly entered upon a period of enforced repose, the direct result of the fascination exercised two years before by Mrs Siddons upon the imagination of a small boy in Ireland. The child, whose name was William Henry West Betty, had been taken to see her play Elvira at Belfast, and had returned to his parents' farm in a condition of stage-struck wonderment. He had pestered his father, and bothered his mother from morning till night to let him be an actor, until, in the words of a contemporary pamphleteer, seeing that 'the Siddonian accents still rang in his ear, and the majestic march and awful brow still filled his fancy,' they had allowed the importunate child to have his own way. He had been examined by the manager of the Belfast Theatre, had spouted some of Elvira's lines 'with the wild and unskilful vigour of untutored genius,' and after some prefatory studies, had been engaged to play for a few nights as Osmin in *Zara*. This had been in August 1803. Ireland was unsettled and alarmed on account of the recent insurrection, and the moment was propitious for a novelty. So it was that '*A Young Gentleman only Eleven Years of Age*' had been billed to appear in high tragedy. The next morning Belfast could talk of nothing else.

The boy Betty had promptly been engaged for nine nights in Dublin; then he had played at Cork; and soon afterwards he had swept the provinces of Great Britain off their feet. At last, London only remained to be taken by storm.

He appeared at Drury Lane in the autumn season of 1804, and in less than no time became the rage. He was accompanied everywhere by a Cerberus of a father who was also his impresario and publicity manager and drove his bargains admirably. His negotiations ended by arranging that his son should appear on the first of December at Covent Garden. A detachment of Guards was required outside the theatre that night; while inside there was a strong body of police officers on whom devolved the task of rescuing those unfortunates who succumbed to the pressure of the surging, clamouring, fighting crowds who were trying to get in to the already overflowing theatre, which, on that occasion, was presenting a tragedy called *Barbarossa*. At last the prodigy, impersonating Selim, a slave, and wearing a russet, fur-trimmed jacket, white trousers and turban, walked sedately on. He was to all appearances an engaging child with a pleasing manner, without affectations or tricks; and with a certain energy and grace in his movements. Although he lacked the experience of the passions he represented, he was very gifted in a precocious way, and had an astonishing intuition and judgement in his ideas of playing. He was able to portray fear in an extraordinary degree; but was unable, very naturally, to grasp the infinite moods of love. Sometimes the poor child became confused and lost the thread of the story, becoming involved in a pathetic tangle of meaningless words. But taken all round he was looked upon as an unparalleled genius, and while in London he played Tancred, Achmet, Octavian, Richard III, Hamlet, and Young Norval.

The rage for Master Betty passed beyond the limits of sense and comprehension. Kemble and Mrs Siddons, lifted up by the tidal wave, and unable to resist, were beached high and dry on the shingle of public indifference, while the hysterical craze spread down from the politicians to the populace. The classic dignity of Kemble, his authority, his experience and his position were all waved aside in the headlong rush to idolize the greatest phenomenon since the youthful Mozart. Mrs Siddons sat back and waited with superb indifference for the frenzy to subside. She referred to 'the baby with a woman's name' and was thoroughly disgusted. 'Mrs Sid begs to know what she is to do with the Puppet – she thinks it will be quite absurd her playing with him . . .' facetiously wrote Patty to Mrs Piozzi. But it was an age of wonders. There was also the rather vulgar Infant Billington, who had made its mark strutting about the stages of Brighton and Worthing; and Kemble, a little later, sought, rather to his discredit, to capitalize the popularity of juvenile marvels by exploiting the talents of a Miss Mudie, aged eight, whose artless efforts, however, raised nothing more than contempt in the breasts of the Covent Garden public. So that neither of these rivals was in any way comparable to the boy Betty; and the combined receipts of his efforts at Drury Lane and Covent Garden that season fell not far short of £35,000. He was a gold-mine to his managers. He received £50 a night, and a whole benefit a week throughout the season. There was no knowing what the wonder would not accomplish next, and serious projects now began to be entertained for the erection of commemorative statues to the Young Roscius. The climax came when Pitt adjourned a sitting of the House of Commons, and members repaired in a body to the theatre to see Betty playing Hamlet. Certain benevolent persons then came forward to interest themselves in his classical studies, and for his special edification the boys of Westminster School performed a play by Terence in Latin, at which ceremony the small guest of honour was introduced to the Archbishop of York. To do him justice Betty was apparently not spoiled by the exaggerated importance that was given to him. The most that could be said against him was that he was inclined to be capricious and touchy, and certainly he was very impatient of remonstrance. Mrs Siddons pigeon-holed him very accurately, when, after she had seen him play – a concession paid to prejudice by her sense of justice – she crushed the eulogies of Lord Abercorn, who was ready to call him the greatest actor in English history. She had found Master Betty much what she had expected he would be: 'My Lord, he is a very clever, pretty boy, but nothing more.'

While Master Betty was stealing her thunder, Mrs Siddons had been engaged in settling herself into the new cottage she had lately bought at Westbourne Green. It was really more of

[218]

a *ferme ornée* than anything else, and was the concrete form of her longing for rest and retirement in the country; that is to say outside London. Its site at present, however, is so distinctly inside London that it is difficult to imagine in the Harrow Road of the mid-twentieth century, the Arcadian surroundings of Westbourne Farm in 1805, when fields, meadows and market-gardens spread their flowery verges away into the distance.[1] But the cottage itself was afterwards demolished in order to make way for Progress and the Permanent Way, although it lasted long enough to bring contentment to Mrs Siddons in her declining years. She was as pleased as a child with her new possession. It fulfilled, though sadly, and rather late in life, the reward that for years she had promised herself. It was her Nook, her Box, 'that dear little spot my home,' with its green laurels, and wooden palings hidden by shrubs and flowers, and scented by the clinging honeysuckle that trailed over her lattice windows. 'A very pretty bird's-nest,' William thought it when he visited the farm in the following year. But he also advocated a snug house in London for the dark, damp winter months.

She had moved in during April, and had begun renovations. Mr Nixon, her London landlord, combined his trades in the most convenient manner, for he was as well an upholsterer and an undertaker. So that besides being cheerfully bespoken by Mrs Siddons to bury her when the time should come, he was also set to work on Westbourne Farm. It was for her the pleasantest of existences; for secure in the devoted, though at times perhaps rather deafening company of the two giggling girls, Patty Wilkinson and Dorothy Place, the large, benevolent, imposing woman felt that the world could be safely shut out of her life for a time. Occasional reverberations from London

---

[1] Westbourne Farm was demolished nearly 100 years ago. Its actual site has from time to time been the subject of speculation, though it now seems definitely established. The late Dr Herbert Friend, whose long professional life had been passed in the parish, and who died in 1942, remembered the house well when it was used as a meeting-place for small societies. He definitely sited it in the area now contained within the rectangle formed by the Harrow Road, Woodchester Street, Cirencester Street and the stone passage linking these last two. The east wing of the cottage, Mrs Siddons's studio, would have stood in line with and almost opposite to the present St Martha's Hall.

there certainly were – it was, after all, only just over a half-hour's drive in her carriage to the West End – and sometimes echoes from the Galindos might be inclined to disturb her serenity. But the time was mostly taken up with Cecy, with letter-writing, needlework, gardening, and with her agreeable recreation of modelling, for which she had built on a studio to the house. In the last few years she had taken to making portrait busts of her family and friends in clay, and she thoroughly enjoyed the hobby. She had presented most of her friends with examples of her craft, and had exchanged some of these with Mrs Damer, Walpole's niece, who had inherited Strawberry Hill. As Mrs Damer's work received some sort of official recognition, it has been thought probable that her talents for sculpture were more competent than those of Mrs Siddons, and Campbell politely refers to Mrs Damer as being the more skilful artist on account of her having 'no other occupation to engross her time.' Then there were occasional tours. In 1805 she visited the Wye Valley with her eldest brother and stopped at Welsh Newton to see the grave of Blessed John Kemble, of whose heroic death she and John Philip were extremely proud, and she, in fact, contributed a small annual sum of money for the maintenance of his grave.

She had reached a period when she was still too active in mind to retire from her profession, but was hampered by the somewhat ageing disadvantages of her now monumental physique. Although she was only fifty, chairmen were already beginning to grumble when they had to carry her, and three years later, when she was playing Queen Katharine, she had the disturbing misadventure of not being able to extricate herself from her armchair; it rose with her. The incident was effectively concealed by the devotion of one of her attendants who busied herself with extra attentions round the Queen until the crisis was past. Its cause remained a source of embarrassment none the less. All the Kembles had a latent tendency towards stoutness in their middle life. Stephen had always been enormous, while Elizabeth, who presently emerged from the New World with her husband, Mr Whitlock, after an absence of sixteen years, was a corpulent and jolly version of her tragic sister. 'A noble, glorious creature very wild and eccentric,' Sarah called her, finding her not so tall as herself, nor so hand-

[220]

some, but, as she generously concluded, her equal if not her superior in every other particular.

From the autumn of 1806 until the beginning of December, Mrs Siddons was acting again. Her appearances for the past four years in London had been spasmodic and irregular, with the exception of the winter of 1803, and during this short engagement she had an unpleasant experience when an apple was thrown at her from the gallery during a performance of *Coriolanus*. Kemble was enraged. He held up the proceedings, and used the occasion as an example in which to remind the public of the respect that was due to his players. 'Ladies and gentlemen,' he thundered, 'I have been many years acquainted with the benevolence and liberality of a London audience, but we cannot proceed this evening unless we are protected, especially when ladies are exposed to insult.' (Interruption from the gallery: 'We can't hear you.') 'I will raise my voice, and the galleries *shall* hear me. This protection is what the audience owe it to themselves to grant, and what the performers, to the credit of their profession, have a right to demand. I have offered, on the part of the proprietors, a hundred guineas to any man who will disclose the ruffian who has been guilty of this act. . . . I hope I shall never be wanting in my duty to the public, but nothing shall induce me to suffer insult.'

After this there was no more trouble, and, from the New Year onward, Mrs Siddons was acting regularly with Kemble's company and earning £30 a night, rising to £50 shortly before her final retirement.

She lost her mother in the spring of 1807. Masterful Mrs Kemble died at Islington, full of years, having witnessed the apogee of her family, yet unable to find life endurable without her genial Roger. The following year William Siddons extinguished his mediocre career at Bath, passing quietly out of his circle of celebrities at the age of sixty-seven. Towards the end of his life, Mrs Piozzi had begun to think him more sinned against than sinning; though why, apart from her capricious tendencies, it would be hard to discover. She evidently heard his side of his domestic trials when he stayed as her guest at Brynbella, and gave some credence to his version that he had been turned out of the house by his wife. Ominously she continued, that the world was beginning to blame her and pity him. But Mrs Piozzi could be dangerously inaccurate.

His last years had been entirely governed by rheumatism and domestic events. Newspaper scares provided him with excitement, and his pleasures lay in small and simple things: Puss and her kittens, taking Cecilia to Worthing, shopping at Bath for Mrs Piozzi, and celebrating national events in a flow of jubilant verse. Trafalgar had given a stirring fillip to his particular muse who had promptly produced an ode upon the victory. His visit to Westbourne Farm had had the same effect, and as it has a period interest and also does justice to the man in his most kindly mood it is given below.

ON MRS. SIDDONS'S COTTAGE AT WESTBOURNE

Would you I'd Westbourne Farm describe,
I'll do it then, and free from gall,
For sure it would be sin to gibe
A thing so pretty and so small.

The poplar walk, if you have strength,
Will take a minute's time to step it;
Nay, certes, 'tis of such a length,
'Twould almost tire a frog to leap it.

But when the pleasure-ground is seen,
Then what a burst comes on the view!
Its level walk, its shaven green,
For which a razor's stroke would do.

Now, pray be cautious when you enter,
And curb your strides from much expansion;
Three paces take you to the centre,
Three more, you're close against the mansion.

The mansion, cottage, house, or hut,
Call't what you will, has room within
To lodge the King of Lilliput,
But not his Court, nor yet his Queen.

The kitchen-garden, true to keeping,
 Has length and breadth and width so plenty,
A snail, if fairly set a-creeping,
 Could scarce go round while you told twenty.

Perhaps you'll cry, on hearing this,
 What! every thing so very small?
No: she that made it what it is,
 Has greatness which makes up for all.

Three weeks before her husband died Mrs Siddons had been on one of her periodic visits to him at Bath, and had left him to fulfil a season at Edinburgh. She cancelled the engagement and hurried back again to the South. She was sincerely saddened by the loss of the petulant and rather nagging old man, and she could think of nothing else but the long years of struggle, difficulty and success that they had faced together. She uttered her feelings in a torrent of emotion to Mrs Piozzi 'May I die the death of my honest worthy husband, and may those to whom I am dear remember me when I am gone as I remember him – forgetting and forgiving all my errors, and recollecting only my quietness of spirit and singleness of heart.' Her sentiments were always generously conceived and spontaneously expressed. Some time before his death there had been some little difference with William as to the disposal of his property in his will. The bulk of it had been earned by her, and yet she asked for no more than would render her independent, and out of the power of any human being in the world. It was, when all was said and done, a reasonable request. Even now, Mrs Piozzi was unable to refrain from exercising her wit at Mrs Siddons's expense. A curious remark appears in the *Thraliana* under the date line of 11th August 1808; though unsupported by further evidence: ' Mrs Siddons is said to be engaged to marry Lord Erskine when her year of widowhood is expired – *I* say she always did continue to shine brightest in her *last Act*, however fatigued before.'[1]

By the time that Covent Garden reopened early in September

[1] Some years earlier she had alluded mysteriously in the same journal: 'Neither Mr Erskine nor Mrs Siddons have their imagination under a very tight rein. – We all three ride it in snaffle'.

1808, she was well enough to resume work. Exactly one week later, on the night of the nineteenth, the fruits of her brother's labours, and much of her own, were entirely obliterated within a few hours. *Pizarro* had been given, during the performance of which a gun had had to be fired, releasing some wadding which had evidently been carelessly left to smoulder among the canvas scenery. By six o'clock the next morning Covent Garden Theatre had been completely gutted. The fire must have begun at about four o'clock in the morning, for Mrs Siddons had been in the theatre until after twelve, and the watchman had left at one, when there was still no sign of alarm.

The catastrophe was complete; for efficient salvage was impossible, although firemen were soon on the scene. The unpractical planning of the building made assistance even more of a problem than it need have been, for the main pipe was at the time under reconstruction, and there was consequently no water to be got. After an hour of furious conflagration some water was procured, and the engines were set to work. But even so the firemen were unable to reach the blazing theatre owing to the ingenuity of its design; for its eastern elevation in Bow Street was entirely masked by two rows of houses which were built up against it leaving only one aperture, the stage doorway, as a means of penetrating to the building. The narrow opening in Hart Street, now Floral Street, on the north side, was also useless as a means of access, and the principal entrance was in the Piazza. The great house, built by Rich, had stood since 1732, and consequently, when a party of firemen rushed through the main entrance, the whole colonnade collapsed upon them. Those who were not killed by the mass of falling masonry were scalded to death by the steam of their own hose-pipes, and the next day twenty-two bodies were recovered from the smoking ruins.

The losses were incalculable. They were estimated at £150,000. All the properties were destroyed. The scenery, dresses, stage-jewellery, and armour, and the wines of the famous Beef Steak Club were totally consumed, while Handel's giant organ, with many of his MS operas and other MS works by Dr Arne, vanished completely with the rest of the musical scores.

Mrs Siddons had her own troubles. Her losses, too, were

[224]

immense and irreplaceable. The costumes, jewellery and lace that she had collected during thirty hard-working years, including a magnificent veil that had belonged to the murdered French Queen, were estimated to be in the neighbourhood of £1,500. In fact the veil alone was worth £1,000. But for Kemble the disaster meant ruin. He was fifty-one and had to begin his life all over again. His loan for his own share in Covent Garden was not yet paid off, and in addition to this he had lost everything. His superb library, collected with scholarship and care, was gone. He had lost everything except his sense of dramatic effect. The next day a friend had called to condole with the ruined proprietor, and found him soliloquizing before his glass as he shaved. 'Of all this vast treasure,' he announced at large, 'nothing now remains but the arms of England over the entrance of the theatre and the Roman eagle standing solitary in the market-place.'

The proprietors were in despair, but they were, at least, insured. They had in any case proposed to reconstruct the theatre before very long, and were now, to a certain extent, provided with a nucleus for rebuilding by receiving £45,000. Then other compensations were not altogether wanting. Lords Guildford and Mountjoy offered to advance Kemble any sum of money by whatever means it could be raised. The Duke of Northumberland contributed £10,000 to the fund for reconstruction, and, with a magnificently ducal gesture, cancelled his bond when the first stone was laid. Plans were immediately set on foot; the building was placed in the hands of Robert Smirke, and before long the public subscription fund had reached £75,000. Mrs Inchbald, fond as she was of the Kembles, and sympathetic to their misfortunes, lamented the disaster to her friends while despising the extravagance of popular sentiment. The Kembles, she decided, were not such objects of pity as they were made to appear, and she felt that the exaggerated comfort which they received from certain quarters was a little absurd. This was true enough, for the most prominent people in the country did their very best to turn the heads of the leading players. Physicians attended them for nothing, and after a visit drove about the town giving the latest news of a spoiled patient. This passion was confined to star players, and of these Kemble and Mrs Siddons were the planets; so that it was usual to refer to 'the *dear* creatures', and it was always customary to inquire for '*dear* Mrs Siddons'. It is therefore not surprising to learn that, when the rebuilding of Covent Garden began, the foundation-stone was laid on 30th December by the Prince of Wales, in great state and abominable weather, before an immense concourse of fashionable people. The entire theatre company was on parade, headed by an invalidish Kemble, who had been hauled out of his sick-bed and obliged to attend the historic occasion inadequately clad for mid-winter ceremonial in white silk stockings and thin-soled pumps. Mrs Siddons was conspicuously present in a large hat with tossing black plumes.

The new theatre, itself not destined to survive even half a century, was opened to the public exactly one year after the calamity. It was an imposing compound of marble and porphyry without, and pseudo-classicism and imitation porphyry within. There was a foyer sixty feet long, adorned with plaster statues and plush sofas, three green-rooms, a vastly increased staff, and accommodation for 2,800 people. Fire had been effectually taken into account, and water-pipes were manifest in every part of the house with 'great brass cocks' which gave a reassuring reminder of their useful presence in the lobbies, and were considered the last word in modernity. Fire, at the time, was present in the mind of everyone, for in February, five months after the disaster at Covent Garden, the epidemic had spread to Drury Lane, and, providing one of the most splendid conflagrations on record as it illuminated the night sky with the vivid reflection of its fury, had ruined the fortunes of Sheridan and reduced the old playhouse to a heap of cinders.

The total cost of building and equipping the phœnix that had miraculously risen within the space of one year from its ashes in Covent Garden came into the handsome neighbourhood of £300,000; even then the proprietors were still in debt on account of the former building, and Kemble's loan had not yet been liquidated. The funds in hand, including insurance and contributions, totalled about £121,000, leaving £209,000 still outstanding. Some privileges had to be accorded to subscribers to the fund, and an arrangement was made giving them admittance for a considerable period on free passes. There was plainly only one way in which to meet liabilities, and this was to raise the prices of the seats. For this step the newspapers carefully prepared the public with judiciously worded explanations, and the opening of the new theatre was awaited with confidence.

At length the first night arrived, and on 18th September the audience flocked in and took their seats for *Macbeth*. The orchestra struck up the National Anthem, loyally accompanied by the entire public, and then Kemble stalked on to deliver an address in verse upon this auspicious evening. But no sooner had he begun to speak than he was howled down by an organized demonstration in which pandemonium was reinforced by every conceivable insult. Nevertheless the play began. As the actors one by one appeared upon the stage, they were applauded, but the moment that they began to speak their words were drowned by hooting and cries of 'Off!' Then began the solemn ritual that during the course of prolonged repetition came to be known as the 'OP' (Old Prices) dance: a rhythmic stamping of feet and sticks to the reiterated monosyllables 'OP! OP! OP!' The demonstration had been superbly organized. Placards were exhibited, some of which were insulting and others indecent, and the pittites got up in a body and stood for the rest of the evening with their backs to the stage as a protest to the increased prices of their seats. Mrs Siddons came on and was greeted with a deafening roar of derision. On her way to the theatre her carriage had been roughly handled by the rioting crowd, and she was not slow in realizing that the greatest share of popular rage was reserved for the Kemble family. She had the good sense to resign her engagement at once, for nothing that the world could offer would induce her to return to the inferno that she had just experienced. As a matter of fact the Old Prices riots went on uninterruptedly from that night for the next three months, and sporadically for nearly a year, until Kemble's resistance was utterly broken down; but not before he had reasoned fairly with the public, submitted the account-books to an independent committee including the Solicitor-General and the Governor of the Bank of England, who confirmed his statements, and hired prize-fighters to deal with the mob in the most summary manner. The demonstrations were so well organized and executed that night after night, as the riots went on, the Bow

Street runners would round up fresh ringleaders, and take them before the magistrates. Finally, Sir James Mansfield, hearing the action of one of the leaders, who sued for false imprisonment, found for the plaintiff with £5 damages. But still Kemble held out. His windows were smashed in by the mob, and for weeks his wife lived in a state of suspense and emergency with ladders placed against the garden windows, ready to be used as a means of escape if their personal safety were threatened.

The chief complaints were on account of foreign singers, notably Madame Catalani, the private boxes, whose ante-rooms were put to the blush by the unequivocal accusation of their being the scenes of 'abandoned and titled sensuality', and the higher price of the pit, which the public concluded was destined to meet the large salaries of the foreigners. Kemble was at last faced with the alternative of abolishing the private boxes or being ruined by his enemies. At his extremity of endurance he decided to give in, upon which the tyrants hoisted a placard of truce with the words 'We are satisfied' written largely across it. With the exception of sporadic outbreaks which took place from time to time throughout the following season, the OP riots were over and had passed into history.

Mrs Siddons was ill from agitation and strain on her brother's account, and although she kept well away from the theatre, she was in constant touch with him and his wife, and her indignation at the dominion of the masses was inexhaustible. But she also spared plenty of indignation for Mrs Galindo's pamphlet, which had meanwhile appeared, and which she looked upon as a rascally attempt to obtain money from her by intimidation. Fortunately, although its sale was brisk, *Mrs Galindo's Letter to Mrs Siddons* was looked upon as an artful method of blackmail, and Mrs Siddons bravely determined to weather the storm of its unpleasant notoriety rather than to shame herself by complying with the Galindos' threats. Public opinion was temporarily entertained by the pamphlet's revelations and privately shocked at the attack. It was, in Captain Burney's words, 'a deed without a name and a work without a reader', and he, believed it to be a scoundrelly book.

NINETEEN

THE Bath set was diminishing. Mr Piozzi had died. Miss Seward had died. The first Mrs Whalley had died. Mrs Piozzi was estranged from Mrs Pennington, preparing to quarrel with Mrs Siddons, no longer on terms with her daughters and involved in perpetual legal disputes in connexion with the lease of Streatham Park. Shortly after his wife's death, Mr Whalley had married a wealthy Miss Heathcote, described as 'gentle, kind and good, and sensible, though reserved'. In 1805 this lady had succumbed to the effects of a chill caught at a crowded Bath assembly, and Mr Whalley had once more been left alone. For a little while he had mourned, and then, throwing caution to the winds, had begun to entertain with feverish prodigality. He was nearly sixty, but, behaving as though he were twenty-six, he bought a house in London, entertained sumptuously, collected paintings, wasted a very great deal of money in buying jewels, and finally in a burst of self-esteem pulled strings through the unwilling medium of Sir Walter Scott in order to take his degree of Doctor of Divinity, and went to Edinburgh to receive it. Whalley was a strong Tory, an amateur musician, wept at a military band and was didactic and absolutely impatient of contradiction. Wilberforce called him the 'true picture of a sensible, well-informed, and educated, polished, old, well-beneficed, nobleman's and gentleman's house-frequenting, literary, and chess-playing divine – of the best sort – I hope beginning to be serious.' Dr Whalley was not beginning to be

[229]

serious. When he was nearly seventy he married a third wife, this time a widow, on the strength of her reputed fortune. Reputation, however, was its only substance. She was encumbered with debts which he found himself obliged to discharge. Quarrels resulted in a legal separation, a great deal of distressing publicity and the old man's eventual withdrawal to the Continent, where once again he surrounded himself by a coterie of appreciative and admiring friends. But he never lost touch with his actress heroine, saw her whenever he was in London, and had outlived her by two years when he died at Versailles in 1833.

Mrs Siddons was an elderly woman. Sorrow, illness and hard work had prematurely aged her, and the goal towards which she had been directing her energies for years past was now within reach. She was looking forward to her retirement with undisguised longing. She had always been constitutionally strong, equipped with a powerful stock of energy and with vital resources. She had besides a useful attribute: an ability to discard very quickly the ill-effects of a complaint, dominating her body by strength of mind and energy of spirit. So that her physique, although constantly shaken by the various shocks that it had experienced, was saved by its surprising recuperative powers.

Since she had come to Covent Garden she had created no new characters, although she had acted frequently in London and the provinces from the stock of her favourite plays. Since the OP riots the whole of the Kemble family had been restored to their former degree of popularity, but Kemble had lately been shelving more serious dramas in a desperate attempt to reimburse the proprietors for the heavy losses that had been incurred through his concessions to the rioters: an average of £10,400 a year. He had therefore turned his attention to box-office 'draws', and had begun to stage extravaganzas in order to attract larger houses. In 1811, his production of *Bluebeard*, with its elephant and its feature of sixteen 'most beautiful horses mounted by Spahis', had gone some way towards rewarding his business-like activities. *Bluebeard* was a magnificent success. It was also a deliberate contribution to popular taste and the decline of interest in acting.

Mrs Siddons's last season in the theatre was a very busy one.

She played indefatigably all her most ample and matronly characters. Preparations for her last appearance were well in hand early in the year, with Patty in full command as impresario and every responsible dramatic critic ready to speed the veteran into her retirement with the utmost eloquence, until, as she herself sadly remarked, she felt as if she were 'mounting the first steps of a ladder conducting her to the other world.' But by the spring of 1812 she was visibly drawing on the reserves of her strange and moving powers. She was looking ill, she spoke indistinctly, and the opening stages of any play were noticeably an effort. Crabb Robinson saw her in April playing Margaret of Anjou in the *Earl of Warwick* and commented on her capacity for triumphing over drawbacks as the play developed and her powers gained strength; finally showing, in every limb, 'the tumult of passion with an accuracy and a face equally impressive to the critic and the man of feeling. Her advancing age is a real pain to me,' wrote this enthusiast of 37. 'As an actor she has left with me the conviction that here never was, and never will be, her equal.'

Later in the same month he saw her as Mrs Beverley, when 'her voice appeared to have lost its brilliancy (like a beautiful face through a veil)" But the ravishing power of her smile and her quick transitions of expression were as youthful as ever. In these she could still enchant.

There was some hesitation about deciding which particular play should have the honour of Mrs Siddons's farewell. *Measure for Measure* was hit upon but then rejected in favour of *Macbeth*. All the seats at Covent Garden had been sold out long in advance, and there was considerable difficulty to procure one of the coveted tickets bearing on its red seal the word 'Farewell' as the twenty-ninth of June drew near: the date of the historic performance which was to be made the occasion of her benefit besides being that of her professional decease. The night arrived at last. Tier upon tier, encircling the auditorium, rose the boxes, in whose bowers of fringed plush, jewelled as though for Court, reclined the languishing, ogling, high-bosomed, white-armed, delicate women of the new Regency. Lord Byron and his genius, Lord Byron and his conduct, the immorality of the waltz, and the improbability that the French army would reach Moscow before Christmas were their principal topics of conversation; and as Thomas Lawrence entered Mr Lyson's immense box, and gazed round the stifling and overcrowded theatre, largely peopled with his own resplendent sitters, he may have dwelt with more than a little pang in his volatile heart upon the tragedy which bound his life invisibly to that of the august woman in whose honour the audience had assembled that night. Joseph Farington, all eyes and ears, sat as near as he could to the stage; the Sheridans were in the orchestra seats, and highly distinguished persons occupied every conceivable place. It is not known what Mrs Siddons wore as Lady Macbeth at her farewell performance. She had lately taken to a Mary Stuart costume of black velvet, wearing with it a large white ruff and a quantity of jewellery. It is possible that she did so now.

At the end of the sleep-walking scene tumult broke out. Among the thunders of prolonged applause a series of incomprehensible sounds emanated from the audience, the meaning of which, as *The Times* observantly noted, was not at first 'distinctly understood, and the house was considerably disturbed for some time'. However, the public's intention was eventually interpreted as a delicate compliment. They wished the play to end then and there with the exit of Lady Macbeth, and after an interval of twenty minutes, the curtain rose slowly on the great moment of the evening. Mrs Siddons, plainly robed in white satin and wearing a veil, was seen seated at a table. Then she rose and gradually moved forward, waited for the roaring applause to die away, and, after pulling herself together, began her farewell address. Her distressing partiality to speeches in verse was as strong as ever, and, judging from the quality of the effusion, it might have been composed by Mrs Siddons herself. It had, in fact, been composed by her nephew, Horace Twiss, MP, who played with literature, dilettantism and politics.

The digression, in rhymed couplets, was heard during eight minutes of profound silence. It concluded with an exhortation to the public that they might continue in future years to think kindly

> *On her who, parting to return no more,*
> Is *now the mourner she but* seemed *before.*

[232]

Herself subdued, resigns the melting spell,
And breathes, with swelling heart, her long, her last farewell.

It was an emotional moment. Very naturally it was deeply felt by the heroine herself. Amid ringing applause Kemble came forward in tears and led his sister off the stage; and, as she moved slowly away, leaning on his arm, she appeared to be sunk in dejection, but Farington, straining forward to notice her expression, could not perceive that she had faltered or showed any signs of weeping. When Kemble returned to inquire whether the play was to continue, the public would have none of it, and the evening fittingly came to an end among tears and acclamations.

So Mrs Siddons passed into retirement after a lifetime of almost uninterrupted and absolutely original work. 'We can only say,' wrote James Ballantyne in panegyric, '. . . that no sculptor or painter, in the sublimest flights of his fancy, ever embodied . . . a creature so formed, so gifted, to agitate, awe, and astonish mankind by her professional powers, as her whose matchless form, face, voice, and eye are now finally withdrawn from our public admiration.'

Yet that very summer her ardent admirer, Crabb Robinson, records seeing her for the first time without pleasure, in *Comus*. Considering her age, her proportions and the fact that the part was written for a girl of sixteen, this is not surprising. Dressed 'most unbecomingly', and wearing a low gipsy hat with dangling feathers, 'she looked old', he declared regretfully, 'and I had almost said ugly. Her fine features were lost in the distance. Even her declamation did not please me'. This fashionable declamation, he had formerly heard from Mrs Abington, relied upon an over-elaborate emphasis given to insignificant words for its chief effect, and was a complete innovation of the Kemble dynasty.

In her time, and largely through the Kemble influence, the theatre had seen great changes, and the position of players was now almost parallel with other reputable professions. Mrs Siddons could look back and remember the days when actors in the rich costumes of crowned kings or peruked lords were to be seen standing about in the wings of the theatre blowing their noses through their fingers. She could also remember the bawling tones of bottle-nosed tragedians, and their prancing gait across the stage, intended to give the impression of a stately walk. Sights like these were now exceptional, only to be seen in the companies of barnstormers who, like Mr Crummles and his troupe, struggled along upon their uncomfortable journeys until well on into the mid-century. The new generation that had arisen brought with it the brilliant, demented genius of Kean, the staid severity of Macready, and the young lady who was expected to fill the vacancy created by Mrs Siddons: Miss O'Neill. But not everyone was at Miss O'Neill's feet. Lord Byron loyally refused to see her in case she should disturb his memories of the one and only Siddons, who was to him, throughout his life, 'the *beau idéal* of acting'.

Some time during 1813 a movement was begun to recall Mrs Siddons to the stage. Byron in his correspondence mentions a subscription book that was 'going about for signatures! (she having lately taken leave, to the loss of ages – for nothing ever was, or can be, like her).' There now appear to have been three of these books, which were placed respectively at Messrs Hookham's and Mr Ebers's, both in Old Bond Street; while another was at the London Coffee House on Ludgate Hill. Subscribers were invited to sign their names, and the lists, when considered by the committee to be appropriately filled with enough influential signatories, were to be presented to Mrs Siddons in the hope of persuading her to return to the theatre. One of the three note-books, small quarto in size, has come to light in recent years. It is bound in red leather, and on the cover is stamped in gold lettering, 'Recall of Mrs Siddons to the Stage'. It contains 518 signatures representing the most distinguished persons in every sphere of the arts and sciences, and presumably the other two volumes were not inferior in the gratifying results which they achieved. Mrs Siddons should have had every reason to be satisfied with the petition; she was, however, not to be deterred from her resolution. She had the strength of mind to refuse temptation and the intelligence to retire while she was still likely to be missed. But she had no intention of being idle. What with the cost of living, that was now doubled, and the Luddites, who were contributing to the alarming insecurity and unrest of the nation, she felt bound to keep going or else to forfeit her one luxury, her carriage. She was desperate to retain her comforts and to move into London before the winter, before the 'sweet nutshell' at Westbourne became too damp and dreary. She resolved to give a series of public readings from her two favourite poets, Shakespeare and Milton. These took place during the winter of 1812–13 at the Argyle Rooms. The Duchess of York headed the list of patrons attending these 'one-man' shows, and the fact that the series of six performances at half-a-guinea a seat yielded a profit of £1,300 is proof of their immense popularity. A typical evening was that in January 1813, when the proceeds were to be devoted to an actor's widow, Mrs Cherry. The audience were in their seats at 8.45 for a reading of *Macbeth*. The orchestra had been hidden from view by a large, red screen, in front of which had been placed a reading-desk, lit up, holding a quarto volume printed in large type. Mrs Siddons, dressed in black velvet with a red coral necklace, and wearing her black hair in a classical fashion, or, as a lady's journal described it, 'in fancy costume', was led on to the rostrum by Horace Twiss, was rapturously applauded, bowed gracefully and began. The experience was altogether delightful. It was almost more popular than her inimitable acting, for if it began as a recitation it turned into a dramatic representation. The intimacy of the moment, the entire absence of stage trickery and illusion gave each spectator the impression of being alone with her. Proximity showed her as she actually was: still beautiful and still youthful, especially in the upper part of the unlined face and smooth skin. She hardly ever resorted to her spectacles, for her memory could supply the words when her dim eyesight failed her, and she used her glasses mostly as an aid to emphasis, waving them airily from time to time in her hand. Mrs Piozzi, who had quarrelled with almost everybody by now, tried her best to find fault with the readings, and wrote off in a humour to her adopted nephew: 'Why she *acted* every word of it – witches and all; and having been ever *slow*, is now *tardy*; so we were kept till 12 o'clock – no music intervening, nor nothing to break the almost monstrous uniformity: for tho' she does vary the tone, she never changes the Key Note, by any Accident; in any character. It was, however, a very great Performance, and . . . her Attitudes and Gestures, and Figure, are incomparable'.

But on another occasion when she was feeling less quarrelsome she gave Mangin, her friend, a very different account. The scene between Malcolm and Macduff had been read by Mrs Siddons so as to break the hearts of her hearers, she told him. In fact the readings were so successful that they became in time a recognized institution. Mrs Siddons took to giving them at her evening receptions after she had left Westbourne and moved into her last London house. By that time she was being looked upon as something more than mortal, and commanded more spontaneous respect than was accorded to an empress. She was regaling her guests one evening with *Macbeth* when Benjamin Robert Haydon was invited among some other acquaintances and celebrities. In the short interval the men got up and chatted together over cups of tea and refreshments. Suddenly, before they had finished eating, their hostess began again. 'It was,' wrote Haydon,[1] 'like the effect of a Mass-bell at Madrid.' In dead silence they all crept shamefacedly back to their seats, some with their mouths still full, others balancing cups and saucers on their knees. Tom Lawrence, still the *enfant terrible*, but lately restored to grace, was there too; and with his mouth full of toast and his eyes full of water from the effort to be quiet, now and then gave a sly crunch, and then pretended to look guilty and awed; pretended, too, to be paying attention to the impressive voice as it boomed dramatically onward . . . 'eye of newt and toe of frog'. And then bit furtively into his toast again. Haydon left, having thoroughly enjoyed his evening. As he went out from the over-heated room on to the landing he paused for a breath or two of air, and listened to the servants in the hall below. 'What!' his own man was saying, 'is that the old lady making such a noise? . . . She makes as much noise as ever!' 'Yes,' replied another, 'she tunes her pipes as well as ever she did.'

Honours abounded for the veteran. She spent a week-end at Windsor, diverting the gloomy life of 'these amiable sufferers', as she called the Royal Family once more under the pall of insanity, and was rewarded by Queen Charlotte with a magnificent jewelled cross upon a heavy gold chain which was fastened round her neck before her royal hearers. Then she was invited to read before the most 'eminent

[1] *Autobiography of B. R. Haydon*, 1853.

[236]

characters' of Oxford and Cambridge. She took Cecilia with her, now a grown-up young lady of nineteen, and Cecilia basked happily in the rays of reverence that were focused upon her adored mother. She was sadly disappointed that Patty was not there to enjoy 'the attention and admiration shown to our *Darling*', at Cambridge where she received a handsome Bible in stereotype from the syndics of the University, before whom in return she delivered the trial scene from the *Merchant of Venice*.

During the suspension of hostilities that preceded the 'Hundred Days' there had been a concerted rush of English visitors into France. Mrs Siddons also took advantage of the lull, and decided on a trip to Paris with Patty and Cecilia. She had never been there before. She had a lot to see, and many people to meet. One of these was the Duke of Wellington, to whom she was introduced, and who was particularly courteous to her. A few days later she met him again at a reception. The two Lions were left together in the middle of the room. The Duke stood there in silence: Mrs Siddons stood there in silence. Neither of them had anything to say, and the company looked on in astonishment and consternation. But Mrs Siddons and the Duke were being true to themselves. She had no social talents; she was never a snob, and conversation had failed her once again. The Duke was, anyway, a man of few words. A more enjoyable experience was a visit to the Louvre, and her first sight of its treasures. She had always been susceptible to classical influences. Years earlier, at the house of the painter Hamilton, her host had drawn her attention to her resemblance to a statue of Ariadne on his staircase. Then and there she had sat down on the stairs in earnest contemplation of the figure. 'Yes,' she had said, 'it is very' – she had meant to say 'like', but self-consciously added – 'beautiful. So very beautiful that I fear you must be flattering me.' Now, however, the stately woman, leaning upon the arm of Thomas Campbell, who was doing the honours of the Louvre, passed heavily down the gallery, and came to a stand before the Apollo Belvedere. As with the Duke of Wellington, she remained in silence for a long time before giving utterance to her impression of the marble youth. When it finally came it was characteristic of herself, and of the religious sense which affected all her reactions to art and life. 'What a great idea it gives us of God, to think that He has made a human being capable of fashioning so divine a form!' Campbell was unluckily too much occupied in being seen in her company by the other visitors to collect any more of these interesting impressions, and as they walked along the galleries, he enjoyed the curiosity that they were exciting; indeed, he added, 'her looks were so noble, that she made you proud of English beauty, even in the presence of Grecian sculpture'.

*　　*　　*

There is another fuller account of this on a later visit to the Louvre recorded by Crabb Robinson, who happened to be there also on the same day. Word had gone round that Mrs Siddons was below and Robinson deserted 'The Raphæls and Titians' to discover the goddess, the glimpse of whom he declared, gave him greater delight than any he had received in Paris. So in search of this ageing muse he went, and he found her below. He had never seen her so close before. He studied her physiognomy carefully as she walked about with her sister, Mrs Twiss, and 'I kept as near as I could with decorum, & without appearing to be watching her; yet there was something about her that disturbed me. So glorious a head ought not to have been covered with a small chip hat. She knit her brows, too, on looking at the pictures, as if to assist a failing sight. But I recognized her fascinating smile with delight, though there was a line or two about her mouth which I thought coarse.'

These frank observations from an enthusiast, partial almost to the point of prejudice, were of infinite value as correctives to undisciplined admiration. Critically, Crabb Robinson retained all his discrimination; he became almost surgically impersonal.

Theoretically, his passion for Mrs Siddons exceeded all bounds of reason. He was to call Boaden's *Life* 'one of the most worthless books of biography ever written', yet which gave him very great pleasure merely because to read such a statement as: 'This evening Mrs Siddons performed Lady Macbeth . . .' had the effect of recalling 'the yet unfaded image of that most marvellous woman, to think of whom is now a

[238]

greater enjoyment than to see any other actress'. Could admiration express itself in more rhapsodical terms?

Such praise bordering on veneration, goes some way toward explaining the nature of the emotions aroused among her spectators, especially those who were capable of being stirred by the extremes of human passion.

The art of Mrs Siddons evidently contained the power of stirring the emotions on a twofold level. By sheer histrionic ability she succeeded, doubtless, in arousing among an audience the feelings she intended. Thus far, she has made herself intelligible to subsequent generations. But that she also possessed a quality lying on a deeper, intenser level, we can be fairly certain, although to interpret its effect in literary terms with any hope of succeeding, must be the despair of biographers, especially those who never beheld her. James Boaden, who, however worthless his works, was so familiar with her characteristics that his evidence is invaluable, affirms that the incomparable pathos of her early London period had, by later life so yielded to force and majesty, that a later generation of theatre-goers was sceptical enough to doubt its ever having come within her range.

Her most tremendous effects were obtained often by simple sentences, inadequate to convey through any means other than her own secret power. Mrs Nugent, a great admirer, recorded in her diary some hint of this indefinable quality. 'I remember her saying to a servant who had betrayed her in some play no longer acted: "There's gold for thee, but see my face no more!"' There is no giving an adequate impression of the might, the majesty of grace she possessed, nor the effect on a young heart of the deep and mysterious tones of her voice.

*   *   *

There was another visit to the Continent a few years later, this time to Switzerland. In 1821, after Kemble's retirement, Mrs Siddons went out to stay with him at Beausite, his comfortable villa near Lausanne. She went there as much for her health as for the pleasure of seeing him, for the headaches from which she had always suffered were now increasingly intense. But the change of air did her little good, although the sight of the snow mountains was in itself a new experience. The Alps made the Welsh hills very insignificant. Both Mrs Siddons and Cecilia were in raptures over the scenery, they could not believe it to be real. They sailed on the lake, ate chamois – a new gastronomic experience for Mrs Siddons – and performed the intrepid feat of mounting a glacier, with the aid of two men who hacked footholds for them in the ice. Kemble was in excellent health and spirits. He worked all day in his garden, held open house to travellers, and since his retirement looked younger and in higher spirits than he had been for a long time. But the strong air had had only a superficial effect upon him. His constitution, shattered by hard work, had done its best to withstand the effects of rich living, and in London he had sometimes dragged through his parts half asleep with drugs and pain. Two years after his sister's visit he died from a stroke, and was buried out in Switzerland.

George Siddons had got married out in Calcutta to a Miss Mary Fombelle, and the first consignment of Anglo-Indian grandchildren – there were seven of them eventually – arrived in England during 1814, accompanied by an ayah speaking nothing but Hindustani, and were deposited with their grandmother at Westbourne. Mrs Siddons was accustomed to looking after grandchildren, for Harry's babies had sometimes stayed with her, and on those occasions she had solemnly done her best to amuse and entertain them, and to get them to love her, for all her rather awe-inspiring appearance. But Harry died in 1815 at the age of forty, the third of the Siddonses to be tubercular. The blow left his wife and family in distressed circumstances up at Edinburgh, for they were entirely dependent upon his success as manager and proprietor of the Theatre Royal, into which position he had been inveigled through the enthusiasm of Sir Walter Scott, which included all the acting members of the Kemble family. Mrs Siddons went up to Edinburgh, and in spite of ill health played for the benefit of her son's family during ten special performances. Harry's loss, although less afflicting than those of her two daughters, was a shock to her nerves and spirits. 'The little that was left of my poor sight is almost washed away by tears . . .' she wrote resignedly to Mrs Fitzhugh. 'God's will be done!'

Throughout her life Mrs Siddons had been sincerely religious. The limits of her philosophy were determined by the

[240]

fences of Divine Will. Within the acreage of her own freedom she had developed powerfully, especially in the upward growth of her more masculine traits, concentration and strength of will. Spiritually, perhaps because she was unimaginative, she had remained static, and without lateral expansion. Her faith was simple, courageous and direct. She had none of the uncertainties of modern minds as to the boundaries between right and wrong; and her fixed attitude towards these problems, less cynical than that of her eighteenth-century contemporaries, was a good deal in advance of her own age. Mrs Siddons, had she come into the world half a century later, would have provided one of the most substantial pillars of Victorian England. The spiritual aspect of her religious feeling was strongly involved with her art. For this reason perhaps her favourite divine poem was *Paradise Lost*, which in 1822 she paraphrased in an abridged edition for her children. *The Story of our first Parents, Selected from Milton's Paradise Lost: For the Use of Young Persons. By Mrs Siddons*, was published by John Murray. It only needed her approbation in order to turn Haydon's exhibition of 'Christ Entering into Jerusalem' from a doubtful enterprise into the most successful painting of the moment. He had already been struggling with it for six years, had repainted the Christ's head six times, had washed his hands of the Academicians and been flouted in turn by them, and was now taking a lonely stand on the success or failure of the monumental painting upon which depended his pledged honour and his existence. In his journal he has recorded the opening day of the exhibition. The room had begun to fill. Artists, duchesses, poets and connoisseurs walked round, gossiped, stared at the picture; and yet no one dared to criticize the unorthodox appearance of the Christ. The verdict on the picture was still undecided at five o'clock in the afternoon, when Mrs Siddons walked in. In respectful silence the company waited to hear her opinion. Sir George Beaumont, who should have known his own mind, at last ventured a timid: 'How do you like the Christ?' There was a pause, during which the fate of the artist hung between insolvency and affluence; success and failure. Judgement came at last in its slow, deliberate tone of conviction: 'It is completely successful'. Haydon was then presented, invited, 'in an awful tone', to call, and complimented on his achievement. Through Mrs Siddons's independent criticism a final seal of excellence was set upon the painting, and its success was established. The story is not given as an example of her æsthetic judgement – she was too clearly playing for safety – but it is a curious proof of the immense authority which she had somehow succeeded in impressing upon the educated classes as well as upon the public. Haydon went home, and with a full heart wrote an almost servile letter of gratitude to his benefactress. He called at her house, and was 'most gloriously received'. The experience seemed to him like meeting the Mother of the Gods. Well might he have felt satisfied with her encouragement. Her enthusiasm for the picture had communicated itself to the public, and from that moment the gallery had been continually besieged, and the exhibition brought him in altogether seventeen hundred pounds. All this was in keeping with her own ideas. Mrs Siddons took herself and her great talent for granted, and she took herself seriously. It would never have occurred to her to doubt the fact that, artistically speaking, she was a wonder. Her attitude might be mistaken for complacency, it was certainly not conceit. As Campbell said of her, she was 'a great, simple being', honest, open and direct in her thoughts and in her words. Without the full realization of this it would be impossible not to smile at the story of the little girl who was taken to see the famous Mrs Siddons in order that she might remember the event in after years. She saw, in fact, a very large, very beautiful, very noble-looking old lady who took her hand, gazed at her, and slowly said, 'Ah! my dear, you may well look at me, for you will never see my like again'.

TWENTY

GAS lighting was new. So were steamboats and engines; and London bridges at long last were augmenting. In 1817 Mrs Siddons left Westbourne, where she had found herself vegetating in the sweet but none too stimulating company of Cecilia and Patty, and took a house in Marylebone. No 27, Upper Baker Street, stood at the very top of the row on the right-hand side nearest to Regent's Park. It was a large house with a back that looked straight on to the country and the new Park which was being surrounded by Nash with palaces of stucco, and the fashionable architect received instructions from the Regent to shorten Cornwall Terrace so that Mrs Siddons's rural prospect should be uninterrupted. It was plainly and almost severely furnished inside, for her tastes had always been simple, and when Mrs Piozzi went there one evening soon after Mrs Siddons had moved in, she described herself as dining 'out of town'. Latterly Mrs Piozzi had been disposed to be antagonistic towards some of her sincerest friends, and in her old age, which was showing signs of rivalling Dr Whalley's in its frivolity, she had been given to enthusiasms for young and recent acquaintances, and suspicions concerning her few surviving contemporaries. 'The Bath People are those who I depend on for my *social* Comforts in future, not the London ones,' she wrote to her nephew. 'Doctor Whalley will last me out, I dare say; and while he lives Mrs Siddons will never be my *open* Enemy. My Fears from them all are as cold as my hopes: they will do me

[243]

neither good nor harm.' The observation is a commentary upon Mrs Piozzi's last years, when bitterness and acrimony, debts and disputes filled the existence of the old cynic. Nothing is known of the reason for her distrust of Mrs Siddons. But the quarrel, if quarrel there was, had been settled before the actress left Westbourne, for Mrs Piozzi was invited to a magnificent luncheon there – which took place at the curious hour of 5 pm – and after the departure of the other guests had stayed on with her hostess, and with Mrs Fitzhugh as go-between the two old ladies had shaken hands and made it up. She died in 1821, thirty-seven years after her immortalizer, Johnson. Mrs Siddons made haste to recover her letters from the executors, and all were returned with the exception of the one in which she had replied to Mrs Piozzi's condolences on the death of Harry. It marked her rapidly approaching state of complete resignation – even of impatience to get through the remaining years. . . . 'The only good thing we can reckon upon with any certainty in this world is, *that one is far advanced upon one's journey to a better.*' Mrs Siddons was never happy after her retirement. With the approach of dusk she would sit at her window, and think of the days when, at that hour, she was due to leave for the theatre. First there had been the anticipation, then the pleasure of dressing for her part. Then there had been the joy of playing it. In 1817, when Kemble had retired from the stage, and had been given a public dinner among more fuss and attention than had ever been shown to her at her own farewell, a spark of the old resentment against injustice had flared up again in her breast. With her eye firmly fixed upon immortality she had turned bitterly and almost jealously to Samuel Rogers with an indignant comment: 'Well, perhaps in the next world women will be more valued than they are in this'. She still fancied that she had enemies who would take pleasure in mortifying her; for, she wondered, how otherwise would they have run after new favourites like Miss Brunton, Miss Smith and Miss O'Neill. So, 'I am not yet extinguished,' she proudly proclaimed.

She was extinguished, none the less. In the same year she appeared in a special performance of *Macbeth* for the edification of Princess Charlotte and Prince Leopold, neither of whom had ever seen her play. The event provoked Hazlitt's superb essay,

[244]

at once an imperishable tribute and an implied rebuke. She should never have acted again after this. But benefits arose from time to time in which she appeared for members of her family or for deserving institutions. For the greater part of the nation she was now such a phenomenon in herself that criticism was out of the question. Even Mrs Trench, who years earlier had carped at her indiscriminate indulgence in paroxysms of agony, could now recall none of her criticisms. Time, for her as for so many people, had obliterated everything but the consolation that a revered personality was still present, and she was now only conscious of the fact that the like of Mrs Siddons would never be seen again. She was fast approaching the sublime state when she was to be numbered among the perfections of history which can never occur more, which the present can never see equalled nor the future envisage. She had become a legend. As late as 1850 Crabb Robinson, inveterate theatre-goer to the last, had seen Rachel and found her wanting; wanting in 'the magical tones, and the marvellous eye, and the majestic figure of Mrs Siddons'.

In 1822, at a party given by Lord Lansdowne, George IV introduced the French Ambassador to a severe old lady dressed in crape, wearing a black veil like a diadem across her dazzling white hair. She appeared to him like a queen who had abdicated. She solemnly greeted Chateaubriand, misquoted three sentences from the *Génie du Christianisme*, and with equal solemnity proclaimed her identity: 'I am Mrs Siddons'. And Chateaubriand declared that he would have believed her had she said she was Lady Macbeth. On the whole, she had not much interest in new acquaintances, and old friends were thinning out yearly. Sir Thomas Lawrence had reached the climax of his career. In 1815 he had been knighted; in 1820 he had been elected President of the Royal Academy, and his list of sitters included most of the royalties who had bargained their way through the Congress of Vienna. He had never left off his philandering habits, and had lightly passed from one beautiful woman to another. With the passage of time his charming, easy manner had increased in decorum, and, like his portraits, had acquired a suavity that was as deliberately cultivated as it was facile. For one of his last victims he returned, after the fashion of sentimentalists, to the cradle of his first loves. This time to Mrs Siddons's young niece. The susceptible man of sixty had not been able to resist charming the adolescent imagination of pretty, precocious little Fanny Kemble, who made a special entry in her journal of his dangerously seductive power: 'He could not answer a dinner invitation without its assuming the tone of a *billet doux*; the very commonest conversation was held in that soft low whisper and with that tone of deference and interest which are so unusual and so calculated to please.' In the end the old charmer even had his way with 'The Immortal' herself. Towards the close of her life her affection for him had gained in strength, and although there was never a return to the old, close intimacy, there were two occasions when they each spoke of one another in a spirit that revealed all the muted sentiments of past years. One day, to her youngest brother Charles, Mrs Siddons had remarked that she would like to be carried to her grave by Lawrence and himself. Lawrence, when he was told of her wish, profoundly moved, had cried, 'Good God! did she say that?' But there was another time when the old *roué* gave himself away as completely as he had ever done. During his elderly flirtation with Fanny Kemble he had presented her with a print of 'The Tragic Muse'. It was elaborately inscribed to the 'niece and worthy successor' of the original. But before giving it he erased the words 'and worthy successor', and as the print was left lying about in his room for a day or two before delivery, he was overwhelmed with sadness. 'Cover it up; I cannot bear to look at it,' he said to his secretary. Nor was he to bear Mrs Siddons to her grave. Fate was ironical. Fate decided that Lawrence should be the first to go. He died suddenly, in his library, early in January, 1830, in his sixty-first year. He was given a funeral of which the splendour must have pleased him. He lay in state at Somerset House, and then, the cynosure of public attention, he was borne to St Paul's Cathedral and deposited near Sir Christopher Wren and Sir Joshua Reynolds.

*   *   *

'Sat two hours with my old friend Mrs Siddons, a majestic ruin.' The line occurs in a letter written by Joseph Jekyll some three years before she died. The only remains of her beauty, he added, were her powerful eyes.

A new generation of Kembles had gown up. Charles had married Miss de Camp, the victim of his brother's attempted indiscretion, and she had presented him with two daughters: Fanny, the Kemble memorialist, and Adelaide. Fanny Kemble was symbolic of the new order. She had no recollection of her aunt's public life beyond being carried through the swarming crowds outside Covent Garden on some occasion when the old lady, 'a solemn female figure in black', had made one of her rare public appearances and was welcomed by a 'tremendous *roar* of public greeting'. In 1831, Fanny, from the eminence of twenty years, surveyed the stage of life, and believed herself able to estimate the achievements of seventy-six. Full of self-assurance she was imparting opinionated confidences to her journal. 'What a price she has paid for her great celebrity!' she wrote, referring to her venerable Aunt Siddons. 'Weariness, vacuity, and utter deadness of spirit. . . . She has stood on a pinnacle till all things have come to look flat and dreary; mere shapeless, colourless, level monotony to her. Poor woman! what a fate to be condemned to, and yet how she has been envied as well as admired!' Yet until recently Mrs Siddons had been fairly active in her life, spending the winters in London, surrounded like some matriarch with grandchildren, nephews and nieces; while her summers were spent on visits to friends or at some watering-place. She had celebrated her seventy-second birthday by staying with Lord Darnley at Cobham Hall, where there had been a fatiguing dinner with twenty-three guests, conversation with Prince Leopold, now a forlorn widower, and with the Duchess of Kent; and the evening had been devoted to music and Shakespeare. Lately, festivities of this nature had become too much for a rather ponderous old lady, and in 1830 she had been troubled with a serious interior inflammation which seems to have had some of the symptoms of colitis. The next year brought back the tortures of erysipelas, which attacked her in the leg, and caused excruciating pain, intense discomfort, and blinding headaches. Intermittently she was well enough to go out for drives in her carriage. The month of May 1831, ended in a spell of wintry weather. Mrs Siddons caught cold during a drive on the thirty-first, and a fierce attack of erysipelas in both legs was the immediate result. That night she had high fever, terrible vomitings, and rigors.

The parting genius was being sent upon her way with much sighing, yet with the gentlest and most patient endurance. Cecilia and Patty never moved away from her. She was, according to Fanny Kemble, the one idea of their whole devoted lives. Dr Leman, whom they had called in at once, sacrificed his patient to the theories of his time. He plied her with physics, and stuffed her with food so that her discomfort was only aggravated; and in treating her gangrened legs he forced her to undergo a protracted torture. On the evening of 7th June, stupor at last set in. Cecilia, brokenhearted at her mother's long agony, was filled with profound relief as she watched her slip gently into a steady sleep. As she held the limp hand the transition from sleep to death was almost imperceptible until at eight o'clock the next morning, a Wednesday, she knew by the irregular flutter of the faint pulse which gradually ceased that the end had been reached.

The news was immediately taken to Charles Kemble, who officially informed the theatre of his sister's death, and with Cecilia superintended preparations for the funeral. On 15th June, as early as nine o'clock in the morning, an immense concourse of persons was collecting in Upper Baker Street. At New Road, round at the Globe, an hour later, appeared the hearse and its attendant mourning coaches, and the business of caparisoning the horses was begun. They were then adorned with funereal plumes, and during this operation the crowd gazed from the tall sash windows, mysteriously shuttered in the June morning, to the sombre plumage of the horses; and then again directed its interest to the windows. At half-past ten the door opened, and the coffin draped in a pall of rich purple velvet was carried out and placed in the hearse, and the procession set off. The attendance was impressive. After the hearse came two coaches-and-four containing the chief mourners. These were followed by fourteen mourning coaches-and-four, each containing representatives of Covent Garden, Drury Lane, and others of the dramatic world. The *cortège* concluded with two gentlemen's carriages. An attempt had been made on the part of the nobility and gentry to ensure that they, too, should be represented, but the idea appears to have been flouted by the Kembles in favour of a 'quiet' funeral. The procession moved on among following and increasing crowds. It passed up the streets by Regent's Park, Alpha Road, and Princes Street to Paddington where, at Mrs Siddons's former church of St Mary's, her remains were deposited in the half rural cemetery. Five thousand people saw her laid to rest, and before the coffin was lowered into the grave there occurred one of those mysterious incidents which are never fully explained. A young woman, heavily veiled, whose identity has never been established, came and knelt beside the bier, giving vent to her grief in the strongest manner. Mrs Siddons had emerged from years of privacy to resume for a brief hour or two her old dominion over the public. Few of those who were present and in tears can have remembered the early griefs of Belvidera and Calista: only those with exceptional powers of imagination may have conceived of the extreme pathos of Isabella and Jane Shore. The imperial dignity of Shakespearian queens had long since become a legend; but the people who had gathered in the streets of Paddington were not unconscious of the magnitude of the occasion. They had lost in Mrs Siddons 'the stateliest ornament of the public mind'.

Had she died earlier in the century she might have been graced with an agreeable headstone, one of the legacies of eighteenth-century elegance. As it happened, she died on the turn of a new age, when Taste was being roughly pushed aside by its headstrong brother, Utility. Therefore, she lies in the most forbidding of tombs. A hard slab pins her underground, bearing the inscription chosen by herself:

Sacred to the Memory of
SARAH SIDDONS,
who departed this life June 8th, 1831,
in her 76th year.
Blessed are the dead that die in the Lord.

In the life of the English Theatre she had ceased for many years to take an active part, although by common consent she had at last been admitted, like some dethroned empress, on to the vaster proscenium of history.

History, however, is not always reverent. Sometimes, holding a grimacing mask against noble features she interprets her captive to posterity with intent to distort, because she is tired, or bored, or merely because she finds her victim has become unfashionable.

Again, equally capricious, she may smother it with gar-lands, or wreathe it with laurel, obliterating its features entirely.

From this treatment our heroine has not entirely escaped. Side by side with Gainsborough and Lawrence, there are Rowlandson and Gillray. Any over-stressing of the solemnity, the sententious mannerisms, the ponderous style, in fact the entire paraphernalia of the later period of amplitude, and the effect can be cumulative to the point of absurdity.

At the last we are left with the eyewitnesses, with tradition, and with our independent judgement; above all with the eloquent, but silent testimony of the incomparable portraits.

APPENDIX A

Mrs Siddons's Repertory at Drury Lane

Season	Character	Play	Author
1782–3	ISABELLA	Isabella, or, The Fatal Marriage	Southerne
	EUPHRASIA	The Grecian Daughter	Murphy
	JANE SHORE	Jane Shore	Rowe
	MRS MONTAGUE	The Fatal Interview	Hull
	CALISTA	The Fair Penitent	Rowe
	BELVIDERA	Venice Preserved	Otway
	ZARA	The Mourning Bride	Congreve
1783–4	ISABELLA	Measure for Measure	Shakespeare
	MRS BEVERLEY	The Gamester	Moore
	CONSTANCE	King John	Shakespeare
	LADY RANDOLPH	Douglas	Home
	COUNTESS OF SALISBURY	The Countess of Salisbury	Hartson
	SIGISMUNDA	Tancred and Sigismunda	Thomson
1784–5	MARGARET OF ANJOU	Earl of Warwick	Franklin
	ZARA	Zara	Voltaire (arr. Hill)
	MATILDA	The Carmelite	Cumberland
	CAMIOLA	The Maid of Honour	Massinger
	LADY MACBETH	Macbeth	Shakespeare
	DESDEMONA	Othello	Shakespeare
	ELFRIDA	Elfrida	Mason
	ROSALIND	As You Like It	Shakespeare

Season	Character	Play	Author
1785–6	THE DUCHESS	*Braganza*	Jephson
	MRS LOVEMORE	*The Way to Keep Him*	Murphy
	HERMIONE	*The Distressed Mother*	Racine (arr. Phillips)
	MALVINA	*The Captives*	Delap
	PORTIA	*The Merchant of Venice*	Shakespeare
	ELWINA	*Percy*	Hannah More
	OPHELIA	*Hamlet*	Shakespeare
	THE LADY	*Comus*	Milton
1786–7	CLEONE	*Cleone*	Dodsley
	IMOGEN	*Cymbeline*	Shakespeare
	COUNTESS OF NAR-BONNE	*The Countess of Narbonne*	Jephson
	LADY RESTLESS	*All in the Wrong*	Murphy
	JULIA	*Julia; or The Italian Lover*	Jephson
	ALICIA	*Jane Shore*	Rowe
1787–8	CORDELIA	*King Lear*	Shakespeare
	CHELONICE	*The Fate of Sparta*	Mrs Cowley
	KATHARINE	*Katharine and Petruchio*	Garrick
	DIANORA	*The Regent*	Greatheed
	CLEOPATRA	*All for Love*	Dryden
1788–9	QUEEN KATHARINE	*King Henry VIII*	Shakespeare
	VOLUMNIA	*Coriolanus*	Shakespeare
	THE PRINCESS	*The Law of Lombardy*	Jephson
	THE FINE LADY	*Lethe*	Garrick
	MARY QUEEN OF SCOTS	*Mary Queen of Scots*	St John
	JULIET	*Romeo and Juliet*	Shakespeare
1789–90	Not engaged		
1791	No new parts		
1791–2	THE QUEEN	*King Richard III*	Shakespeare
	MRS OAKLEY	*The Jealous Wife*	Colman
1792–3	ARIADNE	*The Rival Sisters*	Murphy
1793–4	No new parts		
1794–5	COUNTESS ORSINA	*Emilia Galotti*	Lessing
	HORATIA	*The Roman Father*	Whitehead
	ELGIVA	*Edwy and Elgiva*	Mme d'Arblay

Season	Character	Play	Author
1794–5	PALMIRA	*Mahomet the Imposter*	Voltaire (arr. Miller)
	EMMELINE	*Edgar and Emmeline*	Hawksworth
1795–6	ROXANA	*Alexander the Great*	Lee
	ALMEYDA	*Almeyda, Queen of Granada*	Sophia Lee
	GERTRUDE	*Hamlet*	Shakespeare
	JULIA	*Such Things Were*	Hoare
1796–7	VITELLIA	*The Conspiracy*	Jephson
	MILLWOOD	*The London Merchant*	Lillo
	ATHENAIS	*The Force of Love*	Lee (arr. Tigne)
	ARPASIA	*Tamerlane*	Rowe
	DIDO	*The Queen of Carthage*	Reed
	AGNES	*The Fatal Curiosity*	Lillo
	EMILY	*The Deuce is in Him*	Colman
1797–8	JULIA	*The Rivals*	Sheridan
	MRS HALLER	*The Stranger*	Kotzebue
1798–9	MIRANDA	*Aurelio and Miranda*	Boaden
	COUNTESS OF MONT-VAL	*The Castle of Montval*	Whalley
	ELVIRA	*Pizarro*	Kotzebue (arr. Sheridan)
1799–1800	ADELAIDE	*Adelaide of Wulfingen*	Kotzebue (arr. Thomson)
	JANE	*de Montfort*	Joanna Baillie
1800–1	HELENA	*Antonio; The Soldier's Return*	Godwin
	AGNES	*Julian and Agnes*	Sotheby
1801–2	HERMIONE	*The Winter's Tale*	Shakespeare

Played at Covent Garden 1802–12, but acted no new parts.

APPENDIX B : THE KEMBLE FAMILY

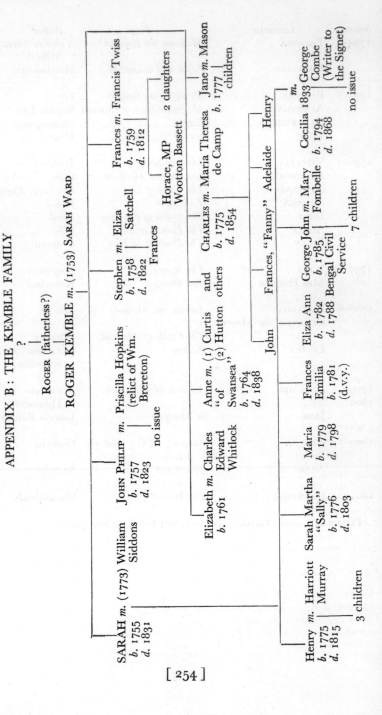

BIBLIOGRAPHY

ANSTEY, CHRISTOPHER. *The New Bath Guide.* 1766.
D'ARBLAY, MME. *Memoirs of Dr Burney.* 1832.
BARBEAU, A. *Une Ville d'Eaux Anglaise au 18me Siècle.* 1904.
BEAUFOY, GWENDOLYN. *Leaves from a Beech Tree.* 1930.
Beauties of Mrs Siddons, The: or, a review of her performance . . . in letters from a Lady of Distinction to her friend in the country. 1786.
Belle Assemblée, La, for 1812.
BOADEN, JAMES. *Memoirs of Mrs Siddons.* 1827.
BOADEN, JAMES. *Memoirs of Mrs Inchbald.* 1833.
BOADEN, JAMES. *The Life of Mrs Jordan.* 1831.
BOSWELL, JAMES. *Life of Johnson.* Ed. G. Birkbeck Hill. 1887.
BOURKE, HON. ALGERNON. *Correspondence of Joseph Jekyll.* 1894.
BURNEY, FRANCES. *Diary.* Ed. C. Barrett, with preface and notes by A. Dobson. 1904–5.
BYRON, LORD. *Letters and Journals.* Ed. R. E. Prothero. 1898–1903.
CAMPBELL, THOMAS. *Life of Mrs Siddons.* 1834.
CANNING, J. H. *Blessed John Kemble.* C.T.S. 1934.
CHATEAUBRIAND, F. R. DE. *Mémoires d'Outre-tombe.* Ed. Biré. (n.d.)
DAVIES, THOMAS. *Memoirs of the Life of David Garrick.* 1780.
DORAN, DR. *Annals of the English Stage.* 1865.
E.H.M. *Recollections of the Past.* 1877.
ENTHOVEN COLLECTION. Victoria and Albert Museum.
FARINGTON, JOSEPH R. A. *The Farington Diaries.* Ed. J. Greig. 1922.
FITZGERALD, PERCY. *The Kembles.* 1871.
GALINDO, CATHERINE. *Mrs Galindo's Letter to Mrs Siddons.* 1809.
GENEST, REV. JOHN. *Some Account of the English Stage in 1660 to 1830.* 1832.
Gentleman's Magazine, The, for 1831.
HARDWICKE PAPERS. British Museum. Add MS 35,350.
HAYDON, BENJAMIN ROBERT. *Autobiography and Memoirs.* 1853.
HAYWARD, ABRAHAM. *Autobiography, Letters and Literary Remains of Mrs Piozzi.* 1861.
HAZLITT, WILLIAM. *Selected Essays.*
HOLCROFT, THOMAS. *Memoirs.* 1810.
JAMESON, MRS. *Characteristics of Women.* 1833.
JENKIN, H. C. FLEEMING. *Papers Literary, Scientific, etc.* 1878.
Johnson's England. Ed. A. S. Turberville. 1933.
KEMBLE, FRANCES ANN. *Record of a Girlhood.* 1878.
KNAPP, O. G. *An Artist's Love Story.* 1904.
KNAPP, O. G. *The Intimate Letters of Hester Piozzi and Penelope Pennington.* 1914.

Lady's Magazine, The, for 1816.
Lady's Monthly Museum, The, for 1813.
LAYARD, GEORGE SOMES. *Sir Thomas Lawrence's Letter-bag.* 1906.
LEWES, CHARLES LEE. *Memoirs.* 1805.
LIVERPOOL PAPERS. British Museum. Add. MS 38,299.
MAUROIS, ANDRÉ. *Meïpe, ou la Délivrance.* 1926.
MERRITT, J. *Memoirs of the life of William Henry West Betty.* 1804.
MORE, HANNAH. *Memoirs and Correspondence.* 1834.
Mrs Siddons. Extract from *The Rheterlogue* by J. N. Ruffin.
Mrs Siddons's First Plays. 1784.
NICOLL, ALLARDYCE. *Eighteenth Century Drama.* 2 vols. 1925–7.
PARSONS, MRS CLEMENT. *The Incomparable Siddons.* 1909.
PENLEY, BELVILLE S. *The Bath Stage.* 1892.
Piozziana; or, Recollections of the late Mrs Piozzi . . . by a friend. 1833.
PIOZZI-SIDDONS LETTERS. English MSS John Rylands Library.
ROGERS, SAMUEL. *Recollections.* Ed. Dyce. 1856.
ROYDE-SMITH, NAOMI. *The Private Life of Mrs Siddons.* 1932.
Secret History of the Green-Room, etc. 1793.
SEWARD, ANNA. *Correspondence.* 1811.
Siddoniad, The. 1795.
SMITH, J. AND H. : *Rejected Addresses: or, the New Theatrum Poetarum.* 1813.
TAYLOR, JOHN. *Records of my Life.* 1832.
The Times Literary Supplement. 9th May 1936.
Theatrical Portrait, The. 1783.
Thespia, Poems to. 1781.
Thespian Dictionary, The. 1802.
Thraliana. The Diary of Hester Lynch Thrale (later Mrs Piozzi). Ed. K.
    N. Balderston. 1942.
WHALLEY, THOMAS SEDGEWICK, D.D. *Journals and Correspondence.* 1863.
WILKINSON, TATE. *The Wandering Patentee.* 1795.
WILSON JOHN (CHRISTOPHER NORTH). *Noctes Ambrosianæ.*
WYNDHAM, H. S. *The Annals of Covent Garden Theatre from 1732 to 1897.* 1906.
YOUNG, J. C. *A Memoir of Charles Mayne Young.* 1871.